SKOLLIE

SKOLLIE

One man's struggle to survive
by telling stories

JOHN W. FREDERICKS

ZEBRA PRESS

Published by Zebra Press
an imprint of Penguin Random House South Africa (Pty) Ltd
Reg. No. 1953/000441/07
The Estuaries No. 4, Oxbow Crescent, Century Avenue, Century City, 7441
PO Box 1144, Cape Town, 8000, South Africa
www.penguinrandomhouse.co.za

Penguin
Random House
South Africa

First published 2017
Reprinted in 2017 and 2018

3 5 7 9 10 8 6 4

Publication © Penguin Random House 2017
Text © John W. Fredericks 2017

Cover photograph © Lindsey Appolis

PUBLISHER: Marlene Fryer
EDITOR: Robert Plummer
PROOFREADER: Dane Wallace
COVER AND TEXT DESIGNER: Ryan Africa
TYPESETTER: Monique van den Berg

Set in 11.5 pt on 15 pt Minion

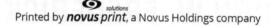

Printed by **novus print**, a Novus Holdings company

MIX
Paper from
responsible sources
FSC® C022948

Penguin Random House is committed to a sustainable future
for our business, our readers and our planet. This book is made
from Forest Stewardship Council ® certified paper.

ISBN 978 1 77609 199 7 (print)
ISBN 978 1 77609 200 0 (ePub)

I dedicate this book to my wife, Una, who walked beside me through the hills and valleys on this journey of life, keeping the faith when days were dark. And in her own words, '*It was a journey to hell and back!*'

Contents

Foreword

I first met John W. Fredericks in 2002 on the steps of the Artscape Theatre in Cape Town.

To be honest, we looked at each other with some suspicion.

He was probably thinking, '*Oh no, not another white guy whose hand I have to shake and never see again.*' And I was thinking, '*Why am I being introduced to this old guy?*'

That meeting was the beginning of a fourteen-year journey that grew into friendship and mutual respect, and which resulted in the South African box-office hit of 2016, *Noem My Skollie.*

The film was South Africa's entry to the foreign-language Oscar awards in 2017 and depicts a part of John's life from teenager to young man.

Now, John's autobiography, *Skollie*, takes the reader through his entire life in a series of fast-paced chapters that show how he survived by combining his streetwise skills with his gift of the gab.

David Wingate, one of Europe's foremost screenwriting experts, reviewed John's writing and described his unique style as more James Hadley Chase than J.M. Coetzee. Indeed, John's writing has the breathless pace and thrilling content of a Chase novel, especially in this auto-biography, but what sets these writers apart is that John is writing about a world in which he actually lived and which Chase could only imagine.

At seventy-one, John still lives in Strandfontein on the Cape Flats and still types with one finger, but he has written a number of plays, film scripts and documentaries that deserve recognition.

Memory is a complex thing that sits somewhere in our brain and which we call upon with varying levels of success at different times in our lives. John has an amazing capacity to remember his past in great detail, perhaps because so many of his experiences were life-changing, life-and-death situations.

But memory can fail and it is always subject to interpretation, and in some cases different memories combine or become distorted. Some are stored away in a locked box in a deep recess of the brain, only to be triggered open by an unexpected life event or from a renewed self-awareness. It is from these memories, both the vivid and the vague, that autobiographies are made.

What persists and shines out from John's memory of his life is his love and respect for family and his deeply felt confidence in the power of the human spirit to prevail over adversity.

This is a man who has not just been concerned with his own survival, but who has also spent most of his life working with young offenders in jails around the Western Cape. His aim is to encourage young people to find a constructive place in society instead of working against it and against themselves.

There is an urgent need to look back on the past so that we can better consider our situation today and plan for a different future, because crime and poverty will not go away of their own accord.

This book, like the film, opens our eyes to one man's life but might also motivate the reader to get to know more about coloured identity and history, not just that created by apartheid, but reaching back to the history of the slave trade and the original people of the Western Cape whose flourishing centres of trade and culture were destroyed by colonialist expansion and whose ancestors were the families that gave root to all humanity throughout the world.

Skollie is both memorable and inspirational, and I encourage everyone, young or old, of any race, colour or creed, to read this book. Be prepared to laugh and to cry, and make sure you find a comfortable place to sit, because once you start reading I guarantee you will not be able to stop.

DAVID MAX BROWN
PRODUCER OF *NOEM MY SKOLLIE*
JULY 2017

Part One

Birth of a rebel

1

In the beginning

My first real memory is of being tucked in under my mother's arm, shivering with cold under the threadbare blanket on the steps of our back porch. I could feel her pain as she cried and prayed softly, her knitting needles stitching rapidly in the dim light.

This was the norm: my dad, Philip, would come home drunk from his day's work as a refuse collector, and we would watch through the windows. If he was staggering, my mom would grab her knitting bag and a blanket and herd me and my five sisters out the back door. We would listen to his drunken shenanigans until he fell asleep. Late at night we'd slip inside and head for our beds. My sisters – three older and two younger than me – slept on a big double bed that took up all the space in the small backroom. I slept on a dilapidated couch in the dining room.

Early in the morning, Dad got up, fed the chickens, harvested eggs for breakfast, made a pot of black coffee, and always, like clockwork, he would bring me a cup. He was different when he was sober, handsome, sunburnt to a dark tan from working in the sun all day. He had long black hair, flashing grey-green eyes and sparkling white teeth. He was ferocious when riled and would not back down from anybody. Born in District Six, he never went to school and spent most of his growing-up days in the Cape Town dockyard where my grandfather had a fishing boat. Dad was a known thug on the docks. He always carried a small light bulb – or globe, as it was known back then – in his pocket, which identified him as a member of the Globe Gang, one of the most notorious gangs in the forties and fifties.

Early one morning, Dad served me a cup of steaming black coffee and went out the back door. A few seconds later the door banged open and he came rushing in, eyes balled in fear. '*Johnnie! Kom gou!*' (Come quickly!) I rushed outside after him and he pointed to the chicken coop where a rooster, feathers bristling, was facing down a huge cornered rat. The hens clucked in fear behind the rooster. Dad gave me a rake and shoved me inside the coop. '*Maak hom dood!*' (Kill him!) I moved slowly towards the rat, rake held low in front of me. '*Watch it.*' Dad murmured again, and then he said, '*Hy gan attack, Johnnie, a cornered rat gan attack!*' (It's going to attack, a cornered rat will attack!) And, indeed, the rat came flying towards me, and I swung blindly in fright, the rake catching it under the belly in mid-air, the teeth of the rake protruding through its back. '*Begrawe dit, Johnnie*' (Bury it), Dad said before heading off to work without any eggs for breakfast. I buried the rat. In just a few minutes I had learnt to face my fears, to kill a rat and that my father was scared of rats.

My mom, Kathleen, a tall, beautiful woman with long black hair, got ready for work at the abattoir, where she had to stand for hours in gumboots on the wet, salt-covered cement floors. Dad was madly jealous of her and would accuse her of all sorts of things when drunk. It was probably also the reason why he saddled her up with a baby every second year. One Saturday the pastor of the church came around to our house to pray with Mom, and Dad lost his cool. He threw an axe at the pastor, barely missing his head, and the pastor fled, leaving his bicycle behind. That day we had great fun riding around on the pastor's bicycle.

Before leaving for work, Mom pointed to a sheep's head in the kitchen sink and told me to clean it after school. I checked out the sheep's head and the flies buzzing around it; there were flies everywhere. The fly catcher on the ceiling, heavy with flies, twirled in the sudden breeze when Mom opened the door. I stared at the buckled piece of brown bread next to half a mug of greasy black coffee and a scraped-clean piece of margarine foil on the wooden kitchen table. Yes! I was the man around here at only seven years old.

We were poor but that was normal, as everybody else was poor in Kewtown, with its multiple courts and alleys, the cream-painted, barrack-like small brick houses, asbestos roofs, each door painted a different shade of pastel. It was probably the first township created by the apartheid regime, with huge blocks of flats to house crowds of people from various creeds and cultures. Poverty and unemployment were rife and could be witnessed by the many people on the streets and men gambling, playing dice or cards, in the alleyways. Drinking and smoking dagga were the norm and a flickering knife was part of everyday life. Women hung over their washing lines, gossiping. It was a cauldron of humanity, each one suspicious of the other. Hair played a big role, and if you had very short hair, people looked down on you. So my sisters, who had very long hair, became targets of jealous, snide remarks. The permanent stench from the sewage plant at the back of the bush hung like a cloud over the township and it was called 'Tietie Land' – for what reason I don't know, but the smell of sewage was ever present.

I was in Sub B at the Methodist school in Athlone, which was quite a distance from our house, and I had to walk to school every day, crossing the main streets of Athlone. I was a malnourished kid with spindly legs covered in warts, and I was the butt of many jokes. Other kids would call me *Johnnie vratjie bene* (Johnnie wart legs). Sometimes they would throw stones at me as if I had the pestilence. So I spent most of my young life on my own, surrounded only by my five sisters. I became a loner by nature, lonely in a crowd. I was embarrassed about myself. This loneliness still walks with me and it moulded me into who I am today.

My sisters and I regularly attended Sunday school at the Gospel Hall on Church Street in Athlone, and I never sang a chorus if I didn't know the words. I would stare at others mumbling along who did not know the words either and I found it funny. At one end-of-year party, the teacher gave everyone toys, beach balls, water guns and toy cars. She gave me a small ten-page book with the title *The Curiosity Club*. I looked at the book and then back at her in disappointment. Many years later I would realise why she gave it to me. I was a curious kid, questioning everything, always looking for the solution to a problem. To while away the lonely hours, I read a lot – old magazines, newspapers, comic books and novels that my dad brought home from the rubbish dump. My storybook characters became my companions. I learnt a lot from them in my make-believe world of cowboys and crooks, cops and robbers, and gunfighters of the American Wild West.

I would write plays, which I would discuss with my sisters, and they would make or find the wardrobe, while I would scout for the props. We would make a poster from cardboard to advertise the play. As the writer, I made sure that I was always the hero or good guy. We would perform to the local kids for one penny each; sometimes even the grown-ups attended. They would cheer and clap their hands at our performance. We brought some life and laughter to the inhabitants of our poverty-stricken community.

I was eight years old and in Standard 1 when my mom bought three donkeys at the abattoir. She felt sorry for them, she explained later. The donkeys grazed in our big backyard and the kids would pay me one penny for a trip around the yard. These kids had to pass through the communal gate that we shared with our neighbour Mrs Lubbe. She was a real dragon, with her miniskirt and short frizzy hair in paper curlers most of the time. She would scream and rant at us. She also had a vineyard in her yard and huge bunches of grapes hung over into our yard. Needless to say, life was great, popping huge baubles of fruit into our mouths, and a good time was had by everyone. Until one day Mrs Lubbe lost her cool, screaming like a banshee, demanding we give the grapes back even though the vineyard in her own backyard was heavy with fruit. I threw the grapes over the fence. She took offence at this, and the next day she went to the council office to report the donkeys.

Mrs Lubbe had a fetish with our straight hair and she would call us *luiskoppe* (lice heads). She succeeded in her request to have the donkeys removed, and they were taken back to the abattoir to be slaughtered. I felt a huge hatred towards her that lingered for decades. I remember her shouting to her two young daughters when we met at the communal gate, *'Bly weg van daai klong af!'* (Stay away from that boy!)

I passed to Standard 2 and had to move to another school, as the Methodist school only had classes until Standard 1. There were no schools in our township, although in that year they had started building a new school in the bush directly behind our house. So I was admitted to Norma Road Primary in Silvertown, the next suburb, and placed into an English class. I could read and write but could not pronounce the English words properly. I became a character to be laughed at, to be made fun of, what with my warts and all. I vividly remember two very pretty girls, the principal's daughter and her sidekick, and the pranks they used to play on me.

One day, after our exercise period, we came back to the classroom to find that the girls were there before us. The janitor had mopped the floor while we were gone and left the bucket of water in the corner, and the girls had moved it under my desk. They were sniggering when I sat down. I stretched out my legs and kicked over the bucket, spilling water over the mopped floor, and they burst out laughing. I fumed at them as the teacher ordered me to mop up the water.

Every morning before school I had to escort my youngest sister Valerie to Mrs Lalla Jones, a neighbour who lived a few doors away from us, who took care of her during the day. Every morning Valerie would bawl her eyes out because she did not like it there and sometimes it felt like my heart would break. She always complained that Lalla's kids ate her food, and when I asked Lalla about this, she would scream at me and send me on my way. I didn't like Lalla, so on a lonely night I sneaked out of the house and threw a stone at her window, breaking it.

I passed to Standard 3 and was admitted to the newly built school behind our house. The school was named Zone A and there was bush all around it. In our sports breaks we were issued with picks, shovels and axes to remove the Port Jackson trees by their roots. It was back-breaking work, but it was fun changing the landscape and seeing a football and netball field emerge. Life was great.

Mom got pregnant again and she gave up her job at the abattoir and started selling sweets and peanuts to the school kids at the back fence of our yard.

As he did his rounds on his refuse cart, Dad collected copper, brass and one-legged Primus stoves, which he would solder and repair. Anything with resale value, which he would sell to the scrapyard at a later stage. Then he started a new venture, bringing home huge bags of dirty empty wine bottles, which he would dump into three 200-gallon drums filled with water. It was my task to clean and wash the bottles and stack them into neat piles. My other chores were chopping wood for the stove and scrubbing and polishing the floors to a high shine on my hands and knees. I also cleaned the blackened pots, a task that was declared men's work by my mom, much to the delight of my sisters. Once a month a distillery truck would come to collect the bottles, and I would watch and supervise when Dad was not present. The driver would hand me the money to pay Dad. We were rich, or so it seemed.

Then the health department officials arrived at our school and my younger sister Cecelia and I were admitted to a convalescent home because we were malnourished. I will always remember the smell of cooked cabbage wafting on the breeze. And standing by the wire fence next to Main Road in Retreat asking passers-by to buy us Wilson's block sweets across the road. I also remember making music on a makeshift drum.

After a month in the convalescent home I returned to school, where I excelled in writing compositions and my teacher would take me around to the other classes to read for them. Dad found a wild plant that gave off a milky juice which he applied to my warts and soon they began to disappear. Now that my school was nearer to my home, I could spend hours at the rubbish dump. Every afternoon after school I would hitch a ride on Dad's refuse cart to go to the dump.

2

The rubbish dump

The dump site was a cacophony of sound as various other carts were already dumping their first loads of the day to the loud banter and insults of the council workers. We entered the dump site and moved slowly towards the dump supervisor, Ballie Honne-oor (Ballie Dog Ears), and his three tan ridgeback dogs gathered around him. For some reason I always felt unsettled when Ballie stared at me from his deep-set eyes. He had thick bushy eyebrows and half of his right ear was missing. Legend had it that he intervened in a dog fight and a dog bit off half his ear. He tugged on a thick dagga zol rolled in brown paper and gave a wracking cough when Dad greeted him: '*Jis! Ballie Honne-oor, waar moet os tip?*' (Where must we dump?)

Ballie's eyes smouldered at this remark, and he spat on the ground. '*Philip, moetie met my fok nie!*' (Don't fuck with me!) He pointed to a gap between two unloading wagons and told Dad to pull up there.

Dad jumped off and dragged a quart of beer from under the seat. I led the horses towards the edge, backed up the wagon, pulled the lever and dumped the load. Dust billowed as human scavengers and mangy dogs scrabbled in the newly dumped load of rubbish. Over the sound of creaking horse carts and jangling harnesses, seagulls squawked as they dipped and dived for titbits of food. Dust swept across the site as it was picked up by the southeaster wind.

I led the horses back towards the two men and commenced to rub down the animals, whispering sweet nothings into their ears. I was uncomfortable under Ballie's stare. His eyes seemed to follow my every move. Ballie dragged on his zol and coughed again as Dad opened the quart of beer with his teeth. He slugged back half in one go, then remarked, '*Djy gan jou nog doodroek van daai dagga, Ballie.*' (You're going to smoke yourself to death from that dagga.)

'*En djy gan nog bekkanker kry van bottels oep byt, Philip!*' Ballie retorted. (And you're going to get mouth cancer from biting open bottles.)

I finished my task as Ballie continued, '*Jou laaitie gan 'n goeie brommer wies, Philip.*' (Your kid will make a good council worker.)

Dad bristled, stepped towards the cart and dragged a battered brown, boxed typewriter from under the seat. He opened it and showed Ballie the typewriter inside. '*My laaitie gan 'n skrywer wies, Ballie!*' Dad told him. (My kid is going to be a writer!)

Ballie gave a guttural laugh. "*'n Skrywer? Whiteys is skrywers! Wie gan hom leer? Djy kannie eens lies en skrywe nie!*' (A writer? Whiteys are writers! Who's going to teach him anyway? You can't even read or write!)

The gathered council workers laughed at this remark and Dad lost his cool. He handed the typewriter to me, dropped his overall straps, and turned on them: '*Vi wat lag julle?*' (What you laughing at?) He went into a boxer's stance and turned on Ballie. '*Kom op, ek en djy, Ballie! Os baklei yt die guns yt.*' (Come on, Ballie, me and you! We fight with our fists.) Ballie's dogs growled softly but Dad was on a roll. The council workers stood mesmerised by the unfolding scenario. Ballie's eyes flickered warily, he spat on the ground, declined the fight, and moved off with his dogs in tow. I stared at my dad in hero worship.

I got the opportunity to handle the reins to ride the cart towards the circle of wagons where the council workers were having their lunch break. I unharnessed the horses and led them to water, then to their stall and feeding cribs. The workers started fires in braziers to warm their food and make coffee. Groups formed to drink, play cards and smoke zol. It was a place of boots and buckles and rough, tough men with strange names. This was my world.

After a while I would go back to the dump site to scavenge for books. The other scavengers knew me well; I was one of their own and a strange relationship existed between us. I always took time out to chat with them and they would always ask me about my school work. They knew about my love of reading and they would gather books by James Hadley Chase, Mickey Spillane and Louis L'Amour and keep them for me.

I took the typewriter home, cleaned it out and spent hours typing on it with different coloured sheets of paper that I scored on the dump. I was in my element. Later, when Dad arrived home, he gathered his accumulated scrap and we set off by bus to sell it to the scrapyard in Black River. Dad bought food and a six-gallon can of cheap wine. Back home he drank wine and played the guitar and we gathered around, harmonising with him.

On a Sunday after a drunken Saturday of fighting with Mom, he sent me to a neighbour's house in Block 2 to pick up a hair-cutting machine to cut my long hair. I was a bit upset with him and in a rebellious mood. Along the way I saw three kids pushing a stalled truck, so I decided to help. We pushed the truck uphill, with the idea that it would start when it rolled downhill. The truck roared into life and we hung onto the back in the hope that it would stop to let us get on board. The driver just kept on going. We hung on for dear life as it picked up speed. My hands slipped, I lost my grip and I hit the ground with a thud. I landed on the back of my head and lost consciousness. I was unconscious for most of that day. I have vague memories of Dad carrying me in his arms through the thick bush and getting into the truck with me when the truck driver returned to take me to hospital. I had to stay home for a few days, but that knock on the head lingered with me for many years to come and I carry the scar on the back of my head to this day.

3

My worst nightmare

At school we played soccer matches with kids from other classes to find the best players to make up the school team. These were exciting times and I got picked regularly as the athletics teacher groomed the team. A few other kids also made the team in every match we played. One of them was Tyrone Felix, a freckle-faced kid with long curly hair. He was a hard tackler and our opponents feared him.

On our school's first outing, a match against North Primary, only a few of us had proper soccer boots, but we played our hearts out. Almost at the end of the match, with no score, the North Primary striker had a clear shot at goal and only the goalkeeper to beat. Tyrone came flying from nowhere with a feet-first tackle. He won the ball and kicked it into midfield to be picked up by the midfielder, a chubby kid named Richard. Richard ran at the defence and passed to the winger, 'Shorty', a small kid who scurried onto the ball and sliced it with his left foot into the net. We won, and, needless to say, we rejoiced. After a pep talk from the coach, a teacher was heard to say about Tyrone, *'Daai klong met die sproete is giftig.'* (That kid with the freckles is poison.) The nickname 'Gif' stuck with him. He was absent from school most of the time, but on match days Gif was there and always got picked for the team. He did not do well at school.

Richard Carelse, the midfielder, was nicknamed Gimba because of his gluttonous eating habits. He always wore nice clothes, had money to spend and had a school uniform too. So we started to hang out together. I liked him a lot because to me he was a rich kid. Every afternoon after school my dad would pull up at the school gates and I would jump on the back step and hitch a ride home. Soon Gimba, Shorty and Gif joined me and our friendship grew. Gif had the knack of whistling like a night bird and we spent hours trying to imitate him. The whistle, with three repeated tweets, became our call sign.

On Saturdays I had to take a train from Athlone railway station to the Salt River fruit and vegetable market to buy a '*halfkroon*' (half a crown or twenty-five pence) special for Mom. The special contained all types of fruit and vegetables, which would last for the whole week. So I got wise. I bought an extra special with my own coins and sold it in the neighbourhood for double the price I paid for it. There were always willing buyers for my fresh produce and I soon had my regular customers. I was all for making money and became a good hawker. Mr Marshall, a fruit and vegetable hawker with a horse and cart, recognised my skills and hired me for the weekends to help him. The people in the area liked my hawking skills, especially the women, and I would sell loads of stuff to them. Mr Marshall paid me well and always gave me a bag filled with fruit and veggies to take home. Sadly, he lost his trust in me when he found out that I was stealing his avocado pears. He fired me on the spot, saying, '*Ek was goed vi jou! Nou steel djy my goed? Fokkof, ek wil jou nie mee sien nie!*' (I treated you well! Now you steal my stuff? Fuck off, I don't want to see you again!)

During the school holidays I would accompany my dad on the refuse cart when he collected the bags of rubbish lining the streets. I sat on the driver's seat handling the reins as the horses plodded along. Dad was at the back emptying the refuse bags as the other workers tossed them into the cart. Then Dad would shovel the refuse to the back. He would be enveloped in dust in the confined space of the cart. Every now and then he would suck on a quart of beer stashed in a brown paper bag. My three newfound friends soon joined me in this adventure.

One Saturday we were collecting refuse along Main Road in Athlone. Gimba was sitting next to me on the driver's seat reading a comic book, Gif on top ogling the girls. Dad was in the back, sorting and shovelling the rubbish. Then a church youth brigade came marching into view playing drums, trumpets and saxophones. The youth in front were holding up placards declaring the goodness of Christ. Shorty was right in front of the pack with a money bag in hand, soliciting funds for the church. Gif spotted him and shouted, '*Hei, kerkdiener ...*' (Hey, church cop ...) Shorty gave him the middle finger, then ducked out of the group and ran in our direction. He jumped onto the back of the cart, tossed his placard inside and joined us up front, still holding onto the money bag. The placard read *Wyn is 'n lawaaimaker* (Wine makes you noisy).

'*Kwaai outfit, my broer,*' said Gif. '*Issit 'n kerk-special?*' (Nice outfit, my brother. Is it a church special?)

'*Fok jou!*' Shorty replied. (Fuck you!)

'*Daai geld behoort aan die kerk, Shorty,*' I reprimanded him. '*Jou pa gan jou hel gee!*' (That money belongs to the church, Shorty. Your dad is going to give you hell!)

'*Te hel met my pa,*' he replied. (My dad can go to hell.)

Gimba stared at the money bag as Shorty pulled out a handful of coins and shoved the empty bag under the driver's seat. '*Hoeveel het djy collect, Shorty? Kom os koep 'n daait.*' (How much money did you collect, Shorty? Let's go buy some food.)

Dad took a swallow from his quart, wiped his mouth with his sleeve and turned to Gimba. '*Gimba, 'n man moet hom nie lat beheer deur sy maag nie.*' (A man should not be controlled by his stomach.)

Gimba glared at the bottle in Dad's hand and held back a retort. Then he jumped off the wagon after Shorty and Gif.

One day, when I was nine years old, I entered our kitchen looking for something to eat. I checked the cupboards, nothing. I turned to Mom, who was sitting at the dining-room table reading her Bible. '*Ma, ek is honger, is daa niks om te eet nie?*' (Mom, I'm hungry, is their nothing to eat?)

She looked at me with weary eyes. '*Gaan na die ashoop toe, Johnnie. Vra vir jou pa vir kosgeld.*' (Go to the dump, Johnnie. Ask your dad for money for food.)

It was payday and the council workers were in a festive mood. They were drinking, smoking dagga, arguing among each other. I looked around for Dad and found him involved in a card game and on a losing streak. They sat around a crate, with a gallon of white wine, dagga zols hanging from their lips. Dad lost a round and pooled some more money. A council worker passed him a big metal mug filled to the brim and Dad slugged back half in one go. He wiped his mouth on his sleeve and picked up his cards as I stepped up to him. '*Pa, Ma het my gestier vir kosgeld.*' (Dad, Mom sent me to get food money from you.)

He turned on me and snarled, '*Kan djy nie sien ek is biesig nie!? Wag totdat die game klaa is!*' (Can't you see I'm busy!? Wait until the game is done!)

I took a step back and watched as he studied his cards. He lost again, pooled some more money, picked up his mug for a last swallow, and I approached him again. '*Pa, daai's nou genoeg. Ma wag vir die geld.*' (Dad, that's enough now. Mom is waiting for the money.)

That's when he lost it. He tossed the wine into my face, snarling, '*Ek het mos gesê djy moet wag!*' (I told you to wait!) I stared at him for a long moment and I saw a dismal look appear in his eyes.

I walked towards the windblown dump site. It was Friday and strangely there were no scavengers on the dump. I wandered around among the huge mounds of rubbish now mostly covered by sand. Lost in thought, I searched the dump, found a book with some pages missing, and discarded it. The southeaster picked up, sweeping dust across the landscape. I heard a dog growl, looked up and saw the stick-like silhouette of Ballie on the skyline. My heart jumped into my throat as the dogs growled again.

'*Ek soek vir boeke, Mr Ballie,*' I shouted at him. (I'm looking for books.)

Ballie kept staring at me and I was overwhelmed by a sudden fear. He wet his fingers with his tongue, held his hand in the air, and said, '*Djy moetie so ver kom nie, Johnnie, die suidooster is 'n vreeslike wind. Djy val en djy skree, maa niemand kan jou hoor nie.*' (You shouldn't come this far, Johnnie, the southeaster is a terrible wind. You fall and you scream but nobody can hear you.)

I was gripped by fear and started to run up the mound of refuse, but the harder I ran, the deeper my feet sank into the rubbish. Then Ballie set his dogs on me and they came charging up the hill towards me. The lead dog caught up with me and brought me down, licking at my face as if it was a game. I heard Ballie breathing hard above me as he unzipped his fly and his aroused penis jumped out of his pants. I screamed. He clamped his big dirty hand over my mouth, muffling my scream. With his other hand he ripped off my shorts and pushed his penis into my butt. He groaned as he pumped into me with vigour. '*Soe djy wil 'n skrywer wies?*' he grunted. '*Ek sal jou wys!*' (So you want to be a writer? I'll show you!)

I lost all sense of time. He eventually got up, zipped up his pants and muttered, '*Die's jou eie fokken skuld ... en as djy iets sê van die, lat ek die honne jou opvriet!*' (It's your own fucking fault ... and if you say anything about this, I'll feed you to my dogs!) He moved off with his dogs in tow. I just lay there with my face in the dirt. Hurt and traumatised, I stumbled back to the laager to find all the wagons gone and Dad snoring drunk under his cart. I was shattered. I helped him onto the driver's seat and handed him the reins. He was confused and just stared at me with his wine-wet eyes.

When I got home Mom wasn't there so I headed straight to the bathroom and scrubbed myself vigorously, washed my shorts and hung them out to dry. Dad came home from work half drunk and penniless. He splayed himself across the couch and almost immediately began to snore. I looked at my sisters and was overwhelmed by a feeling of hopelessness. I had a few coins in my pocket so I gave my sister Francis a tickey to buy a packet of broken biscuits at the nearby shop.

Later Mom arrived home with a parcel of fish and chips as Dad was waking up. He screamed at her, '*Djy's laat! Waa was djy gewies!?*' (You're late! Where were you!?) I cringed. Mom put some fish and chips on a plate and put it on the table in front of him. He swiped the plate onto the floor in one vicious move, snarling, '*Moenie vi my kak gie nie!*' (Don't give me shit!)

Mom grabbed her bag of knitting and a blanket, and we escaped through the back door. We sat on the back stoep under the blanket and I decided to tell Mom that Ballie had raped me. She was crying softly, the tears streaming down her face, and I did not know where to begin. '*Ma, iets het gebeur op die tip vandag,*' I stuttered. '*Mr Ballie ...*' (Mom, something happened on the dump today. Mr Ballie ...)

Mom gave me a wan smile. '*Mr Ballie is 'n goeie man, Johnnie, net baie eensaam nadat sy vrou afgesterf het.*' (Mr Ballie is a good man, Johnnie, just very lonesome after his wife died.)

A sob caught in my throat and for a moment we were in total darkness as a small cloud covered the moon.

I went inside, took a big knife from the kitchen drawer and came back outside. I stood next to Mom for a while, trying to hide my tears.

'*Hoekom is jy so rusteloos, Johnnie?*' she asked. '*Kom sit.*' (Why are you so restless, Johnnie? Come and sit down.)

'*Ek gan kyk gou vir hout om 'n vuurtjie te maak, Ma,*' I replied. '*Ek's nou terug.*' (I'm going to find some wood to start a fire, Mom. I'll be right back.)

I slipped out the gate and stuck to the shadows as I made my way to Ballie's house. I took up a position behind a wall opposite his house. I watched his house, sharpening the knife against the brick wall as Ballie's dogs howled at the moon. I trembled when he appeared in the doorway, looking weird with a nightcap on his head. He strode outside his gate, looked up and down the street, and I scooted out of there. I was scared silly. From that day onwards, I had recurring nightmares of being raped by Ballie.

The next day was Dad's day off and he was quiet for most of it. He gathered his scrap and was on his way to the scrapyard when he turned to me. '*Gan djy nie saam scrapyard toe nie, Johnnie?*' (Aren't you coming with me to the scrapyard, Johnnie?)

I felt like dying. '*Nie vandag nie, Pa.*' (Not today, Dad.)

He continued, '*Wat makee djy dan vandag?*' (What's wrong with you today?)

I think I hated him then. '*Niks vekeerd nie, Pa. Ek moet nog vloere skrop.*' (Nothing wrong, Dad. I must still scrub the floors.)

Soon after that, as I was coming through the bush near Main Road in Athlone, I spotted the truck from which I had fallen coming down the road. I picked up a half brick and threw it at the truck, shattering the windscreen. The truck came to a screeching stop as I ducked into the bush and scuttled away. I felt vindicated, but there was an eyewitness who saw me. On Sunday morning a Detective van Wyk came to our house and I was really scared. The detective and my dad discussed the stoning of the truck in our yard. Dad gave him two of our brooding hens and the detective left, never to be seen again. Dad was quite upset;

he grabbed me by the scruff of my neck, unbuckled his army belt and lashed me viciously across my thighs and buttocks, screaming, '*Is djy 'n fokken skollie?!*' (Are you a fucking skollie?!)

Mom came dashing out the back door, shouting, '*Daai's nou genoeg, Philip. Los hom nou!*' (That's enough now, Philip. Let him go!)

Dad glared at her and spat bullets of profanity at her. '*Gan djy vir die fokken windscreen betaal!?*' (Are you going to pay for the fucking windscreen!?)

I took the gap, ran inside and slid under the bed in the backroom. I lay there, whimpering in pain. After a while, Dad came into the room and he coaxed me from under the bed. He said he understood but that I mustn't do it again.

I never went back to the rubbish dump.

4

Lessons in life

My grades dropped in Standard 4 and I just managed to pass to Standard 5. Gimba and Shorty also passed, but Gif stayed behind. Gif just faded from school. He had no support, so he took to the streets to try to make a living for himself. Most of the time he could be found playing dice with older men in alleys or on street corners. He became streetwise and never played soccer again.

Mr Woodford the class teacher was a real ladies' man, a handsome hunk in a tailored suit and with long, shiny, slicked-back black hair. We all lived in fear of him. He didn't believe in sparing the rod and his thick cane with a red, taped handle hung against the wall behind his desk. We had to do our homework diligently or there would be hell to pay. When he came to school with a cow's lick of hair hanging over his forehead we knew he was in a bad mood, and most of the time he was on our case. One day after school, Dad pulled up at the gate with the empty refuse cart, blocking the access just as Mr Woodford was about to drive off. We jumped into the cart as Woodford hooted continuously. He got out of his car, strode over to the cart and shouted at us, '*Klim van die wa af!*' (Get off the cart!)

Dad pulled up the brake and jumped off the cart. '*Het djy miskien 'n problem met die kinners?*' he asked mildly. (Have you perhaps got a problem with these kids?)

'*Die seuns is onnet en het geen disipline nie!*' Woodford ranted. (These boys are scruffy and undisciplined!)

Dad took exception to this and his eyes flashed in anger as he stepped up close to the teacher. More learners gathered and I was quite embarrassed by the scene unfolding. I tried to intervene. '*Pa ...*' I murmured. But Dad was past listening and snarled into Woodford's face, '*Luister, meneer, jou job is om die laaities te leer, my job is om jou robbies skoon te maak! Soe leer djy, en ek sal jou kak optel! Is djy by my!?'* (Listen, sir, your job is to teach these kids and my job is to clean up your rubbish! So you teach, and I'll pick up your shit! Are you with me!?) Woodford stood speechless as Dad looked at him deep down.

The next day at school when Woodford arrived, the cow's lick was hanging over his forehead. He was simmering with anger and the learners went diligently about their tasks, too scared to breathe. Woodford took his cane from the wall and banged it across his desk. I almost jumped out of my skin at the sound. *'Sit neer julle penne en luister mooi!'* (Put down your pens and listen nicely!) he commanded, and we complied. He explained that we were going to start writing an English composition that day and that we had two days to finish it. The learners groaned and shuffled their feet. I was excited. The one year in an English class stood me in good stead.

When I got home from school that day, I immediately started on my story and continued until dusk. I started a fire in the Welcome Dover coal stove. I remember we were having horse meat that night that Mom had got at the abattoir. A tough, sweet-tasting meat that took hours to cook.

On the Friday when I arrived at school, Shorty and Gimba were there already and they had not done their compositions. *'Julle ouens is in groot moeilikheid,'* I told them. (You guys are in big trouble.)

Shorty grabbed Woodford's cane and threw it out the window into the long grass.

We handed in our compositions and Woodford was really impressed with my story and called me up front. He told me that he wanted me to read my story to all the Standard 5 classes after school. I cringed.

I had never stood in front of a crowd, and the whole day I was worried sick about the reading. The last bell sounded and my classmates shuffled outside and gathered in the courtyard. They murmured and shuffled their feet, unhappy that they had to stay behind. Some teachers stood around the perimeter; they too were unimpressed as Woodford strutted proudly onto the podium. I stood right at the back, trembling in trepidation.

Woodford strode to the lectern and announced, *'Vandag gaan een van my leerlinge sy opstel voorlees. Gee 'n hand daar vir John Fredericks,*' he shouted. (Today one of my learners is going to read his composition for us. Let's give a big hand there for John Fredericks.)

The learners cheered as I made my way to the podium, shouting, *'Johnnie! Johnnie! Johnnie!'* I looked at them, then at my composition, and the words became a blur. My throat constricted and I could not utter a word. I rubbed my throat, indicating to Woodford that I couldn't read. The learners jeered. Woodford grabbed me by the scruff of the neck and frogmarched me to the classroom. We entered and he headed straight towards the cane on the wall and found it missing.

Woodford changed like a chameleon as veins appeared in his face. His neck tendons went tight with anger, and for a moment I thought he was going to punch me. I trembled as he stared at me for a long moment until his anger subsided. He picked up a notepad, scribbled on it, sealed it and handed it to me, saying, *'Gee daai vir jou ouers.'* (Give that to your parents.)

When I got home, Dad was in a bad mood. He was sitting on the couch strumming his guitar, a half bottle of white wine on the floor beside him. Mom was at the table knitting. I handed the note to Mom, but Dad intercepted it and tore open the envelope and scanned the note. Without much ado, he unbuckled his belt and whacked me across the thighs. *'Djy bly oek innie kak!'* he screamed at me. (You're always in shit!)

Mom intervened. *'Los hom, Philip! Jy kan nie eers lees nie. Laat ek die nota sien.'* (Let him go, Philip! You can't even read. Let me see the note.)

She took the note and read, *'Jou seun is goed in stories skryf, maar hy moet ophou om grapjas te speel by die skool.'* (Your son is good at writing stories, but he must stop acting like a clown at school.) Mom found this funny and burst out laughing, much to the chagrin of Dad, who left the room in a huff and went out the back door.

During the Easter holidays, Gif, Shorty and I set off for Gimba's house to give him an unexpected visit. We knocked on the front door but nobody answered, so we went around to the back gate, which was slightly ajar, and slipped inside. Almost immediately we were confronted by

Hobo, an old tattooed gangster. His face was blue with tattoos, with the number 26 displayed prominently on his neck. '*Wantoe is julle reis!?*' he rasped. (Where are you off to!?)

The guy was scary and I stuttered, '*Os ko vi Richard besoek ...*' (We've come to visit Richard ...)

He glared at us. '*Gimba?*' he rasped again. '*Hy's biesig!*' (He's busy!) He pointed to a bench in a corner of the yard. '*Wag daa tot hy klaa is.*' (Wait there until he's done.)

We sat on the bench and scanned the yard. Gimba and a man I assumed was his father were rolling dagga sticks at a big table with a huge pile of dagga on a newspaper. They were having a competition to roll the most sticks of dagga in a short period of time. Old gangsters stood around chugging at chalices of dagga. They watched father and son compete. Mr Carelse, aka Mr C, was winning. He wore a wide-brimmed Stetson that shielded a 26 tattoo on his forehead, and he grinned broadly, the sun bouncing off his gold dentures.

Hobo stepped up to him and said, '*Hies drie laaities om vi Gimba te sien, Mr C.*' (Here's three kids to see Gimba, Mr C.)

Mr C looked towards us, scanned us once, and dismissed us in a blink of an eye. '*Hulle kan wag,*' he growled. (They can wait.) Gimba's eyes flickered towards us, and with a glum smile he continued with his task. The whole scene grabbed my imagination. This was a totally different world. It was the dark side.

We listened as the gangsters spoke in 'sabela', the prison slang, sharing their gang and prison escapades. They came in all shapes and sizes, but each one of them sported a 26 tattoo. Foxy, a runner with broken dentures, entered with a brown bag with roasted chickens and some loaves of fresh bread. He plonked it down on a side table and looked at Mr C.

'*Vat vi jou 'n stukkie om te iet, Foxy,*' said Mr C, '*en gie soema daai drie laaities oek 'n stukkie.*' (Grab yourself a piece to eat, Foxy, and give those three kids a piece too.)

As Foxy handed us some bread and chicken, Gimba glanced at us, losing his concentration and spilling some dagga onto the sandy floor. All of a sudden his dad hit him with a '*tenner*', smacking him against the ears with the palms of both hands. I flinched as tears jumped into Gimba's eyes. Mr C grinned at Hobo, saying, '*My laaitie gan 'n 26 wies as hy groot is, Hobo.*' (My laaitie's going to be a 26 when he's big, Hobo.) I flinched again.

Hobo begged to differ. '*Jou laaitie hettie die pluck nie, Mr C, plus hy vriet te veel!*' (Your kid doesn't have the pluck, Mr C, plus he eats too much!)

Mr C bristled at this remark. '*Wat wil djy vi my sê, roebana?*' he asked harshly, lowering Hobo's status. (What are you trying to tell me, robber?)

'*Ek vondela net om te kan sê jou laaitie het mos nie nodig om an die nomme te vat nie, Mr C,*' Hobo answered warily. (I'm just saying that your kid doesn't have to take on the number, Mr C.)

Mr C taunted him: '*Salute! En wat wil djy nog vi hom sê, Hobo?*' (Salute! And what else do you want to share with him, Hobo?)

'*Net … net die basics, Mr C,*' Hobo stuttered. '*Hy moet nooit ienage iets van 'n anner bandiet vattie.*' (Only the basics, Mr C. He must never take anything from another convict.)

Mr C turned to Gimba and asked him, '*Het djy die boodskap, Richard?*' (Do you get the message, Richard?)

At that point a truck pulled into the yard, loaded with bags of dagga, and Mr C took control. '*Okay, manne, laai gou die sakke af!*' (Okay, guys, unload these bags!) The gangsters got to work.

Then he turned to us. '*Julle ouens moet nou vi julle yt die kol yt vat,*' he commanded (You guys will have to leave now) – and off we went.

On our way home, Gif split away from us. Shorty and I walked on in silence for a while, then he suggested, '*Ko saam my hys toe, Johnnie, dan kry ek gou vi os 'n juice.*' (Come home with me, Johnnie, and I'll get us a juice.) Shorty's dad was a blue-collar worker and he earned more money than most of the locals. This could be seen from all the modern electrical appliances around the house. They also had a coloured maid and the house was spanking clean. I waited in the lounge while Shorty went to the fridge in the kitchen.

Then his mother appeared, a long-faced woman, with her hair in green plastic curlers and a cigarette in her mouth. Her eyes pinched when she saw me. She said nothing but went after Shorty in the kitchen. '*Vir wat bring jy daai klong na ons huis toe, Martin?*' (Why did you bring that boy into our house?)

'*Wat's dan vekeerd met hom, Ma?*' said Shorty. '*Hy's my vriend.*' (But what's wrong with him, Mom? He's my friend.)

Mrs Jacobs raised her voice. '*Hulle is happy clappies! Hulle dans en sing in hulle kerk en sy pa krap in ander mense se vullisdromme. Bly weg van hom af!*' (They're happy clappies! They dance and sing in their church and his father searches through other people's dirty dustbins. Stay away from him!)

I cringed at this remark and I heard Shorty say, '*Maar dis sy pa se werk, Ma.*' (But that's his dad's job, Mom.)

'*Dit maak nie saak nie!*' she said. '*Bly net weg van hom af!*' (It doesn't matter! Just stay away from him!)

Deeply hurt, I slipped out the door.

On a hot summer's day while I was washing bottles in the yard, Gimba, Gif and Shorty paid me a visit. Gimba checked all the dirty bottles waiting to be washed, grinned at me and said, '*Die biesigheid tel op …?*' (Business picking up …?)

I was glad for the visit and for the helping hands. '*Julle ouens kom asof julle gestier is – ek het help nodig.*' (You guys came as if you were sent – I could use some help.)

Gimba and Shorty each grabbed a makeshift bottle brush and got to work. We washed the bottles vigorously, splashing water, while Gif hung around idly.

Mom arrived with a plate of sandwiches and put it down on an over-turned crate. As Gif helped himself to two sandwiches, Mom turned to him and said, '*Gaan jy nie help om die bottels te was nie, Tyrone?*' (Aren't you going to help with the bottles, Tyrone?)

Gif swallowed a bite before replying. '*Nie vi'dag nie, antie Kettie, ek moet nog library toe gan.*' (Not today, Auntie Kettie, I still have to go to the library.)

Mom chuckled with mirth. '*Library …? Maar jy's dan nooit op skool nie, Tyrone.*' (Library …? But you're never at school, Tyrone.)

Shorty dried his hands and took two slices of bread and said solemnly, '*Hy gan aandskool, antie Kettie. Hy kannie soe goed lies innie dag'ie.*' (He goes to night school, Auntie Kettie. He can't read so well during the day.)

That set Mom off on a new wave of mirth. Still chuckling, she went back into the house. I remember thinking that I hadn't heard her laughing in a long time.

Gimba grabbed his share of the bread and snarled at Gif, who was on his second helping. '*Pak die bottels, Gif, djy kan mossie soe fokken lui wies'ie!*' (Stack the bottles, Gif, you can't be that fucking lazy!)

Gif grabbed another slice of bread and ducked for the gate, shouting, '*Nie vi'dag'ie … later.*' (Not today … later.) Then he was gone.

On a Thursday night after Mom had left for a church meeting, three of my sisters and I were listening to the radio while Dad, in a drunken stupor, was sitting on the couch strumming his guitar. He had sent my second eldest sister Grace to the shop to go buy cigarettes and was waiting impatiently for her to return. Minutes later the front door burst open and Grace rushed in with tears streaming down her face. Dad looked up at her, ready to explode at her long delay. Then he saw that she was crying. '*Wat makeer, Gracie?*' (What's wrong, Gracie?)

Grace stuttered, '*Mr Wilton, Pa … hy het my geklap.*' (Mr Wilton, Dad … he slapped me.)

Dad seethed. '*Hoekom, Gracie?*' (Why, Gracie?)

'*Die winkel was vol, Pa … toe bars iemand in die lyn in voor my, toe klap ek hom … en toe klap Mr Wilton vir my.*' (The shop was full, Dad … somebody jumped the queue in front of me so I slapped him … then Mr Wilton slapped me.)

Dad stomped to the backyard and returned with two axes. He shoved both of them behind his army belt like double guns. Then he took two knives out of the kitchen drawer and stuck them in my belt. He walked to the front door, opened it, and said, '*Kom, os gan na die winkel toe.*' (Come, we're going to the shop.) So we followed him – Grace, Francis and my two younger sisters, Valerie and Cecelia, holding onto my hands – marching behind Dad out through the communal gate.

Mrs Lubbe was standing at the gate wearing a miniskirt and paper curlers in her short frizzy hair. I thought that Mrs Lubbe had a thing going for Dad. '*Naand, Philip,*' she said coquettishly. (Good evening, Philip.) Dad brushed past her, ignoring her completely. We marched past without greeting her, following in Dad's footsteps. We were on a mission.

Mrs Lubbe spluttered, '*Julle kinners mettie lank hare dink tog julle is boe uit soes wit katte!*' (You kids with the long hair think you're on top of the log like white cats!)

We ignored her, but Dad didn't take kindly to her remark and turned on her. '*Hare!? 'n Hond kak hare! Hoeko gan was djy nie jou hare nie? Kry 'n lewe!*' (Hair!? A dog shits hair! Why don't you go wash your hair? Get a life!)

Wilton's, the only shop in the community, was crowded with locals as usual when we entered. Dad headed directly towards the owner, Mr Wilton, and snarled at him, '*Djy! Hoeko klap djy my kind?*' (You! Why did you slap my girl?)

Mr Wilton's eyes dilated with fear, and he stuttered, '*Sy ... sy ...*' (She ... she ...) He was at a loss for words. Dad whipped out his axe and Mr Wilton screamed, '*Security!*'

A big Zulu security guard came running with a short, spiked knobkierie in hand. Dad swung the axe at him and he parried the blow. Dad swung again and the guard, a trained stick fighter, parried again and whipped the axe out of Dad's hand. He had both the axe and the kierie in hand and he laughed at Dad.

Big mistake. Dad whipped out the other axe, jumped over the counter and went after him, striking out at him. The guard fled, with Dad close on his heels, and the crowd screamed as Dad swung again, smashing the marble top of a long freezer in half. Mr Wilton stared in disbelief at the shattered marble top. Dad looked at me, pointed to the fresh meats and rolls of cheese, and said, '*Wat wil djy hê?*' (What do you want?) I pointed to a roll of cheese and Dad took it out and handed it to me and off we went.

Later that night the cops came round and arrested Dad. They put him into a police Land Rover, while the locals jeered at the cops, who were ready and willing to use their guns. When Mom came home, we told her the whole saga.

'*Hy kan daar bly totdat hy môre hof toe gaan,*' she said, almost in relief. (He can stay there until he appears in court tomorrow.)

Mom made a stack of stolen cheese and tomato sandwiches and we had a feast. Dad was released the following day and ordered to pay a fine, which Mom paid from her meagre income. Dad was in a bad mood most of the time after that.

5

Down on the corner

More local boys had joined our group. There were two dark-skinned brothers named Solly and Chip, and Robbie, a loose-lipped boy who was a habitual liar. The three of them were into housebreaking. They dressed nicely and always had money to throw around. Sydney 'Tanne' Nicolson was a brash, handsome sixteen-year-old with sparkling white teeth and a devil-may-care attitude. He operated with the Apache Kids in Athlone's Main Road. He was on the run from the law for robbery and hung out with us to evade capture. The local wannabe gangsters feared him and he was sort of our protector. He was quick with a knife and he was also a dog whisperer. He could entice any ferocious dog to eat out of the palm of his hand. We were gathered on our corner shooting the breeze one day when we heard a voice screaming, '*Fight!*'

Tanne shouted, '*Lat os dala!*' (Let's go!) We hurried towards the scene of the fight. It was happening in Koodoo Street, where I lived. Two muscled old street fighters, Mr Axe and Jubal, were facing up to each other. They had stripped off their shirts, exposing their tattooed bodies. They circled each other as the crowd gathered. Mr Axe, big and black, threw a punch at Jubal and smashed him in the mouth. Jubal spat blood, wiped his mouth with his hand and came onto Mr Axe again. Smelling blood, Mr Axe swung wildly and Jubal, slim and lithe, danced out and in. He ducked under Mr Axe's flailing arm and hit him with a left in the solar plexus and a terrific right uppercut, and Mr Axe hit the ground with a thud, his head hitting the curb painfully.

Mr Axe was dazed and stared around him. Jubal took him by the hand and pulled him up. The crowd cheered as the two fighters embraced and shook hands. I was mesmerised by the scene. They played to the crowd. They provided entertainment in the dreary streets of the township. On another Friday night the same shout of *'Fight!'* went up. I hurried to the scene to find Jubal on the ground, bleeding from a stab wound to his heart, and Mr Axe standing over him with a bloody knife in his hand. I felt deeply saddened and disappointed.

Dad was a good guitarist and the Minstrel bosses headhunted him to join their troupe. They paid him a stipend and he got a free uniform. Dad loved it because he could also drink for free. On a Saturday night, Dad came swaying down the court in full Minstrel's regalia, his face painted black and white. He was playing his guitar and singing, *'Julle kan vi my ma loe, julle kan vi my ma loe ...'*, loosely translated as 'What you looking at ...?'

People jeered at him. Solly burst out laughing and said, *'Hie kom jou dronk toppie, Johnnie.'* (Here comes your drunk dad, Johnnie.)

I hit him in the mouth, splitting his lip. *'Moetie kom kak praat van my ou nie!'* (Don't talk shit about my dad!)

Solly was shocked at my sudden violence. *'Ek maak maa net 'n joke,'* he said. (I was just joking.)

I glared at him. *'Djy maak kak jokes.'* (You make shit jokes.)

His brother Chip, a sharp-faced dude, bristled and stepped up to the plate. *'Djy kan mossie my broer soe moer nie.'* (You can't just hit my brother like that.)

Shorty whipped out his knife. *'Ek seconds daai, Johnnie. Djy praatie soe van family nie. Respek die mense!'* (I second that, Johnnie. You don't talk like that about family. Respect the people!)

Tanne, paring his nails with his knife, chuckled at the exchange while Robbie sucked on the tail end of a joint. Gif looked at him in disgust. *'Gooi weg daai fokken ding, Robbie, jou lippe is te lank.'* (Dump that fucking thing, Robbie, your lips are too long.)

Gimba chortled at the remark and Robbie changed the conversation. He told us that he had passed a house where he could have scored big time, except that the people had a big black German shepherd in their bathroom.

Tanne was all ears. *'Waa is die joint?'* (Where is this house?)

Robbie gave him the directions and Tanne turned to me. *'Kom, Johnnie, gan saam met my!'* (Come, Johnnie, come with me!)

I really did not want to go. '*Vat vi Robbie saam, hy wil mos by die hys inbriek.*' (Take Robbie with you, he wants to burgle the house.)

Tanne was insistent. '*Nei man ... nemma byt die hond sy lip af, of is djy bang?*' (No man ... just now the dog bites off his lip, or are you scared?)

I was scared alright, but I couldn't show my fear as Gimba goaded me, '*Johnnie issie bang nie, Tanne. Hy't 'n pluck!*' (Johnnie's not scared, Tanne. He's got pluck!) So I went with Tanne.

The house was in darkness when we got there. We jumped over the fence and sidled towards the house, keeping in the shadows as we approached the slightly open bathroom window. A dog growled softly. Tanne indicated for me to stay back and whispered to the dog, '*Ringo ... Ringo ... come boy ...*' Ringo came and stuck his head out the window and Tanne rubbed his head, whispering sweet nothings into his ears. Ringo jumped through the window into Tanne's arms and we left with the dog in tow. It was uncanny. I asked him how he knew the dog's name was Ringo.

Tanne grinned at me. '*Al die honne wat ek steel se name is Ringo.*' (All the dogs I steal I name Ringo.) He chuckled some more and asked me for my belt. I handed it to him and he looped it around Ringo's head. He told me I could have the dog. I didn't want it, but I felt empowered by the fact that Tanne trusted me.

The guys were amazed when we arrived at our corner with Ringo in tow. They were excited and Robbie exclaimed, '*Nei, julle is kwaai ouens.*' (No, you guys are good.) I basked in their admiration.

Later, after we split up, I was left standing with the dog that I did not want. I pondered the situation for a while. I knew there would be questions asked, and Mrs Lubbe would surely be suspicious if I suddenly became the owner of a dog. I hit on an idea and set off for Ballie's house.

I hung out across the road. Ballie was feeding his dogs – I could hear them growling viciously in a feeding frenzy. Ringo was hungry and his ears were like antennas, as he could hear them too. I picked up a stone and threw it onto Ballie's roof. Ballie's dogs stopped growling and howled. The back gate opened slightly and Ballie appeared, peering around. I let Ringo go and he bounded over the distance like a bullet from a gun. He ran head first into the gate as Ballie tried to close it. He rebounded and dashed inside the yard, knocking into Ballie, who stumbled and fell. Ringo attacked the three ridgebacks. The dogs growled horribly as they fought and Ballie had no idea where Ringo came from. The next evening, I overheard Dad telling mom that two of Ballie's dogs had been seriously wounded in a fight and had to be put down.

'*Fooitog*,' said Mom. (Shame.)

I felt vindicated.

Another sixteen-year-old called 'Mobster', a close companion of Tanne's, came to congregate on our corner. He was a funny chap who just wanted to be a tough guy. He was very talkative and laughed at his own feeble jokes. I didn't like him much because he was so full of himself. Early one Saturday night we were hanging on our corner when Tanne suggested, '*Ko os gan Road toe*.' (Let's go to the Road.) The main street in Athlone was called the 'Road'. I knew Tanne was wanted by the cops and that he was tempting fate, but he had a long panga pushed down his trousers.

The Road was crawling with people as we weaved through the crowds to get to our destination. A police car pulled up next to the curb and a white cop got out, gun in hand, which he pointed at Tanne. '*Nicolson! Staan vas!*' (Hold it!)

We stopped, but Tanne was having none of that. '*Fokkof!*' he said and took off, weaving between the pedestrians.

The cop went after him, shouting, '*Nicolson, stop!*'

Tanne turned, whipped out his panga and attacked the cop, slashing him across the head. The cop pressed his gun against Tanne's heart and shot him at point-blank range. Tanne dropped dead.

Mobster stood straddle-legged over Tanne and screamed defiance at the law. More cops arrived and beat Mobster with sjamboks, ripping the shirt off his back. They handcuffed him and threw him into the back of the van, where he lay bleeding and moaning in pain. I shoved a couple of cigarettes through the wire mesh of the van. We were sobered by the sudden death and violence that had ensued.

The following week, the township was abuzz with the news of Tanne's death, and his mother, an uppity woman who had always pleaded his innocence, was shattered. At his funeral on the Saturday there was a bus going to the graveyard, so seven of us jumped on. At the graveyard, the mourners gathered around the grave site, singing gospel hymns. Several gang members arrived, including the Apache Kids. The leader, Apache, a stout light-skinned dude with a thick plait of black hair hanging down his back, walked right up to the coffin with five other gang members. All of them were dressed in black chalk-stripe suits and black Stetson hats. The mourners murmured as they gathered around the coffin with the wreath on top. Silence fell as Apache plucked a flower from the wreath and said, '*Os iet 'n blommetjie by sy graf.*' (We eat a flower at his grave.) His followers followed suit, taking a flower each, putting it into their mouths and eating it. Then they turned and walked away, towards a big black car parked in a lane. They got in and the car kicked up dust as they drove off at speed.

On a cold winter's night, I left Mom and my sisters sitting on the back porch and sneaked away to our corner. Gimba and Shorty were gathered around a fire brazier. I was fuelling the fire with tomato crates when Gif arrived with a big parcel of red penny polonies. Gimba's eyes glittered at the sight and he plucked three polonies from the string. '*Jirre, Gif, djy's 'n baas.*' (Jeez, Gif, you're a boss.)

Shorty took two. '*Djy's ytgevriet, Giemba, djy gryp soema drie?*' (You're a glutton, Gimba, why did you grab three?)

Gif and I took two each, stuck them on short pieces of wire that we hid in the long grass and held them over the flames. The polonies crackled and popped, the fat dripping into the fire making a soft hissing sound. Gimba finished off his first polony and concentrated on the next one. '*Ek het 'n kwaai Western gewatch vi'dag innie bies. Die stuk se naam is Shane.*' (I watched a cool Western in the bioscope today. The film is called *Shane*.)

I was feeling glum and not really interested in what he was saying. '*Djy's gelukkig, vi'tel os 'n bietjie.*' (You're lucky, tell us about it.)

Gif chortled. '*Hy'sie gelukkig nie, sy pa vi'koep dagga!*' (He's not lucky, his dad sells dagga!)

Gimba swung a wild punch at Gif, which he evaded. '*Djy bly fok met my, Gif!*' (You're always fucking with me, Gif!)

'*But your Dad does sell dagga,*' said Gif. Gimba grabbed him by the shirt front and they went into a scuffle, rolling around in the long grass.

Shorty got irritated with them. '*Los jou kak, Gif, lat hy die fokken storie vi'tel!*' (Stop your shit, Gif, and let him tell the fucking story!)

They let go of each other and Gimba stared into the flames of the fire. '*Aag, fok'ie storie!*' (Aah, fuck the story!) We sat in silence for a while, then Gimba's eyes lit up. '*Ek onthou nou 'n kwaai lyn.*' (I just remembered a cool line.) He embraced Shorty and mimicked the character in the film. '*A gun is only a tool, Marion, you must remember that.*' Gimba made as if he was going to kiss him and Shorty pushed him away.

'*Fok weg, Gimba! Vi'tel djy aaire 'n storie, Johnnie, die ding kan mossie stories vi'tel nie.*' (Fuck off, Gimba! Why don't you tell a story, Johnnie, this thing can't tell a story.)

I was in no mood to tell stories. '*Ek'it niks stories vi'dag nie,*' I said. (I got no stories today.)

Gimba took a battered joint from his shirt pocket and lit it by the flame of the fire. He sat back and coolly sucked at the joint.

Gif got all excited and asked for a puff. '*Gie 'n skyf daa, Gimba?*'

Gimba ignored him, tugged at the joint again and blew the smoke into Gif's face. None of us had ever smoked dagga and it was a new experience.

I asked him, '*Gan djy die hele pil ytroek, Gimba?*' (Are you going to smoke the whole joint?)

Gimba passed the joint to me and I took a leisurely tug and almost coughed my lungs out. They cackled with laughter. I tried again and the hit made me dizzy, so I passed it on. I peered into the flames as the joint made its round. '*Hoor julle dromme...?*' I asked. (Do you hear drums...?)

Shorty gave me a strange look. '*Watte dromme? Djy's geroek, Johnnie! Vi'tel 'n fokken storie.*' (What drums? You're stoned, Johnnie! Tell a fucking story.)

Well, I thought I heard drums and I tapped a beat on the tin drum I was sitting on. '*Okay! Verbeel julle, os is innie woud en os sien 'n ou daar by 'n vuurtjie sit, hy is besig om ghoemadromme te maak. Dan tel hy sy eie ghoemadrom op en slaan so 'n stadige ritme... Dan skielik verskyn*' *daar 'n meisie oppie toneel … 'n lekker meisie …'* (Okay! Imagine we are in a forest and we see a guy sitting by a small fire, he is making ghoema drums. Then he picks up his own drum and starts to beat a slow rhythm … A girl suddenly appears on the scene … a sexy girl …)

Shorty gave a low whistle. *'Ek sal mos likes om soe 'n kin te meet.'* (I would like to meet a girl like that.)

'Maa djy kan dan nie eers stryt pee nie, Shorty,' said Gif. (But you can't even pee straight, Shorty.)

'Hou jou fokken bek, Gif, djy likes om kak te praat!' (Shut your fucking mouth, Gif, you like to talk shit!)

Suddenly four gangsters stepped into the firelight. Their leader was a rotund thug with the words 'Kannie Worry' (Can't Worry) tattooed across his forehead. Behind him were 'Boy Terror' and two others. Both Kannie Worry and Boy Terror wore shiny black cowboy boots. The stench of dagga smoke hung on them like an invisible cloud.

Kannie Worry eyeballed my polonies on the wire and demanded, *'Ek's honger, gie daai worsies hie!'* (I'm hungry, hand over those polonies!)

I stood up and backed off. *'No ways …'*

His right boot shot out and struck me in the belly, winding me, and I slumped to the ground.

Gif went for his knife and Boy Terror kicked him in the ribs, sending the knife flying. Then he hit Gif with a knuckleduster in his face, splitting his lip and sending Gif sprawling. Gimba shoved his last polony into his mouth and the third thug smacked him so hard that he spat out polony pieces and went crashing into Shorty, and both of them went down.

Kannie Worry gave a guttural laugh, put his boot on my back, pulled my shirt out of my pants and cleaned his boots with it. *'My boots makee 'n polish.'* (My boots need a polish.) Then they robbed us of our polonies and moved on, laughing as they went.

Gif scrambled up, found his knife and was about to go after them. His eyes were crazy mad.

'Vang jou tyd, Gif!' I said. *'Osse tyd gan kom!'* (Hang on, Gif! Our time will come!)

Gif screamed into the night, waving his knife in the air. *'Daai fokken*

Kannie Worry sal nou moet begin worry! Ek gan hom kry!' (That fucking Kannie Worry must start worrying now! I'm going to get him!)

Gif's lip was bleeding, so I took a cloth out of my pocket and dabbed at the blood. Up close and personal, he smiled as he looked into my eyes and whispered, *'Djy's my broer, Johnnie ...'* (You're my brother, Johnnie ...)

I looked at him deep down and I could see the loneliness in his eyes. *'Allie tyd, my mieta, allie tyd ...'* (All the time, my friend, all the time ...)

Shorty gave Gimba a hand up and grinned at his polony-splattered jersey. *'Soe, djy het jou cut weg, Gimba?'* (So, you had your cut, Gimba?)

'Fok jou!' Gimba said.

Part Two

The Young Ones

6

The bicycle

A new gang called the Invaders flourished in Block 1 of the flats situated a short distance away from where we hung out. One night a group of ten Invaders cornered me on our turf. 'Green Eyes', a barrel-chested dude with short, thin legs, told me, '*Kykie, djy en jou brasse moet same os koppel.*' (Look here, you and your brothers must join us.)

I was not interested. '*Nei, os is olraait soes os is.*' (No, we're alright as we are.)

Green Eyes snarled at me. '*Wie de fok is djy om vi my te vi'tel julle's olraait?*' (Who the fuck are you to tell me you're alright?) Then he slapped me and his henchmen joined the fray, kicking and beating me in a frenzy of violence. I lay comatose on the ground and Green Eyes had the last word. '*Next time skop ek jou dood!*' (Next time I'll kick you dead!) I simmered with pain and fury.

I sat down on our corner holding my head, and then I whistled our call. In the distance I heard two replies and soon Gif and Shorty came racing each other down the alleyway. They fell silent as they saw my swollen face. '*Wiet jou soe gemoer, Johnnie?*' Gif asked. (Who fucked you up like this?)

Gimba arrived, his head bowed in despair.

I snarled at them, '*Waa de hel is julle ouens as 'n man julle nodig het?*' (Where the hell are you guys when I needed you?)

Gimba was morose. '*Ek moes my toppie help by die joint.*' (I had to help my dad at home.)

I spat blood. '*Jou toppie gehelp? Kyk hoe lyk ek! Die is soema kak die, os moet 'n pact sign!*' (You had to help your dad? See how I look! This is bullshit, we must sign a pact!)

'*Ek seconds daai,*' said Shorty, '*dan kan os staan soes 'n family.*' (I second that, then we can stand as a family.)

Gif whipped out his knife. *'Ek wil die enforcer wies!'* (I want to be the enforcer!)

Gimba added, *'En ek wil 'n groot merchant wies, groter as my fokken pa!'* (And I want to be a big merchant, bigger than my fucking dad!)

Shorty said, *'Ek sal die money man wies, soe daai mean Johnnie trek die vrag.'* (I'll be the money man, so that means Johnnie is the leader.)

I liked that. *'Salute! Os kan os eie kroon kyk en os moer enige ding wat os pla, maa as djy eers in is, kan jy nie weer ytkom nie!'* (Salute! We look for our own money and we fuck up anybody who bothers us, but once you're in, there's no way out!) Then I added: *'Nog iets! Dis man vang, man staan! Stem julle?'* (Another thing! If you get caught, you take the rap! Do you agree?)

They nodded their agreement. We used Gif's knife and made a small cut on our wrists and put our hands upon each other's. We were family.

'Soe,' said Gimba, *'is die anners ouens oek betrokke innie pact?'* (So, are the other guys also involved in this pact?)

Gif answered in gangster slang, *'Hulle's nie nou hie nie, soe hulle moet net dala soes os hulle wys!'* (They're not here now, so they've just got to do what we dictate!)

One day Dad came home with an old bicycle that he had salvaged on the rubbish dump. *'Hie's 'n bike, Johnnie, miskien kan djy dit regmaak.'* (Here's a bike, Johnnie, maybe you can repair it.)

I got all excited and started stripping it immediately. I got some emery paper and sandpapered the frame. After I was done, Dad gave me a brush and a small tin of blue paint that he had salvaged and I lovingly gave it a coat of paint. I left it to dry before I tackled the spokes, cleaning them shiny bright. The distillery truck came to fetch a load of cleaned bottles so I bought new tyres, repaired the punctures and – *voila* – the bicycle was roadworthy. Mom was so proud that she bought me a bell and a light. So started a new adventure and my sisters had to pay me to ride on my bike.

Then Dad decided on a new venture. He had made a connection with Mr Ahmedia, a shop owner in Rylands Estate, to sell Christmas hamper stamps. I was appointed as the salesman. Dad summoned me to sit down, gave me a book of stamps and explained, '*Djy begin eeste by familie en mense wat os ken, en hulle sal vi anner mense vi'tel, soe gan die biesigheid groei.*' (You start with family and friends we know first, and they will pass on the word, that's how the business will grow.)

On Friday nights I would fly through the township streets on my bike, selling stamps and collecting money. It was exhilarating and a great experience. One Friday night I made my last stop at my Aunt Siesie's place in Silvertown. I came to a sliding stop at the curb and was about to push my bike onto the porch where two of my older cousins were chilling with beers, but my cousin Deon told me to leave it at the curb, because it would be safe there. They looked big and tough sitting there dressed in shorts and white vests. They were seafarers and they were seldom at home when I went there. Silvertown was always my last stop because my aunt always gave me biscuits and a cool drink and sometimes a parcel of fresh fish that my cousins had brought home from the sea.

I left the bike at the curb and went inside, where my aunt welcomed me with biscuits and cool drinks. Aunt Siesie knew all about my dad's drunken actions. '*Hoe gaan daarby die huis, Johnnie? Is jou Pa darem nugter?*' (How are things at home, Johnnie? Is your dad sober?) Every Friday she asked the same questions and I gave the same answer. '*Hy's olraait, antie Siesie …*' (He's alright, Auntie Siesie …)

Suddenly I heard a commotion from outside. I jumped up and ran to the front door to find a pockmarked thug smashing my bike in the street. He picked it up again and smashed it to the ground. His three drunken cronies cackled with laughter as the front wheel deserted the frame and rolled down the street. My two cousins sat frozen in fright. I ran into the street, shouting, '*My bike! Ek gan 'n saak maak!*' (My bike! I'm going to lay a charge against you!)

Pock Marks gave a derogatory chuckle as they swaggered off. '*Fokkie Law!*' (Fuck the Law!)

I stared in disgust at my cousins through a blur of tears. They were scared.

I ran off, leaving my shattered bike in the street. At the bus stop, I got onto a Golden Arrow bus heading for Black River and got off at the

Athlone police station. I entered and stood uncertainly in the doorway. There was a lone white policeman behind the counter, hanging onto the phone. On a bench against the wall, a knife victim was clutching a bloody rag to a neck wound. A drunk was horizontal on the floor. He had wet himself right up to his armpits. I sidestepped the drunk and stood at the counter, clearing my throat to attract the cop's attention. The cop scanned me once and carried on his conversation on the phone.

I knocked lightly on the counter. '*Meneer...?*' (Sir...?)

The cop glared at me, covered the mouthpiece with his hand and snarled, '*Wat soek jy!?*' (What do you want!?)

'*My bike...*' I said.

He put the phone down and got into my face and snarled again, '*Fokkof! Sê vir jou ouers hulle moet hierna toe kom!*' (Fuck off! Tell your parents to come here!) Then he added, '*Meneer... Fokkof!*' (Sir... Fuck off!)

I retreated in fright. I stopped at the door and said, '*Fok jou oek!*' (Fuck you too!)

The cop jumped over the counter as I dashed out the door. Eyes blurred with tears, I jaywalked between the oncoming traffic to evade the cop. My hatred for white men was born.

At home I explained the whole episode to my parents. Dad was raging: '*Jou fokken cousins is cowards!*' (Your fucking cousins are cowards!)

The perimeters of our township were surrounded by thick Port Jackson bush and people had made several footpaths through it to reach the main street of Athlone. The police Land Rovers had also made a wider path on their patrols through the area. Frustrated by the loss of my bike and by the way the police had treated me, I started my own private vendetta against the law. At night I would hang out in an alleyway until a Land Rover drove slowly through the wide pathway. I would pelt the van with stones then disappear down the alley, flying over high walls and sagging fences. I was high on danger.

Every Wednesday, the Empire Cinema (which everyone called the 'Oubaas') had 'tickey' (two and a half cents) bioscopes and Cliff Richard's movie *The Young Ones* was screening. So my friends and I gathered our coin and went to the matinee show. We bought our tickets and went upstairs, where most of the audience were gangsters from the community and surrounding areas. The air was thick with dagga smoke, and chalices of dagga flickered like fireflies in the dark. We found our seats and settled down with a Gold Dollar filter cigarette each as the title *The Young Ones* appeared on the screen.

Suddenly a figure appeared in the light of the projector and stood blinded and confused in front of the balcony as his eyes searched for a seat. A voice shouted, '*Hei! Ballie Honne-oor! Fok yt die pat yt!*' (Fuck out of the way!) There was a sudden awakening inside of me and I slid down the aisle, grabbed Ballie by his turn-ups and tilted him over the balcony. Ballie screamed as he flew over the balcony before crashing into the seats below. A woman shrieked when Ballie landed.

I slipped back into my seat as the ushers attended to Ballie's broken leg. Gimba whispered to me in shocked surprise, '*Daai's hectic! Wat het hy gemaak?*' (That's hectic! What did he do?)

'*Dit was 'n ongeluk,*' I said. (It was an accident.)

Gimba gave me a strange look. '*Moetie met my kak praat nie, Johnnie.*' (Don't talk shit to me.)

After the bioscope came out, I was on a high from wreaking vengeance on Ballie, so I started singing the chorus of *The Young Ones* and the others joined in as we swaggered down the main street.

We stopped at a shop where four girls were window-shopping. The tallest of the four jumped back as we stopped. Shorty chuckled, '*Sy's 'n bietjie nervous …*' (She's a little nervous …) Shorty threw his arms around her and picked her up. '*Ko os march met die kind!*' (Let's march with this girl!) We burst out laughing at the sight of him trying to hold the tall girl above the ground. The girl screamed, attracting the attention of the passers-by.

'*Lossie kin, Shorty!*' I snarled at him. (Let the girl go!)

'*Djy's vol kak, Johnnie,*' Shorty said as he let her go. (You're full of shit.)

We swaggered on down the main street. On our way home we passed the Pentecostal church and we heard the choir singing. I knew my mom attended the church and did not want to linger.

'*Ko os gat in,*' said Gif. (Let's go inside.)

I wanted nothing of that. '*Nei man … my tanie gat hie kerk … kom os gooi ve'by.*' (No man … my mother attends this church … let's move on.)

'*Is djy bang, Johnnie?*' Gimba said. '*Ko os gat jol 'n bietjie.*' (Are you scared, Johnnie? Let's go dance a little.)

'*Ja man, os gat in!*' said Shorty. (Yes man, let's go inside!) He led the way inside and I followed reluctantly.

Inside the church the band was in full swing, with a banjo and a guitar. The congregants were running around in circles, clapping their hands and stamping their feet to the rhythm of the beat. Gif joined the circle, twisting and turning and doing high kicks in the air. Shorty and Gimba roared with laughter and joined in as the banjo man glared at them. I tugged at Gif's arm as he twirled past. '*Die ou met die banjo watch julle, kom os gooi.*' (The guy with the banjo is watching you, let's go.)

Gif was having none of that and pulled out of my grasp. '*Hoeko? Ek wil jol!*' (Why? I wanna dance!)

My eyes searched for my mom. I latched on to her sitting in the front row, her hair covered with a scarf. She held her Bible close to her bosom, her lips moving in silent prayer. Suddenly she got up and whirled and twirled her way towards the centre of the running circle, her long hair tumbling and covering her face. She spoke in a strange tongue. A babble of words poured out of her mouth. The music stopped and the circle of congregants came to a standstill and sang the Lord's praises. Mom translated the prophecy and I was shocked by this new phenomenon. She brushed back her hair and I saw she had a black eye.

The pastor, a stocky dude, put down his guitar and picked up the microphone. '*Yes, Lord! This is a foot-stomping, devil-chasing, gospel explosion!*' The crowd roared and Gif, Gimba and Shorty slipped out the door, when Mom laid her hand on my shoulder. The pastor continued his tirade. '*Die Here praat met hierdie jong man vanaand! Hy moet hom bekeer voordat dit te laat is!*' (The Lord is speaking to this young man tonight! He must repent before it is too late!) The crowd closed in on us, praising the Lord. I swallowed hard as I reached for her hand. '*Kom, Ma, lat os hys toe gan …*' (Come, Mom, let's go home …)

Mom was silent on our way home, so I took the Bible from her hands. '*Ek sal die Bybel dra, Ma.*' (I'll carry the Bible, Mom.)

At home, she sat down at the table and opened her Bible. '*Kom sit, Johnnie, lees vir my Genesis 37 vanaf vers 3.*' (Come and sit, Johnnie, read Genesis 37 from verse 3.)

I read: '*En Israel het Josef meer lief gehad as al sy seuns, want hy was vir hom 'n seun van die ouderdom, en hy het vir hom 'n lang rok gemaak …*' (Now Israel loved Joseph more than all of his children, because he was the son of his old age, and he made him a dress of many colours …)

I pondered that for a moment. '*'n Rok?*' (A dress?)

Mom described with her hands. '*Dis 'n tipe van oorjas, Johnnie, amper soos die salaah-doeke wat die Muslim-mans dra.*' (It's a type of overcoat, Johnnie, almost like the prayer garb that Muslim men wear.)

I did not understand where this was leading to but I resumed reading. '*Toe sy broers sien dat hulle vader hom meer as sy ander broers liefhet, het hulle hom gehaat en kon nie vriendelik met hom praat nie. Ook het Josef 'n droom gehad wat hy aan sy broers vertel het. Daaroor het hulle hom nog meer gehaat …*' (And when his brothers saw that he loved him more than all of his brethren, they hated him and could not speak peacefully to him. And Joseph dreamed a dream and told it to his brethren and they hated him yet the more …)

Mom held up her hand for me to stop. '*Daai's genoeg, Johnnie.*' (That's enough, Johnnie.) I stopped and we sat in silence for a while. Then Mom whispered, her voice barely audible, '*Jy moet waaksaam wees, Johnnie … jy het 'n hoër roeping.*' (You must be watchful, Johnnie … you've got a higher calling.) Mom slipped an amulet from inside her bosom and hung it around my neck. She said it would keep me from harm.

I passed to Standard 6 and I was sent to Belgravia Secondary, a school that had recently been opened. Mom and Dad had scraped together some money and bought me a spanking new school uniform. There was not enough money for a decent pair of shoes, so they bought a cheap pair. Those shoes were a big problem and one night while running home from the shop, I lost a heel. I searched for the heel for most of the night but I could not find it. The next day, I walked as if I had a limp with my one heelless shoe. I was embarrassed, and during the school break I kept to myself instead of joining the other boys for a game of soccer.

7

The hawker

Mom was worried about me, so when the school closed for the June holidays she sent me to stay with her sister 'Sies Lucky' and Uncle Piet in Mara Avenue in Athlone, where they had a smallholding. Uncle Piet, aka 'Piet Linkie', was a towering man with a fierce temper and the gangsters feared him. He and Sies Lucky had about ten sons and three daughters. Three of them, Frankie, Lenny and Joey, were older, Tolla was my age and immensely jealous of the attention I got from his parents, and the others were all younger than me. Also in the house were Uncle Piet's parents, Ama and Apa, who slept on a high bed, plus his slightly deranged brother Manna.

All three of my older cousins were hawkers and each one had a horse and cart. Sometimes they sold fruit and vegetables, '*kreefdoppies*' (crayfish shells), '*snoekgrate*' (the spine of the snoek stripped of meat) and '*snoekkoppe*' (snoek heads). They had a lucrative business. In their yard they had racing pigeons, chickens, geese, ducks, goats, pigs, a monkey and lots of dogs. Lenny always wanted me to hawk with him, much to Tolla's chagrin. Lenny told him, '*Djy hettie style nie, Tolla. Johnnie kan vi'koep. Ry djy maa met Frankie.*' (You've got no style, Tolla. Johnnie can sell. You rather go with Frankie.) Frankie and Lenny were both gang members affiliated to the Vanguard Kids, who operated in Lawrence Road.

I liked Lenny: he was a smooth talker and a ladies' man. We would sell whatever load we had in a short period of time and we always returned to the yard first. I loved the horse-cart ride on the scenic route along the coast to Kalk Bay to go buy snoek at the harbour. While waiting for the boats to come in with their catch of the day, we would go swimming in the sheltered bay. When the boats came in, we would head back to the jetty and Lenny would barter with the fishermen until he got a good price and would buy a whole shipment of snoek. We would then head back to the township to sell our fish.

Lenny taught me how to blow the copper fish horn and I would blow my lungs out and the people would gather. Lenny would 'flek' the snoek with a large, sharp fish knife and take out the guts and roe. Most of the time he would hold back the roe for us to enjoy after the day's work was done. I loved the roe and fresh fish we ate.

Sies Lucky also taught me some philosophies. She told me to always wash my face with hot water in the morning before I went out to hawk, and she would supply a small tub of water. I stuck to that practice for most of my life.

I had a great time with Lenny. He had served time in prison, and after smoking a dagga joint or two he would share his prison experiences and wisdom with me. '*Een ding, Johnnie, djy moet nooit tronk toe gan nie, maa as djy eendag daar kom, moet djy nooit enige iets van 'n anner bandiet vat nie, en djy het oek nie norig om an die tronk nomme te vat nie.*' (One thing, Johnnie, you must never go to prison, but if you ever get there, never take anything from another convict and you don't have to join the prison number.)

He had a 28 tattoo between his right thumb and forefinger and I was curious about it. '*Nou hoeko het Lenny dan daai tronk nomme, Lenny?*' (Then why have you got the prison number, Lenny?)

He looked at me and said softly, '*Want ek was dom toe ek innie tronk kom, toe vat ek oek annie nomme. Nou loep die nomme same my en ek kannie daar yt kom nie.*' (Because I was stupid when I went to prison, so I took the number. Now the number walks with me and I can't get out.)

After we sold our load, Lenny would pay me, give me a 'fry', a parcel of fresh snoek and some roe, and drop me off at home. And indeed the number walked with him until he was stabbed to death in a dice game in Elsies River. I felt a great loss, as Lenny was my hero.

Shortly after that, Uncle Piet's property was confiscated and they moved to Via Kewtown, near Athlone Stadium and the 'Tickey Blokke', a set of four triple-storey flats. He sold two of his horses and carts and was left with only one horse and cart.

Via Kewtown was a new extension to the township and provided a new bus route that passed by the Tickey Blokke, where a gang called the Road Devils hung out. Joey, idle without his horse and cart, hooked up with the Road Devils, who specialised at jumping onto speeding buses, which had open platforms at the back. They would run alongside the bus, banging on the side to control their jump, grab the pole on the open platform and jump on. They would swing around the pole, rob the passengers and then they would do the 'backstroke' off the speeding bus – jumping off back to front – which took skill and perfect timing. If you mistimed it, you could be killed or maimed. The game was called 'chicken'.

When I visited them, Joey and Tolla, who was also a member of the Road Devils, always tried to initiate me into their gang. '*Komaan, Johnnie, join osse gang*,' Joey would say. (Come on, Johnnie, join our gang.) I wasn't interested but Joey still taught me the skill of jumping the bus. This skill I taught to my buddies and we would have great fun playing 'chicken' on Sunday nights, although we didn't rob any passengers.

Two more guys joined our group, Ebie and Hima. Ebie became quite good at taunting the bus drivers and became a known face to them. The drivers watched for us, and as soon as we jumped on the bus they would drive close to the lampposts along the way in an effort to shake us off. One night Ebie got unlucky: he swung around the pole, in and out, and his head smashed into a lamppost and he fell off. The ambulance arrived and took him to hospital. Two days later he walked out of hospital with a dent on the side of his head and his nickname became 'Smash'. He was never the same after that.

One sunny day I came home and found Grace and Cecelia washing blankets in a bathtub in the backyard. They were soaking wet. Mom was knitting on the porch. She put down her knitting and stomped over to them. She pulled up her dress, tucked it into her panties and got into the tub and told them, '*Soe moet julle dit doen*.' (This is how you should do it.) Grace and Cecelia got into the bathtub and stamped the blankets with their feet. Their laughter rang out in the clear air.

Suddenly Mom became serious and looked at me. '*Ek het vir Francis winkel toe gestuur, Johnnie. Gaan kyk waar maak sy so lank*.' (I sent Francis to the shop, Johnnie. Go and see what's taking her so long.)

The shop was crowded as usual. I looked for Francis there but could not find her. I searched for her among the crowd on the long porch outside the shop. I found her trapped in Boy Terror's arms in a secluded corner, with his cronies standing around, covering for him. I ran straight at them, shouting, *'Los my suster!'* (Let go of my sister!) Boy Terror turned smoothly on the heel of his cowboy boot and kicked me viciously in the belly. Winded and doubled over in pain I stumbled away, and Francis seized her chance and ran off. I ran around the corner of the shop and spotted an empty beer bottle, which I picked up, and I ran back towards Boy Terror and his cronies.

They were zonked and in stitches with laughter at my cowardice when I rushed at Boy Terror and smashed the bottle over his head. He hit the ground bleeding from a gash on his head and I jumped onto his chest. I held the jagged edge of the broken bottle against his throat and he pleaded, *'Asseblief…'* (Please …) I pushed harder, drawing blood, and Boy Terror screamed.

A police Land Rover, with sirens wailing and blue lights flashing, came to a screeching stop. I threw the bottle head on the ground, shattering it, as the siren blew out its last breath. Two white cops hung with guns got out and descended on the milling crowd. The first cop grabbed me by my wrists and pulled my arms painfully behind my back and brought out his handcuffs.

Dad came rushing onto the porch, sucking at oxygen. He pointed to Boy Terror and said, *'Wag nou! Die fokken gangster wil my dogter verkrag het!'* (Hold on! This fucking gangster wanted to rape my daughter!)

'Hy kan nie die wet in sy eie hande vat nie!' said the cop. (He can't take the law into his own hands!)

Dad tried to pull me out of the cop's grasp. *'Die's soema 'n klomp kak die!'* (This is a lot of bullshit!)

The cop whipped out his baton and smacked Dad on the head and he crashed into the bystanders. *'Fokkof, ou man!'* (Fuck off, old man!)

The crowd murmured when they put me into the back of the police van.

At the police station, the cop who had hit my dad took out a clean sheet of paper and took down my details. *'John Fredericks, jy word aangekla van aanranding met die doel om ernstig te beseer!'* (John Fredericks, you are being charged with assault with the intent to commit grievous bodily harm!)

'Maa hy wil my suster geryp het!' I protested. (But he wanted to rape my sister!)

The cop signed the document with a flourish. *'Jy kan dit vir die magistraat vertel môre in die hof.'* (You can tell that to the magistrate when you appear in court tomorrow.) He took my fingerprints and I had to hand in my belt and shoelaces, before he took me to the cells at the back of the police station. I was scared.

The cop unlocked the cell door and thrust me inside. Blinded for a moment, I stood with my back against the wall. When my vision cleared I saw four gangsters sitting on their bed of mats and blankets. I recognised them as the Apache Kids who I saw at Tanne's funeral. Apache himself lay on a high bed with a tight bandage around his naked torso. Above his head, written on the wall were the words *'They shot me in the back, they thought I was one-eyed Jack!'* Apache had been shot in the back.

Gammie, a short, slim dude with a scar across his upper lip, got up and smacked me a quick one-two across the face and lisped, *'Wie's djy!?'* (Who are you!?)

'Ek is Johnnie Fredericks,' I answered.

'Wat het djy gebring virrie ouens?' (What did you bring for us?)

'Niks.' (Nothing.)

Apache raised himself onto his elbows. *'Los hom, Gammie.'* (Let him go.) Apache beckoned me to come closer and he looked at me deep down. *'Is djy nie Tanne se tjommie nie?'* (Aren't you Tanne's buddy?)

I was tongue-tied and nodded wordlessly.

'Okay, Johnnie Boy ... vi'tel my waavoo is djy hie.' (Tell me why you're here.)

'Vi ... vi aanranding,' I stuttered. (For assault.)

He asked me who I had assaulted.

'Ek het vi Boy Terror aangerand, hy wil my suster verkrag het.' (I assaulted Boy Terror, he tried to rape my sister.)

Apache burst out laughing, clutching at his chest in mirth. *'Boy Terror, die cowboy?'* (Boy Terror, the cowboy?)

The other gang members also found it funny and joined in the laughter.

Gammie lit a tobacco joint and handed it to me. '*Nei, djy's daai ou, Johnnie Boy. Iemand moet al lankal vi Boy Terror gemoer het.*' (You're the man, Johnnie Boy. Somebody should have fucked up Boy Terror a long time ago.)

'*Onthou, Johnnie Boy,*' said Apache, '*as djy môre oppie hof verskyn, dan pleit djy onskuldig.*' (Remember, Johnnie Boy, when you appear in court tomorrow, you plead not guilty.)

The next day we went to court in Wynberg and were placed in the big holding cells beneath the courthouse. There were lots of prisoners being held there, from various communities and with different gang affiliations. Violence lurked and the place smelt of urine, tobacco and fear. Gammie and the other two Apache Kids robbed everyone in the cell. The frightened prisoners milled around. Two convicted prisoners, holding onto their leg irons, shuffled into the cell. They were 'Further Charges', men with further charges pending. They were dressed in blue checked prison suits.

Their chains rattled ominously as they dragged them along the cement floor and headed in my direction. Apache was standing in a corner and beckoned me over. '*Staan diekant toe, Johnnie Boy.*' (Stand this side, Johnnie Boy.) I took up a position behind Apache.

The first convict took exception to Apache's intervention. '*Aweh! Wie's djy dan vi'dag?*' (Aweh! Who are you today?)

'*Ek is Apache 26 sterk bene son-op,*' he said, using code words of the 26s. (I'm Apache 26 strong legs sunrise.)

The two convicts were also 26 prison gang members, so they gave each other the thumbs-up salute and started to sabela the number.

A court orderly appeared and called my name. Apache gave me the thumbs-up. '*Kyk vas, Johnnie Boy.*' (Heads up, Johnnie Boy.)

I entered the juvenile courtroom from the holding cells below and looked fleetingly at the gallery. My mom was there, clutching her Bible close to her bosom.

The magistrate, a skinny, thin-lipped white dude with small round glasses, entered the courtroom and everyone stood up. He tugged at his robe and sat down. He looked at me fleetingly before reading the file. My knees trembled. I was on my own.

He looked up and addressed me. '*John Fredericks, jy word aangekla van aanranding met die doel om ernstig te beseer. Wat pleit jy?*' (John Fredericks, you are accused of assault with the intent to do grievous bodily harm. How do you plead?)

'*Hy wil my suster verkrag het, u edele.*' (He wanted to rape my sister, your honour.)

The magistrate looked at me over the top of his glasses and snarled, '*Antwoord net die vraag!*' (Just answer the question!)

'*Onskuldig, u edele ... my suster ...*' (Not guilty, your honour ... my sister ...)

He cut me off. '*Het hy jou suster verkrag!?*' (Did he rape your sister!?)

'*Nee, maar ek ...*' (No, but I ...)

The dude was in a bad mood and he cut me off again. '*Hy het nog nie jou suster verkrag nie, maar toe vat jy die reg in jou eie hande?*' (He did not rape your sister, and yet you took the law in your own hands?)

My stomach rumbled and I had a sudden urge to go to the toilet. I looked to the prosecutor but there was no help from his side, as if he too was scared of the magistrate. I felt as if I was going to shit myself, but I retorted, '*Moet ek dan gewag het totdat hy haar verkrag het?*' (Should I have waited until he raped her?)

The magistrate lost it. '*Jy is 'n swaar asem; ek vind jou skuldig en vonnis jou tot ses houe met die ligte rottang!*' (You are a troublemaker; I find you guilty and sentence you to six lashes with a light cane!)

I was taken back down the stairs to the holding cells and deposited into a smaller cell. There were other juveniles present who were also waiting to get lashes.

An older boy was sitting on the floor with his pants off, his bare butt on the cold cement. I stared at him and he grinned at me. '*Trek jou broek af en vries jou gat, dan is dit nie soe seer nie!*' (Drop your pants and freeze your butt, then it won't hurt so much!)

All eyes were on me and I hesitated momentarily, plucked up my courage, dropped my pants and suppressed a shiver as I sat down on the cold floor.

A white male nurse and a coloured cop entered the cell. The nurse pulled up his nose at the smell of faeces from the blocked toilet. The coloured cop, big and strong with a strong smell of liquor on his breath, had no problem and went about his task of dealing out lashes with a smirk on his face.

The six lashes did not hurt so much, and when I was released Mom was waiting for me outside the court. '*Ek hoop jy het nou 'n les geleer, Johnnie.*' (I hope you've learnt a lesson now, Johnnie.)

Dad was not so forthcoming. '*Hy gan nie nou hoor nie, Kettie; hy't mos nou tronk geproe.*' (He's not going to listen now, Kettie; he's had a taste of prison now.)

I was fourteen years old and halfway through Standard 7 when I was expelled from school. I was labelled a troublemaker, a skollie. Suddenly I had status among my fellows and Boy Terror gave me a wide berth.

I was at a crossroads in my life. Mom was on my case all the time, so I stayed at home and I had a lot of chores to do every day. I fed the chickens, cleaned the coop, chopped firewood, and scrubbed and polished the floors, with Mom breathing down my neck.

One day she decided that I had to go and find a job. She told me to go to the labour bureau in Cape Town and see if I could find work.

I was glad to get out of the house, so I took a train from Athlone railway station to Cape Town and walked to the labour bureau. The waiting area was packed with unemployed coloured people from all walks of life. A guy came out of an office with a sheet of paper in hand and announced that a building company needed six men to do bricklaying. Ten men got up and showed him their papers. He selected six of them, took down their names and sent them on their way. Three gangsters walked in and hustled everybody for money and robbed a guy of his wristwatch. Nobody did anything to stop them.

I hung around until late afternoon when the office guy appeared again. He said that Lyons Green Label Tea in Observatory was looking for five young men for casual work. This seemed like a good enough way to earn some money and I was selected with four other boys from various townships across the Cape Flats. We had to report at the factory the following day and Mom was very happy when I got home and gave her the news.

I arrived at the factory early the next morning to find the other boys already there and we started work inside the warehouse. We had to stack boxes of tea right up to the ceiling but I was happy doing it. The reason why they hired us in the first place was that they were launching a new brand of tea into the market. The new brand was Seven Seas Tea and we were transported to a township where we had to hand out leaflets and small samples of the tea.

The people then had to stick the leaflet onto their windows, and when we came back three weeks later, whoever was still displaying the leaflet won a beautiful serving tray with a ship painted on it with the Seven Seas logo. They also got boxes of tea as part of the prize. It was exhilarating, and for the next three months we covered several townships across the Cape Flats. We got paid less than ten rand a week, but Mom was happy and I was glad that I could make her smile again. She also liked her pink tea and I always brought home bags of samples and she would drink tea to her heart's content.

A downside of the job was that we had to wear yellow oilskin coats, like the fishermen wore at sea, even in the heat of summer. Plus there was Norman the supervisor, a wannabe wrestler who would wrestle the other guys during our lunch break, which could be anywhere, at a shop or an open field. He would wrestle them to the ground and stuff dog poo into their mouths. He didn't bother with me much, as I was always sitting to one side reading a book. I always carried a book in my back pocket, plus a knife.

One Friday afternoon he threw caution to the wind, grabbed me from behind and wrestled me to the ground. The memory of Ballie on top of me seared through my brain. As he tried to shove the dog shit into my mouth, I whipped out my knife and stabbed him in the arm. He screamed as the blood spurted from the wound. The police were called and I was arrested again. They also docked my week's salary. Mom was shattered.

In juvenile court I appeared before the same magistrate as before, who almost gleefully sentenced me to another six lashes with the light cane.

8

Street life

The alley corner where we hung out was at the entrance to our township, so we were sort of gatekeepers. The alley divided six courts of semi-detached houses in half, and most people used it to get to their homes. From our corner we could see everyone and everything entering the township.

Many of the pedestrians lingered on our corner on their way home from work. We were homeboys, and if you showed us love we would show you love back. We greeted everybody but if you didn't acknowledge our greeting or our presence, you became a target for abuse and profanity, or you might even be robbed. We would also help the elderly with their groceries and carry it home for them. Some of them would give us a tip or some fruit. Our crew grew. Some guys were bookworms who loved reading, and those who came to exchange books with me were always welcome. We would tell stories and discuss books and authors. We also loved to sing. After smoking some 'slow boats' we would harmonise until late at night. Sadly I was never welcome in their homes; to their parents I was the original 'bad company'. So I was always on the outside.

Then Shorty's dad got him a job at a plant nursery as a bicycle messenger delivering plants and invoices to various companies. After a while they trusted him to do the banking too. One night while the four of us were smoking a joint around the fire brazier he told us about his escapades for the day and the amount of money that he had deposited in the bank. Shorty was a money lover and his eyes lit up when he spoke about it. '*Ek het tienduisend rand in my hand gehet vi'dag, my broerse.*' (I had ten thousand rand in my hands today, brothers.) He spoke with his hands, indicating the magnitude of the money.

Gimba gave a low whistle. '*Daai's 'n moerse klom geld, Shorty. Djy kan mos weghardloep met die pak!'* (That's a lot of money, Shorty. You should run away with the package!)

An idea was born.

'*Os kan jou mos rob, Shorty,*' I suggested. '*Djy moet net sê wanne.*' (We can rob you, Shorty. You must just say when.)

Shorty was game. '*Os kannit Maandagoggend soe omtrent tienuur doen, dan vat ek die hele weekend se takings bank toe.*' (We can do it on Monday morning about ten o'clock, because then I have to deposit the whole weekend's takings.)

I liked the idea and I set out the plan. We would wait for Shorty opposite the bank, I said. If he had the money, he would light a cigarette as a sign. We would overpower him and Gif would scratch him with his knife to verify that he was robbed.

Gif grinned at Shorty. '*Salute! Net 'n krappie.*' (Just a scratch.)

Gimba brought forth another slow boat and we sat and smoked in silence. Four storybook characters planning a robbery.

Early Monday morning Gif, Gimba and I jumped a bus and hitched a ride to Mowbray. Each of us had a knife and a balaclava in our pockets. We were five minutes early and we hung out outside a clothing store across the street from the bank and pretended to do window-shopping. The minutes ticked by agonisingly slowly. We were high on danger. Then Shorty arrived on his delivery bike with its box in front. He pushed the front wheel into a bike slot, chained it, and lit a cigarette.

We pulled the balaclavas over our heads and dashed across the street. As Shorty reached for a satchel of money in the box, we struck.

Gimba threw his arms around Shorty, and I went for the satchel of money. Shorty reacted violently, holding onto the satchel and resisting us. That was not in the script, and Gif stabbed him hard in the arm, which wasn't in the script either. Shorty screamed in pain at the sight of his flowing blood. We took off. We were fleet-footed and got away with the money before anybody could react. Our first robbery had been a success.

We hid the satchel of money and lay low for the whole day until Shorty arrived after spending time in hospital to have his wound stitched. The cops had taken his statement, but Shorty had stuck to his story that he could not recognise any of the robbers. He was pissed off with Gif. *'Djy het my nogal fokken regtig gestiek, jou fokken rot!'* (You fucking stabbed me for real, you fucking rat!)

'Maa djy wil dan nie die fokken geld lossie!' Gif protested. (But you wouldn't let go of the money!)

Our haul was R20 000 and we split it four ways, but Shorty was unhappy. *'Ek moet mere kry yt die deal yt, ek was met die mes gestiek!'* (I should get more out of the deal, I was stabbed with the knife!)

'Fok jou, daai's jou eie skuld!' said Gimba. (Fuck you, it's your own fault!)

I intervened, telling Shorty that he would have to keep a low profile at work, and not to advertise his newfound wealth but to behave like a robbery victim. Alas! Shorty was put on sick leave for two days and he went to the Hat Centre in Plein Street in Cape Town and bought himself a new wide-brimmed Stetson hat.

He went back to work wearing the hat, which immediately aroused his boss's suspicion. The guy called the cops and Shorty was arrested, but he refused to give us up and took the rap. He was sentenced to ten lashes and lost his job and we bought ourselves some fancy clothes.

One night Gif, Shorty and I were on our corner. Gif and Shorty were on their haunches, boning their shoes. A small metal plaque high on a wall read 'Spitting Prohibited'.

I watched as a police Land Rover climbed over the curb and entered the bush. I picked up a couple of stones and threw them at the van. The van swerved and drove into a tree stump. The wheels kicked up sand as the driver tried to gain traction.

Gif jumped up. *'Wat de fok?'* (What the fuck?) He picked up a couple of stones and thumped them against the van. Shorty giggled gleefully and followed suit.

A cop jumped out of the van and fired a flurry of shots in our direction. We ducked into the alleyway and fled, jumping over walls and hedges. The cop fired more shots and gave chase. The bullets ricocheted off the walls of the houses. The cop was hard on our heels and gaining on us when we reached Gimba's place. We went clattering over the corrugated-iron fence and jumped into the yard.

Mr C and Gimba were busy rolling dagga sticks. Mr C grabbed the newspaper loaded with dagga, bundled it up, and gave it to Gimba. '*Shaft'it daa agter!*' (Shaft it at the back!)

Gimba disappeared around the back of the house as Mr C grabbed us and pulled us into the shadows as the cop ran past. He had a gun in his hand. He waited until the cop's boots faded into the distance before putting the safety on. '*Waamee is julle bymekaa?*' (What are you up to?)

I tried to catch my breath. '*Die boere, Mr C, os het net daa oppie hoek gestaan toe skiet hulle op os!*' (The cops, Mr C, we were just standing there on our corner when the cops opened fire on us!)

Mr C bared his gold dentures in a ferocious grin. '*Moetie met my ko kak praatie! Ek het oek an 'n gang behoort toe ek 'n laaitie was!*' (Don't talk shit to me! I also belonged to a gang when I was a kid!)

Mr C's premises were littered with empty dagga papers. '*Moetie soe rondstaan nie,*' he said. '*Kry vi julle man-man 'n biesem en maak die jaart skoon!*' (Don't just stand around. Grab a broom each and sweep the yard!)

We grabbed a broom each and started sweeping while Mr C sat down at a table and counted his money, his gun close at hand. I glanced enviously at the stacks of money. He caught my eye and read my mind. '*Guns en kroon gie vi jou krag ... maa ees moet djy jouself bewys!*' (Guns and money give you power ... but first you have to prove yourself!)

Gimba, always trying to please his dad, queried, '*Os kan osself bewys, Pa.*' (We can prove ourselves, Dad.)

Mr C looked at us for a long moment as if contemplating an idea. He tapped on his wristwatch with his finger. '*Nie nou al nie, met tyde saam ...*' (Not now, sometime soon ...)

From then on, we roamed the streets and hustled for money every day. We would walk into a clothing store, intimidate the workers, take clothing from their shelves and leave without paying for it. We took risks. One night we stopped at the Ole, an Indian restaurant, and smelt the curry wafting out the door, so we decided to go inside and take a table. The owner, who spoke in broken English, looked at us in suspicion and approached us. '*What you want ... you have money to pay ...?*'

I showed him a roll of money and addressed him in posh English.

'*Can we have four plates of curry and rice please, and a milkshake each?*' The guy was still unsure about us but the money convinced him. He turned away and I spoke again. '*Sir, could we have eight samosas for starters, please?*' He seemed to like my tone of voice and wrote down the order. The food came and we devoured it in quick time under the owner's watchful eye. But I had my eye on the wall clock that read 8:55. I knew that a bus passed the restaurant at 9:00. I cleaned up my plate and sipped on my milkshake, while the others all watched me. At 8:59 I got up, took out my money and approached the owner as if I was going to pay the bill. He went to stand behind the cash register and I dashed out the door. The others scrambled after me with the owner in hot pursuit, screaming abuse at us in his own tongue.

The bus careened around the corner at full speed and we lined up in a row on the pavement. We banged on the side of the bus with both hands as it flashed past, grabbed the pole and swung aboard, leaving the restaurant owner stranded on the street.

Soon after that I got a message from Mr C that he wanted to see us. When I arrived there, my three buddies were sitting at a small table, playing cards. There were a lot of older gangsters in the yard imbibing expensive liquor. I joined my buddies and after a while Mr C walked over, put his gun onto our table and spoke in whispered syllables. '*Dis tyd dat julle ouens moet bewys.*' (It's time for you guys to prove yourselves.)

I was all ears as I stared at the gun.

Mr C continued. '*Hippy en sy 28 broerse smokkel oek nou en hulle trek ál my customers.*' (Hippy and his 28 brothers are also dealing now and they are attracting all my customers.) His words hung in the air and we waited in anticipation. '*Soe, Hippy moet val.*' (So, Hippy must fall.)

Mr C took hold of the gun and spun it, and when it stopped the muzzle of the gun was pointed between me and Gimba. Gimba seized the moment to please his dad and went for the gun. '*Ek kan dit doen, Pa.*' (I can do it, Dad.)

His father stopped him. '*Minute, Richard, volgens nomme, die gun wys mee na Johnnie toe.*' (Hold on, Richard, as the number dictates, the gun is pointed more at Johnnie.)

Gimba's eyes flashed angrily at me. I stuck the gun down the front of my pants and we left for Hippy's yard.

When we got there, we were stopped at the gate by Miley, a thug with rotten teeth. *'Wat's julle molefisie?'* (What's your business?) He looked scary.

'Os soek 'n paa stoppe dagga om hie te roek.' (We're looking for a few sticks of dagga to smoke.)

He gave us a once-over and pointed us to a guy with frizzy hair hanging over a stable door. Frizzy Hair took our money in return for four sticks of dagga.

We walked past Hippy, a long-faced dude who was counting money in a secluded space, as we headed for a corner. Gif found an empty quart bottle, smashed it and salvaged a chalice with a long jagged edge. Gimba prepared the dagga while Shorty rolled a diamond filter from cigarette foil. Gif stuffed the chalice and gave it to me, and Shorty struck a match, which flickered and died. Twice more we tried to light the pipe and failed. Hippy appeared in the yard and strode over to us. He took the pipe from my hand. *'Lat ek julle wys hoe om 'n pyp te roek!'* (Let me show you guys how to smoke a pipe!)

Hippy lit the chalice himself, took a long tug, and the pipe crackled as the dagga glowed red. He exhaled through his nostrils and handed the red-hot chalice to me. My hands trembled as I took it from him and the gun slid down inside my trousers, the barrel peeping out beneath my turn-up. Hippy grinned at me as I tugged at the chalice. Then I stabbed him in the eye with the chalice. Hippy screamed as he tugged at the chalice embedded in his face. As his bodyguards rushed at us, I picked up the gun and pulled the trigger but the gun jammed. Gimba and Gif stabbed the two thugs, Shorty grabbed Hippy's money off the table, and we scooted out of there.

Back in Mr C's domain, we found him and the gang elders waiting for us. We gave him the stolen money and the gun. A slow grin spread across his face as he stared at me. *'Het djy hom afgehaal?'* (Did you kill him?)

My stomach fluttered at the question. *'Ek is nie sieke nie, Mr C, maa ek het hom darem goed karnuffel.'* (I'm not sure, Mr C, but I hurt him badly.)

Mr C's smile faded for a moment then he burst out laughing and shouted at Hobo, '*Hobo, stiek hulle 'n tjap daa!*' (Hobo, give each of them a tattoo!)

Hobo led us to a secluded corner and, using a ballpoint pen, drew the words 'Mr Crime' on our left forearms. He produced his tattoo outfit, a matchbox containing a thin sewing needle stuck between three matchsticks with only the point visible, tied tightly with cotton. Then he took out some torch-battery dust, put it into a bottle top, spat into it and mixed it into a paste. He dabbed the point of the needle into the mixture and tattooed our arms. When he was finished, he squeezed out the blood and wiped it with a wet cloth. We had status.

One day, Shorty and I were standing on our corner when Gif arrived and showed us two sets of red dice. One set was 'bombaais' – fake dice. '*Check'it yt!*' (Check it out!) He rattled and rolled the bombaais several times and they always landed on seven or eleven, which was called a 'nick'. Every time you threw a 'nick', the pool would be yours. Cheating like this was a very dangerous game; if you were caught out you could be maimed or even killed. Shorty got all excited. '*Ko os gan soek 'n dice game!*' (Let's go find a dice game!) So we set off in search of one.

We found a dice game going at the entrance of Block 8. The confined space was heavy with dagga smoke as the players had a few chalices making the rounds. They were older and established gang members. The pool was huge and I had butterflies in my stomach when Gif entered the game.

A one-eyed gangster called Oeg rattled and rolled the dice and lost. It was Gif's turn and he took out the pair of real red dice, threw some money into the pool and enticed them to bet more money while rattling the dice. '*Bob I nick?*' The gangsters put money into the pool. Gif rattled and rolled and lost. He bent down to pick up the dice and Oeg rasped, '*Los die fokken dice!*' (Leave the fucking dice!) Gif left the dice as Oeg continued, '*Ek hou vi jou dop, jou fokken skollie!*' (I'm watching you, you fucking thief!)

The other gang members chuckled inanely and Oeg played to the crowd. He looked up at a tall dude, Faraway. '*Faraway, het djy gewiet die laaitie was gebore innie tronk? Hy't tyd gestoot van 'n baby af!*' (Faraway, did you know this kid was born in prison? He pushed time since he was a baby!)

Faraway replied drily, '*Dan het hy sieke baie tette gesuig ...*' (He probably suckled a lot of boobs ...) More inane laughter from the zonked group, and Gif smiled at them but the smile never reached his eyes.

The game continued and then it was Gif's turn again. He pooled his money, then rattled the dice while soliciting them again. '*Bob I nick ...*' The members pooled their money and Gif very subtly switched the dice. He rolled and they came up seven, so he took some of the pool money and stuffed it into his pockets. He started over again. '*Bob I nick ...*' The gangsters pooled their money, Gif rolled again, and this time it came up eleven. As he picked up the money to put it into his pockets, he fumbled and both sets of dice landed on the ground. Oeg growled, '*Jou tief!*' (You bitch!) Oeg went for his knife but Gif was faster and stabbed him in his seeing eye. Oeg screamed and Faraway caught him before he fell. We set off running before the zonked gangsters could react. Gif gave us some money on the run and then we split up.

Later that evening I met up with Shorty and we headed for our corner, where I could see a fire going in the brazier. When we reached our corner it seemed deserted, but there was a small metal bathtub next to the brazier. Curious, I went to investigate and four men appeared out of the darkness. Faraway and three of his cronies. I tried to run and Faraway threw me with a brick in the back. I scrambled away and dived under the fence, but Faraway grabbed hold of me and dragged me back. He had an axe in his hand, which he pressed against my neck. '*Waar's Gif? Praat gou of ek kap jou fokken kop af!*' (Where's Gif? Talk quickly or I'll chop off your fucking head!)

I was shit scared. '*Ek wietie, Mr Faraway.*' (I don't know, Mr Faraway.) Shorty was being held in a headlock by a second thug. Faraway banged the axe against the wall next to my head and pointed to the metal tub. '*Ek gan jou fokken kop afkap en in daai bad gooi!*' (I'm going to chop off your fucking head and throw it into that bathtub!)

I had to think fast and blurted, '*Ek kan jou 'n sak dagga kry, Mr Faraway.*' (I can get you a bag of dagga.)

Faraway held the axe above his head but he was interested. '*Waa gan djy 'n sak dagga kry?*' (Where are you going to get a bag of dagga?)

'*Daa by Mr C, Mr Faraway.*' (At Mr C's place.)

He contemplated for a moment. '*Okay, maa jou chommie bly hie. As djy slice, dan slice ek sy kop af!*' (Okay, but your friend stays here. If you slice, I will slice off his head!)

Shorty's eyes were balled in fear.

'*Ek sallie slice nie, Mr Faraway, God se waarheid.*' (I won't slice, Mr Faraway, God's truth.) Faraway let me go and I set off on a mission.

It was late and Mr C's yard was in darkness when I arrived there. I looked and listened for any sounds but heard only a distant snoring. The corrugated-iron fence shrieked briefly when I jumped over. I sat on my haunches and panned my surroundings. Hobo was sitting in a dilapidated armchair guarding the gate, but he was fast asleep and snoring softly. Others were sleeping around a dying fire brazier under an awning. They were dead to the world, so I sneaked into the shed where I knew the dagga was stored. I tugged at a bag but it refused to budge. I tugged harder and a bag slipped out, thudding softly on the ground. Suddenly Hobo sat up. He had a gun in his hand, which he swivelled from left to right, his eyes searching the gloom.

I was soaked in sweat. A rat scuttled across the yard and the barrel of the gun followed it until it disappeared into a hole. Hobo cursed softly, put the safety on and relaxed into his armchair. I waited for a few minutes until he started snoring again and then made my escape.

I returned to our hangout and found them dozing around the embers of the fire brazier. I walked into the firelight and Faraway awoke with a jerk. '*Wat de fok?*' (What the fuck?)

'*Dis ek, Mr Faraway. Ekkit die dagga gebring.*' (It's me, Mr Faraway. I brought the dagga.)

Faraway looked at me in amazement. '*Djy het …?*' (You did …?)

I gave him the bag of dagga and they let Shorty go.

That's when we started to become runners for Mr C. It was a dangerous business delivering parcels of dagga to smaller dealers affiliated to his gang. We had to be focused, as we moved on foot and we had to get to our destination at our own risk. So we ran at speed, taking turns carrying the dagga, the one with the shipment always running behind the other three. We delivered the parcels of dagga, collected the money and raced each other out of the area.

Late one night after finalising a dagga deal, we decided to buy some food and entered a corner shop, with a lone Muslim guy behind the counter.

'*Ko os rob die winkel!*' Shorty whispered. (Let's rob this shop!)

The old shopkeeper's nostrils flared at the sight of us and fear jumped into his eyes. I gave him my most innocent smile. He was unsure of us and said, '*Die biesigheid is maa swak.*' (This business is not making much money.)

I ignored him and took out a roll of money and asked him to give us two packets of biscuits, a packet of cigarettes and a big Coke.)

The 'baai', as we called all Muslim shopkeepers, complied and put my order on the counter. He stared as I riffled the money. ''*n Halwe brood is beter as niks brood nie, nè?*' (Half a loaf is better than no bread, hey?) The guy was greedy for money.

I pulled out some bills and held them in my hand and asked him also for a bottle of fish oil and a packet of butter. The baai happily complied and hurried to the back.

I jumped over the counter and grabbed chocolates and packets of cigarettes off the shelves. Gimba took off with the goods on the counter, while Shorty riffled through the cash register. The shopkeeper rushed back with a long knife in his hand and stabbed at me, screaming, '*Julle fokken skollies!*' (You fucking skollies!)

Gif slid his knife across the counter, shouting, '*Stiek hom, Johnnie!*' (Stab him, Johnnie!) I grabbed the knife as the baai lunged again and I struck out blindly, stabbing him in the arm. Blood spurted and he screamed, '*Allahu akbar!*' (God is great!) We hurtled out the door and ran off.

'*Wat het daai baai gesê ...?*' Gif asked. (What did that baai say ...?)

'*Hy sê dankie dat os hom gerob het!*' Gimba replied. (He said thank you for robbing him!) They cackled with laughter as we jumped a bus. But I felt regret at what we had done.

Soon the cops came knocking at our door, and we were wanted by

Hippy's crew, so we went on the run. We went to stay at a friend's flat in Kensington. We had money to burn and the girls were hanging around outside the flat, much to the chagrin of the local gangsters. The Casbahs and the Mongrels were involved in a gang war, so we stayed close to the flat and only went out at night to look for a score. After two months on the run, I felt the need to go check up on my family.

I reached home safely but Mom wasn't there, only two of my sisters and a younger brother. Mom had made crayfish curry, so I warmed a plate and stood at the open back door, ready to flee if the cops arrived. I did not even hear them arriving. I was watching my little brother through the gap of the kitchen door and I saw fear jump into his eyes and I knew it was the cops. I slipped out the door and jumped over the wire fence and continued jumping fences until I reached the last house. Then I walked to the gate, glanced down the street and saw three police vans parked outside my house. I strolled out the gate as if I lived there and walked off.

Someone saw me and a shout went up, '*Daa gan hy!*' (There he goes!)

I bolted down an alley, took a right turn down Ixia Court and dashed towards the blocks of flats. I was too quick for the cops and I got away. I ran through Block 2 and just as I approached the entrance a group of thugs cornered me. My only way out was through them and I was filled with fear.

The leader of the pack was a big wannabe street fighter and he reckoned to me, '*Kom op, os baklei yt die guns yt!*' (Come on, let's fight with our fists!)

Another voice in the shadows shouted, '*Hy't 'n mes, vat sy mes af!*' (He's got a knife, take his knife!) They did so, and the leader went into a boxer's stance, circling around me, and peppering my face with a flurry of blows. He danced out, and in again, and I whipped out my second knife and stabbed him in the head, the blade crunching through bone. I tugged at the knife and the handle broke off. The thug screamed and ran off with the knife blade embedded in his forehead like a bleeding horn. Two police vans came screaming onto the scene. There was nowhere to run and I was arrested.

I appeared in court the next day and was remanded into custody at

Roeland Street Prison in Cape Town to await trial. It was November and the courts sent most of the prisoners to await trial there over the festive season. Needless to say, Roeland Street Prison was packed to the rafters. About twenty of us entered the notorious 'Groot Kamer' (Big Room), a huge cell where the most dangerous criminals were gathered, including 'public enemy number one' Agmat Hartley and his co-accused Norman Fisher. (Hartley had been acquitted of murder the previous year when his co-accused took the rap and was sentenced to death. Now he was accused of murder again, and he and Fisher were sentenced to death a year later.)

We had to strip naked and stand at the door, and we were ogled by all and sundry. It was embarrassing, but I acted as if it was normal to stand naked in front of a crowd of predators. We then had to delouse. Ten prisoners, each armed with a tin of greasy soft soap, formed a sort of guard of honour. We had to run naked through them on our way to the ablution block. As we passed them, we were slapped with handfuls of soft soap. That hurt.

As I came out of the shower, a hoarse voice shouted, '*Kyk innie hoek, daa's koek!*' (Look in the corner, here's cake!) I looked to the corner and saw the familiar tattooed face of Hobo. My spirit lifted. Hobo had a high ranking in the hierarchy of the prison gangs and I was under his protection.

When I appeared in court a month later, I was found guilty on two counts. Eight lashes for stabbing the boxer and six more for house-breaking. The mood was sombre when I got home. With my painful butt, I could hardly move around much and hung around at home. I felt bad for disappointing my mom again. After two days I realised that Mom wasn't mentioning me in her prayers any more. I approached her about this. '*Ek hoor nie meer Mamma bid vir my nie ...*' (I don't hear you mentioning me in your prayers any more, Mom ...)

She gave me a wan smile. '*Nee, Johnnie, die Here het vir my gewys ek moet nie meer vir jou bid nie, want jy wil nie hoor nie.*' (No, Johnnie, the Lord showed me that I should not pray for you any more, because you don't want to listen.)

9

Sliding board to hell

I was seventeen, and one Friday night the four of us, dressed to the nines with our tailor-made outfits, entered a dance club where a live band was performing. All of us had short haircuts except for Gif, who was vain about his looks and his hair was always slicked back with Brylcreem. Gif checked himself in a mirror in passing and patted his hair in place. I smiled at him. '*Awe! The good looking guy with the bad ideas...*'

He gave me that boyish grin that masked his lethal capabilities. He would knife you in a blink of an eye. '*Live fast, die young and make a good-looking corpse,*' he answered, taking a line from a story I had once shared with them around the fire.

The band was playing a Chubby Checker number and a twist-and-shout session was in full swing. Brash and full of bravado, we swaggered onto the dance floor and let it all out. The teenaged girls congregated around us and we switched partners as the song changed. Most of the girls avoided dancing with Shorty, which pissed him off greatly and he hung out at the bar raging all the while and getting drunk.

One girl with long legs clung to me during a long blues version of the Beatles' 'Hey Jude'. When the song ended, she didn't want to let go of me. Her boyfriend, a long-necked dude with wet curly hair sticking out from under his Stetson hat, did not like this one bit. He pulled her roughly out of my grasp, tearing her dress, and I intervened. '*Djy, lang nek, los die kind!*' (You, long neck, leave the girl alone!)

Long Neck drew a knife. I flipped out my own knife. I went into a knife-fighter's stance and did a slow dance shuffle around him. In and out I shuffled. Then I hit him with a 'two feet', swiping his feet from under him in one smooth, practised move, and he hit the ground with a thud. Gimba grabbed his hat, stabbed it full of holes and tossed it back at him, snarling, '*Daai's 'n kak hoed!*' (That's a shit hat!) and burst out laughing. Long Neck got up as his buddies gathered in a circle around us. Shorty rushed from the bar and dived in a wild slide on his butt and entered the fray.

We assumed the pose from a scene in one of my stories and stood back-to-back to each other, turning slowly, our knives poised. Gif taunted the crowd, throwing his knife from hand to hand. '*Kom op, hie's julle ding…*' (Come on, here's your thing…)

Long Neck's friends reacted warily until a big dude moved in on Shorty, thinking he was a soft target because he was small. Shorty proved him wrong: he jumped into the air towards the big guy and plunged the knife into his shoulder. Blood spurted from the wound and all hell broke loose as the crowd screamed and scrambled for the exit.

The bouncers came running towards us, batons at the ready. They were older gangsters, rough, tough men who had carved a name for themselves among the gangster fraternity and who could control any crowd. They were the '*Manne vannie Road*' (Men of the Road). They had respect.

The crowd retreated as the bouncers arrived. The bouncers stopped at the sight of our back-to-back move. '*Live fast, die young and make a good-looking corpse,*' Gif murmured again. We were caught up in a situation that was heading for a bad ending. We circled and I recognised Apache as one of the bouncers. He was older and wiser now. They also knew that death took no sides and we were bloodthirsty and on a roll. Apache gave a lopsided grin when recognition dawned in his eyes. '*Johnnie Boy, watte fok vang djy an?*' (Johnnie Boy, what the fuck are you up to?)

I relaxed and pointed at Long Neck. '*Is die ding mettie lang nek, Apache. Hy ruk en pluk soema sy kin hie voo my en ek vattie kak van kabouters nie!*' (It's this thing with the long neck, Apache. He pushed and pulled his girl around right in front of me and I don't take shit from dwarfs!)

Apache contemplated for a moment, assessing the situation. '*Okay, ek dink djy en jou maatjies moet julle yt die kol yt vat. Julle is 'n problem.*

Kry vi julle 'n bottle whisky by die bar en verdwyn. Moet oek nie wee trug kom nie. Is julle by my?' (I think you and your mates must get lost. You are a problem. Get yourselves a bottle of whisky at the bar and leave. And don't come back. Are you with me?)

We nodded that we understood. As we left the club, I threw a last dart at Long Neck. *'En djy moet ophou jou hare soe nat maak, of jou nek gan nog langer groei!'* (And you must stop wetting your hair like that, your neck is going to grow even longer!) We cackled with laughter as we exited.

Outside the club we spotted a short dude dressed in gangster apparel taking a leak in the alley next to the club. Gimba approached and hustled him for some money. The guy complied, slipped his member inside his pants and went for a knife in his back pocket. I saw the move and rushed forward with my knife drawn. *'Watch it, Gimba, hy't 'n mes!'* I shouted. (He's got a knife!)

The guy saw me coming and stumbled forward, and as I was about to stab him I realised that he was a cripple. He had a high boot on his short right leg. Gif screamed, *'Stiek hom, Johnnie, stiek hom!'* (Stab him!) But I couldn't do it.

We let the guy go and swaggered down the street swigging from the bottle, singing badly out of tune. Gimba taunted me for not stabbing the guy with the big boot. *'Djy's nogal 'n bang laaitie, Johnnie.'* (You're actually a scared kid, Johnnie.)

'Die ou is cripple, Gimba. Ek stiek nie cripple mense nie.' (The guy is a cripple, Gimba. I don't stab crippled people.)

Gif stabbed at the air with his knife. *'Fok cripple, soe sal ek hom stiek!'* (Fuck cripple, this is how I would stab him!) He proceeded to show us how he would have stabbed the guy.

A dust devil kicked up and whirled towards us. The wind picked up and it started to drizzle. We made a dash for shelter onto the porch of a big furniture store. We sat down to finish the bottle, except for Gimba, who stared through the shop window. There was a row of transistor radios on a shelf inside the shop. *'My toppie sal mos soe 'n radio likes,'* he muttered. (My dad would like a radio like that.) He rattled the door and found that it was dodgy. *'Kykie ... die slot issie reg toe nie. Kom os kraak die winkel!'* (Check here ... this lock isn't closed properly. Let's burgle this shop!)

I was reluctant. *'Die winkel het 'n silent alarm wat afgaan by die polisiestasie.'* (The shop has a silent alarm that goes off at the police station.)

Gimba threw me a taunting look. *'Is djy bang, Johnnie? Os gryp die radio's en gooi, in en uit.'* (Are you scared, Johnnie? We grab the radios and run, in and out.)

I checked the others and they were eager to take the risk. *'Okay,'* I agreed. I took off my socks and pulled them over my hands and Gimba did the same.

I took charge. *'Gif, vang djy 'n pos hie voo die deur. Shorty, djy vang 'n pos om die draai en gooi die call as djy die boere sien.'* (Gif, you take a post here in front of the door. Shorty, you find a post around the corner and whistle the call when you see the cops.)

'Salute!' Shorty replied and set off to take up his post. Gimba and I grabbed a door handle each and tugged open the door as Shorty disappeared around the corner. We slipped inside and hurried straight towards the transistor radios. Out of the corner of my eye I saw the word CASHIER on a desk and changed direction and whispered to Gimba, *'Diékantoe, Gimba.'* (This way.)

Gimba joined me at the cashier's desk and we stuck our knives into the drawer and forced it open. Jackpot! Bundles of money tied with elastic bands were neatly stacked inside the drawer. We tried to rip out the drawer but it wouldn't budge. I did a quick scan for a bag for the money and my eyes flipped up to the window and I saw police helmets flitting past towards the front door. *'Boere,'* I whispered hoarsely and slid on my belly towards an open door, with Gimba in tow. We slipped inside and closed the door softly behind us. It was a small tearoom with barred windows and no way through the roof. We were trapped. I felt sick to my stomach as reality dawned.

I peeped through the keyhole and saw a helmeted black cop with a baton sitting on a chair guarding the front door.

'Een diephoed byrie deur,' I said. (One helmet at the door.)

'Kom os rush hom,' said Gimba. (Let's rush him.)

I looked at him and saw the fear lurking in his eyes. '*Is djy befok? Wat as os hom wit bene maak?*' (Are you fucked up? What if we kill him?) I checked through the peephole again. Two detectives, one white, the other coloured, entered the shop with the white store manager in tow. Both cops were armed with shotguns, which they held close to their chests. '*Twie speurders en nogge wit ou, Gimba,*' I informed him again. (Two detectives and another white guy.)

The detectives moved from one office door to another and the white cop banged on each one with the butt of his gun and shouted, '*Julle hier binne, as julle roer stuur ek julle bokveld toe!*' (You inside, if you move I will kill you!)

The manager then unlocked the door of the office next to the tearoom where we were hiding and it was flung open with force. They moved in, coming our way, and I had a sudden urge for nicotine. I patted my shirt pocket and found one battered cigarette. '*Gie 'n light daa, Gimba.*' (Give us a light, Gimba.)

Gimba shrugged. '*Ek het fokkol nie.*' (I've got fuck-all.) I put the cigarette in my mouth. We were going down and I was willing to go quietly. The white cop shouted another warning, the door to the tearoom banged open, the detectives pointed their guns at us, and I reckoned to the coloured detective, '*Hettie ou nie miskien 'n light daa vi my nie?*' (Do you perhaps have a light there for me?)

The detective was caught off guard by my request and the raging manager stepped up and slapped the cigarette out my mouth, grinding it underfoot. My hatred for all white people exploded. I went after him, grabbed him by the shoulders and headbutted him in the face, twice in succession.

The white detective slammed me in the kidneys with the butt of the shotgun and I hit the ground face first. Gimba stood transfixed by the sudden violence. The coloured cop hauled me up, handcuffed us together and frogmarched us outside. A crowd had gathered, some in their night clothes. The flickering light of the police car, a green Studebaker Lark, threw weird shadows across the curious crowd. Shorty appeared and mingled with the onlookers. Our eyes locked for a long moment. I indicated with my eyes that he should tell my parents.

Shorty nodded that he understood. The police car roared off as a live band across the way rendered a Beatles song, 'This Boy'.

At the police station we were charged and fingerprinted, then escorted to a big cell. We entered to find Gif already there, his mouth swollen and bloody. Gimba ranted at him, '*Djy't bos gelos, jou tief!*' (You squealed on us, you bitch!)

Gif took offence and snarled at him, '*Moetie ko kak praatie, Gimba, die boere het gewiet julle's daa innie die winkel!*' (Don't talk shit, Gimba, the cops knew you were inside the shop!)

I stepped into the fray. '*Lossit, Gimba, os twie staan man virrie saak. Gif was byte, os was binne, soe os kennie vi hom nie.*' (Leave it alone, Gimba, we take the rap for this case. Gif was outside, we were inside, so we don't know him.) Gimba was not happy so I reminded him: '*Man vang, man staan, my mieta.*' (You get arrested, you take the rap, my friend.)

We appeared in court the next day and were remanded back to the cells at Athlone police station for three weeks so that the cops could investigate if we were connected to any other burglaries. For the next few days, every prisoner who was brought to our cell was searched for tobacco or any other valuables and substances in their possession, which we would confiscate. Most of the prisoners gave it up without any resistance when approached by Gif. He was mean and prone to violence.

Late one Saturday night, the key grated in the lock and a soaking wet old drunk was thrown into the cell. He reminded me of my dad, with the same build. He stumbled over Gif's legs and Gif kicked out viciously and sent him sprawling. Then Gif got up to hand out more punishment.

'*Lossie toppie, Gif!*' I shouted at him. (Leave the old guy.) But Gif was beyond listening. He kicked the old man in the mouth, and the guy's top dentures got stuck on the bridge of Gif's bare foot as the old man fell on the cell floor. I grabbed Gif and headbutted him in the face, making him stagger back with blood dribbling from his nose. '*Ek het mos gesê djy moet die toppie ytlos!*' (I told you to leave the old guy alone!)

Gif slunk to his bed on the floor, mouthing obscenities. I tended to the old man and gave him a mat and three sleeping blankets. I took out a ready-made tobacco joint, lit it and handed it to the old man, who took a drag and stared gratefully at me through the drifting smoke, then said softly, '*You will go through deep waters but you will survive ...*' He took a wet, folded gospel tract out of his jacket pocket and handed it to me. It read, '*I am lost, please find me.*'

On a hot, sweaty Wednesday afternoon, two big black guys were put into our cell. They swaggered around, speaking in their own tongue, lit up cigarettes and ignored us as if we weren't there. This pissed us off greatly. Bored out of our heads, we had cleaned and shined the cell floor. We watched as they dumped their cigarette butts onto the floor and left them smouldering. I muttered to Gif and Gimba, '*Kom os seil hulle.*' (Let's sail them.)

They caught on immediately. Each of us proceeded to fold a blanket into a square. We got up, slid the blankets across the floor, jumped on them and surfed towards the guys. We crashed into them and sent them sprawling. Then we put the boots in and robbed them of their valuables and cigarettes. We were full force and they showed some respect.

After three weeks in the cell, we appeared in court. As I entered the courtroom from the holding cells below, I did a quick scan of the gallery and saw my parents, Gif's aunt, Shorty and Mr C, who was at the prosecutor's table probably trying to bribe him. The prosecutor waved him off and he slunk towards his seat. Mom was holding her Bible close to her breast, her eyes closed in silent prayer while Dad stared straight ahead of him.

The magistrate entered, perused his file then looked up at us. '*John Fredericks, Richard Carelse en Tyrone Felix, julle is aangekla vir huisbraak en diefstal. Wat pleit julle?*' (John Fredericks, Richard Carelse and Tyrone Felix, you stand accused of housebreaking and theft. How do you plead?)

'*Skuldig, u edele,*' I said. (Guilty, your honour.)

'*Skuldig, u edele,*' said Gimba.

'*Onskuldig, u edele, ek ken nie die mense nie,*' said Gif. (Not guilty, your honour, I don't know these people.)

The magistrate looked at me over the rim of his glasses. '*Is dit reg wat hy sê, ken julle hom?*' (Is it true what he's saying, do you know him?)

I looked at Gif as if seeing him for the first time. '*Nog nooit vir hom ontmoet nie, u edele.*' (Never met him before, your honour.)

The magistrate nodded his head and scribbled in his file. He knew we were lying. He turned to Gif, '*Jy mag afstaan, mnr. Felix.*' (You may stand down, Mr Felix.) Gif left the dock with a tight smile on his face but happy for freedom.

The magistrate addressed the prosecutor and told him to go ahead.

The prosecutor checked his file and addressed the court. Because the two accused had pleaded guilty, he said, the case could now be finalised if it pleased the court.

The magistrate nodded his head and told the prosecutor to continue. The prosecutor gathered his thoughts, then said, '*Ek vra vir 'n skuldigbevinding, u edele. Twee jaar gevangenisstraf en ses houe met die swaar rottang.*' (I'm asking for a guilty verdict, your honour. Two years' imprisonment and six lashes with the heavy cane.)

The magistrate stared pensively at us and then said that accused number one (which was me) looked very timid and that two years in Porter Reformatory would do me good.

The prosecutor begged to differ, pointing out that accused number one was in fact a few months older than accused number two. We were both seventeen years old.

The magistrate scribbled in his file some more, looked at us for a long moment, then declared: '*Beskuldigdes nommer een en twee, ek vind julle skuldig aan huisbraak en diefstal. Ek vonnis julle tot twee jaar gevangenisstraf en ses houe met die swaar rottang.*' (Accused number one and two, I find you guilty of housebreaking and theft. I sentence you to two years' imprisonment and six lashes with the heavy cane.)

My body whipped in shock at the mention of lashes with the heavy cane, which I'd heard older gangsters speak about with trepidation. They said that one lash was the equivalent of one month. I blurted out, '*U edele, ek sal eerder nog ses maande verkies in plaas van die ses houe, asseblief.*' (Your honour, I would rather have six more months than the lashes please.)

The magistrate looked at me in disgust. '*Ek het klaar gepraat, jy mag afstaan!*' (I've finished speaking with you, you may stand down!)

With tears streaming down her face, Mom gripped my hand as we were led down the well of the court. We were loaded into a big yellow truck and we set off for Pollsmoor prison. I stood at the back of the truck, holding onto the small window bars, and watched the outside world go by. The truck pulled into the yard of the prison. A sign read 'WELCOME TO POLLSMOOR'. I was filled with dread of what lay ahead.

Part Three

Pollsmoor

10

Belly of the beast

It was raining when we entered the reception area of the old Pollsmoor prison. We handed in our valuables and were stripped of our civvies. Our clothes were stuffed into a canvas bag with our names attached and put into storage until our release. We were then body-searched, and the warder seemed to take great pleasure in shoving his gloved hand up our butts as if we were animals.

We were given prison clothes: short pants, navy-blue shirt, jersey and jacket. No underwear or shoes. They gave each of us a 'katkop' (half a loaf of bread with a dollop of jam) and a monitor, a trusted prisoner with an 'M' badge attached to his shirt, escorted us across the yard to our section. My pants were too big and I held them up with one hand while the other clutched the katkop. I had a bad cold, and I had to swipe my runny nose on the sleeve of my jacket. Convicted prisoners hanging out the cell windows gave wolf whistles and a convict shouted at Gimba, '*Hei, ronne hol!*' (Hey, round butt!) Another pointed at me. '*Djy gan nog in my arms lê!*' (You're going to lie in my arms!) I tried to control my trembling as I stepped between the puddles of water.

As we passed a lone warder on guard duty, Gimba brushed against him and the warder smacked him viciously, dumping him into a puddle of water. '*Fok daai kant toe, bandiet!*' the warder shouted. (Fuck that way, convict!)

Gimba scrambled up, still clutching his katkop. We moved on and the monitor murmured, '*Daai's Koegedam. Die bandiete het hom geryp op Kougadam se tronk …*' (That's Koegedam. He was raped by convicts at Kougadam prison …)

The monitor handed us over to another warder, who unlocked the gate and took us to our section. The keys rattled as he unlocked the cell door. He shoved us into the cell and shouted, '*Twee Krismis-hampers!*' (Two Christmas hampers!)

We entered and a voice shouted, '*Staan op stimela!*' (Stand by the door!)

We waited there and my eyes scanned the scene in front of us. There were men playing dominoes, dice, and snakes and ladders, and others just staring at us. In the corner, four convicts, their heads hooded with blankets, were sitting in a circle, deeply involved in a sabela conversation.

A white-haired old convict with a towel slung around his neck approached us. He stopped in front of us and grinned, showing smoke-yellowed teeth. He tugged at a tobacco joint and blew smoke into my face and reckoned, '*Djy lyk vaagweg bekend ...*' (You look vaguely familiar ...) He looked at me for a long moment as if trying to remember where he had seen me before. Then he focused on Gimba. '*Djy's 'n mooi laaitie. Die agge gan jou jag om jou 'n wyfie te maak ... en hulle passellie hie. Die sesse hulle roof en plunder en hulle soek soldate wan hulle is maa min hie.*' (You're a pretty boy. The 28s are going to hunt you to make you a concubine ... and they control this cell. The 26s rob and plunder and they need soldiers because there's only a few of them here.) He whipped the towel from around his neck, exposing a '27' prison gang tattoo with the words 'The Kid Loves Blood'. '*My naam is Timer,*' he said, '*en ek vat bloed!*' (My name is Timer and I take blood!)

The four hooded convicts got up and walked towards us as I wiped my running nose again. I felt like a small kid again, a frightened kid at that. They stopped in front of us, and I looked at the one who was clearly the leader, a slim, dark-skinned dude with a '28' tattooed across his throat. He had purple gums and a lone tooth stood guard at the side of his mouth. '*Wie's julle vi'dag!?*' he barked at me. (Who are you today!?)

I trembled. '*Os issie Young Ones ...*' (We are the Young Ones ...)

He hit me viciously in the face and tears sprung into my eyes as he screamed at me, '*Die Young Ones beteken fokkol hie nie!*' (The Young Ones mean fuck-all here!) He came at me again and I stood my ground, locking eyes with him, and he stopped. '*Soe ... djy's sterk gevriet? Os sal sien vanand!*' (So ... you're a tough guy? We will see about that tonight!)

One of the 26 gang members, named Ghost, pointed to Gimba and addressed Gums. '*Die een is Mr C se laaitie, soe hy's onner osse protection.*' (This one is Mr C's kid, so he's under our protection.)

Gums's eyes lit up at the revelation. '*Mr C se laaitie? Daai vark het my swak gemaak op Barberton se tronk!*' (Mr C's kid? That pig made me weak at Barberton prison!)

'*Os kan altyd die ding stryt maak, Gums,*' said Ghost. (We can always sort it out.)

'*Stryt maak?*' Gums replied. '*Hoe gan djy dit stryt maak, roebana? Djy het dan fokkol nie! Tong en lip beteken niks; bewysstuk, daai's die nobangela!*' (Sort it out? How are you going to sort it out, robber? You've got fuck-all! Talk is cheap; demonstrating, that's the thing!) More 28 members gathered around, and Ghost and his fellow 26 brother, Sampie, backed down.

The cell was a long room with beds on both sides, each made up of a straw mat and three blankets, folded into a bundle. In the middle was another row of mats and Timer pointed us there. '*Julle slaap oppie eiland,*' he said. (You sleep on the island.)

We found an open space on the island and sat down. Gimba gobbled up his katkop. I felt ill and had no appetite so I hung onto mine. Minutes later a lackey arrived and told us, '*Gums roep julle … julle biete gou kom voo julle op julle moer kry!*' (Gums is calling you … you better come quickly before you get fucked up!)

'*Ko os gan hoo wat hy wil hê …?*' Gimba said. (Let's go find out what he wants …?)

I was going nowhere. '*Gan djy!*' (You go!)

Gimba got up and walked towards Gums's 'ranch'. I followed, still holding onto my katkop.

The 28 gang hierarchy in the cell was gathered at Gums's huge double bed made from a stack of mats and blankets. An evil-looking convict with 'Call Me Dog' tattooed across his forehead leered at us. The lackey was busy making an 'andalabak', a cake made with crumbed bread, sugar and a dollop of jam mixed together in a flat tin that he held over a 'vet lampie' (fat lamp) to warm it.

Gums indicated to us to have a seat. '*Sit daa …*' (Sit there …)

I sat down as Gums tugged on a thick dagga zol. He blew smoke into

my face and offered me the zol. I refused the offering. '*Nie dankie,
ek roekie dagga nie.*' (No thank you, I don't smoke dagga.) The Dog
chuckled hoarsely while Gums fumed and offered the zol to Gimba,
who accepted eagerly. Gimba tugged at the joint and held his breath,
savouring the hit and trying to impress.

Gums cut off a piece of cake and offered it to me. '*Iet 'n stukkie koek.*'
(Eat a piece of cake.)

I remembered my cousin Lenny's advice that I should never take
anything from another convict and that I didn't have to join the number.
I showed Gums my katkop. '*Nei ... ek is olraait, ek het nog my katkop.*'
(No ... I'm alright, I've still got my bread.)

The Dog found it funny and chuckled again. Gums bit angrily into
the piece of cake with his one molar and offered it to Gimba. I looked
at Gimba and admonished him with my eyes, but he ignored me and
ate the cake. Suddenly Gums shoved a small amount of tobacco into
Gimba's shirt pocket, took his hand and read his palm. '*Relax ... djy
gan nog 'n lang future het same Gums.*' (Relax ... you're going to have a
long future with Gums.) Gimba's eyes flashed at me as the reality of his
situation hit home.

Gums turned his attention to me. '*Soe djy's 'n clever? Die clevers is
byte, die moegoes is binne! Djy slaap hie vanaand!*' (So you're a clever?
The clevers are outside, the stupids are inside! You sleep here tonight!)

I let him hang for a few moments as his crew waited for my response.
'*Ek dowel mossie vi daai club nie ...*' (I don't play for that club ...)

Gums exploded and beat and kicked me in a frenzy of fury, screaming, '*Jou fokken tief!*' (You fucking bitch!)

I scampered away as Gums turned on Gimba. '*Djy, Elvis! Druk 'n
number!*' (You, Elvis! Sing a song!)

I lay on my bed and listened to Gimba singing in a falsetto. The bell
rang for lights-out and Gums shouted, '*Toe mettie kop en oep mettie hol!*'
(Close your heads and open your bums!)

I waited for Gimba to return to his bed, but I heard a couple of
thuds and Gimba pleading. Soon his pleading turned to moaning and
I knew that he was not returning to bed.

I lay on my back and stared up at the bare rafters and the dew forming droplets on the corrugated-iron roof. I tried to stay awake but I succumbed to sleep. I don't remember how long I slept, but I know I was dreaming of the long-legged girl at the dance. I dreamed that she was caressing my thighs and it felt almost real. My eyes popped open and I stared at the roof. I suddenly realised that there was somebody behind me under the blankets who was caressing my thighs. I whirled in shock and fear, grabbed the perpetrator by his shoulders and headbutted him twice in succession and blood gushed out his nose. It was Gums!

Gums staggered back and clutched at his nose, snarling, '*Jou fokken tief!*' He turned to Dog. '*Dog! Gie my 'n goemba!*' (Dog! Give me a weapon!)

Dog threw him a mug with a leather belt threaded through the handle. He wrapped the belt around his wrist and came at me swinging. I had nowhere to run and tried to cover my head and face as the mug thudded against my upper body. I staggered and fell and a silent scream escaped from my lips as Gums swung the goemba to deal out the death blow. The weapon stopped in mid-air and inexplicably Gums walked back to his bed. I moaned in pain.

The next morning, the cell door banged open and a huge Zulu warder named Babba Jan walked in, followed by Koegedam.

'*Caps off! Folla twie-twie!*' Babba Jan shouted. (Caps off! Form up in two lines!)

Koegedam swung his baton with wild abandon, lashing out at us, and we scampered into line. Babba Jan chose thirty convicts, me included, to go and work in the woodcamp to chop logs for the wood-burning stoves in the prison kitchen.

Some of us had to saw logs into smaller pieces to be chopped into firewood by others. Gimba had a luxury job of stacking the wood. My body ached from the beating of the previous night and I was feverish with cold as I struggled with a saw embedded in a log. Gimba walked over and took hold of the other side of the saw. '*Kom ek help jou.*' (Let me help you.)

'*Ek hettie jou fokken help nodig nie!*' I spat. (I don't need your fucking help!)

Gimba gave me a sad smile and walked off.

A big Zulu monitor guarding the perimeter of the woodcamp strode over, a fighting stick in his hand. He was a mute, and he had a dent in his forehead from stick fighting. He grabbed the other side of the saw and pushed and pulled vigorously. The saw bent and jumped out, cutting me across my left thumb and forefinger. The mute looked at me with a foolish grin on his face as my blood dripped into the thirsty soil, and I lost it completely. I grabbed a pick handle and swung at the mute, who parried the blow with his fighting stick just as Babba Jan entered the fray. My blood splattered chest high across Babba Jan's neat prison uniform. Time stood still and even the insects held their breath as the convicts shuffled into a circle. The mute dropped his guard and I whacked his head with the pick handle. He staggered back and I followed up, beating him mercilessly on the head and shoulders. Babba Jan floored me with one blow of his baton to the head, shouting, '*Jou fokken sprinkaan!*' (You fucking grasshopper!)

I lay there in the dust, my nostrils blowing little holes in the sand. Babba Jan escorted us back to the prison. I had to go to the infirmatory to have my fingers stitched.

The next day was washing day. We had to wash all the prison clothes in the ablution block by hand and the water ran continuously. I was exempted from this task because of my wounded fingers, so I stayed in the cell with two other injured convicts. I watched through the window and saw Gimba and another convict pushing wheelbarrows filled with washing to hang on the lines. Suddenly Gimba appeared at the window and threw a pair of pants at me. '*Shaft'it, Johnnie.*' (Hide it, Johnnie.) I took the corduroy pants and tucked them into my bundle of folded blankets. But the mute monitor had seen the whole move and spoke to the Babba in sign language.

The cell door banged open and the Babba found the pants and dragged me outside towards the ablution block. Other work gangs arrived for their lunch break and all of them were standing in a circle in the block. The Babba pulled me into the circle and produced a rubber hose. '*Wie't die broek vir jou gegee, Sprinkaan?*' (Who gave you these pants, Grasshopper?) All eyes were on me, and although everybody knew who the culprit was, the Babba still wanted me to finger Gimba. The Babba whipped me with the hose and I ran around in circles as he beat me. The convicts just watched and waited for me to squeal on Gimba, and I knew that I had to take the rap or be labelled a coward. I slipped on the wet floor and slid into the wide water gutter. Babba Jan sucked at oxygen as he towered over me. '*Staan op, jou fokken Sprinkaan!*' (Get up, you fucking Grasshopper!)

I staggered to my feet. My whole body ached and my head felt as if it was going to explode.

I was taken to the sick bay with a high fever and stayed there for two days. When I returned to my cell, my left arm cradled in a sling, the inmates became strangely quiet. I sat down on my bed as Timer walked over to me and gave me a postcard. '*Pos vi jou.*' (You got mail.)

I turned my back to the other inmates and read the postcard. '*Dear Johnnie. I trust that you are well. I don't care what other people say about you because I know that under that Beatle haircut ticks a master mind. I love you and pray for you. Be strong! Love, Mom.*' My eyes blurred with tears and I made a silent vow that I would never return to prison again.

11

Hard time

The prison was old and dilapidated and the powers that be had decided to build a more modern and bigger prison a short distance from where we were held. So convict labour was used and it was not because we had any choice. Every morning the same thing happened. The key rattled in the lock, the door flung open and Koegedam would enter, swinging his baton, shouting, '*Folla twie-twie!*' (Form up in two lines!) The convicts would mill around in an effort to dodge his baton and avoid being among the thirty convicts chosen for a work gang. I wasn't scared of hard work so I was always in the first group of thirty. Gimba was under Gums's protection so he never made it into the building group and most of the time he avoided my eyes.

We trudged down a gravel road. I had piss blisters on the bottoms of my feet so it was painful to walk properly. I hobbled to the toolshed and chose a pick and shovel. I figured that I should go for the toughest job on the site. I was wary of showing weakness and having another convict offer to help me and wanting my butt in return. Others grabbed brooms or rakes and were immediately identified as 'slackers'. On arrival at the building site, we had to dig trenches to lay the foundation of the new Pollsmoor prison. The warder who oversaw us was known as Spy Thirteen, a vicious blue-eyed white dude with a long nose. Spy Thirteen did not talk a lot; he just stood around chain-smoking. An older convict digging in front of me took a breather and the Spy whacked him on the head with a baton. '*Sak, bandiet. Diesie jou ma se huis nie!*' (Dig, convict. This is not your mother's house!)

The old convict, wise in the ways of prison life, handed his prison card to the Spy, who took the card and whacked him a couple more times on his head and shoulders, snarling, '*Drie maaltye vir jou, bandiet!*' (Three mealtimes for you, convict!) What he was saying was that on

Sunday the convict would be locked in an isolation cell and would lose all three meals of the day. On Monday morning he would be released from isolation, eat his porridge covered with bluestone coffee – which he would pee out a minute later – and go back to work on the building site. He would be weak from hunger. I was a skinny guy and could not afford to lose any meals, so I kept my head down and dug deep.

It was back-breaking labour and at night I was so tired that I just wanted to sleep, but that was out of the question. I had to keep my wits about me and I only went to sleep when I was sure that everybody was sleeping. My body ached.

As soon as the foundation was laid, we had to fill it with sand and then we had to whack it solid. The 'whackers' were 25-gallon drums filled with concrete and a thin iron pole in the middle that served as the handle. We stood in a row in the baking sun and whacked the ground, with the Spy shouting, '*Lig dit kniehoogte!*' (Lift it knee high!) So we lifted it knee high to the rhythm of 'Shosholoza' that was sung by a black convict.

Blisters formed in the palms of my hands and burst open and started to bleed, but I held onto that thin pole and whacked. My bloody hands stuck to the pole. I knew if I let go to ease the pain it would be more painful. Many convicts, unable to take the pace, handed in their cards and were sentenced to lose three meals on Sunday. A convict dropped from heatstroke, but that didn't bother the Spy much. I let go of my whacker and tried to drag him into the meagre shade and the Spy exploded. He beat me with his baton on my head and shoulders. '*Los die fokken hond, bandiet!*' (Leave the fucking dog, convict!)

I tugged at the convict one last time and got him into the shade.

The convicts stopped working and gathered around as the Spy came after me, swinging his baton. '*Ek het mos gesê jy moet hom los!*' (I told you to let him go!)

I tried to cover my head and face with my arms, and as he swung the baton I grabbed it in mid-air. '*Die bandiet het water nodig, ware ...*' (The convict needs water, warder ...)

The Spy fumed at my audacity. The convicts murmured and shuffled their feet and the Spy came to his senses. '*Drie maaltye vir jou, bandiet, en gee my jou fokken kaart!'* (Three mealtimes for you, convict, and give me your fucking card!)

I gave him my card but I kept on working. A convict murmured, *'Die laaitie gan 'it nie maak nie ...'* (This kid is not going to make it ...)

When we arrived back at the prison, I was taken to the infirmatory for a knob on my head that I had sustained during the beating at the Spy's hand. The medical orderly gave me the once-over. *'Jy bly ook in die kak! Wat is dit met jou?'* (You're always in shit! What's wrong with you?)

I returned to my cell and sat down on my bed. The convicts were strangely quiet. I looked up and saw them watching me and I queried the silence. *'Wat gan an? Lyk ek dan soes Vader Krismis?'* (What's up? Do I look like Father Christmas?)

Timer gave a guttural laugh. *'Nei ... djy lyk soes 'n kakgat laaitie, maa djy het pluck!'* (No ... you look like a shit-arse kid, but you got pluck!) He turned to the inmates in the cell and shouted, *'Bring die andalabakke, my broers, bring die zoek. Let's celebrate!'* (Bring the cake, my brothers, bring the dagga. Let's celebrate!)

Two inmates scurried forth to bring the required items and Timer gave me a huge dagga zol and a piece of cake, much to the chagrin of Gums, who stared at me with hate-filled eyes.

On the Sunday morning, my name was called for the isolation block as I had been sentenced to go without food for the day. The other inmates were from different sections and they quickly overpowered the weaker convicts. Luckily for me, some of the work gang were among them and they showed me respect.

The next day, after an hour of whacking I became so weak and dizzy from hunger that I had to stop and hold onto the whacker for support. I saw the Spy coming my way and braced myself for an onslaught, but instead he gave me a water bucket and ordered me to fetch water. It was a relief as the tap was some distance away. I figured the Spy had a soul after all.

After another week of hard labour, my and Gimba's names were called for a visit. The visitors' section was a cacophony of sound as the visitors shouted to be heard by their loved ones behind bars. I spotted Gif and Shorty in the milling crowd so we headed their way. The two of them were looking good, all dressed up in suits and Stetson hats.

Gif gave me a boyish grin. *'Awe, Johnnie, hoe change hulle hie binne?'* (Awe, Johnnie, what's changed inside here?)

'Die wêreld moer my hie binne, Gif, maa ek survive.' (The world is fucking me up inside here, Gif, but I survive.)

My hair was cut short but Gums did not want Gimba to cut his hair, which was quite long. Shorty stared at Gimba's hair and chortled, *'Djy het daam 'n kwaai hairstyle, Gimba, is daai 'n tronk special?'* (You've got a nice hairstyle, Gimba, is it a prison special?)

Gimba blushed so I changed the subject. *'Wat het dan daai aand gebeur toe die boere os gemang het, Shorty?'* (What happened that night when we were arrested, Shorty?)

Shorty hung his head in shame. He said I was right about the silent alarm. He was still on his way to the lookout when the cops passed by him.

I looked at Shorty deep down and saw the regret lurking in his eyes, so I decided to let him off the hook. *'Daa'sie pyn nie, Shorty, soe is soe ...'* (There's no pain, Shorty, shit happens ...)

Shorty's eyes lit up with relief.

Gimba checked out Shorty's wardrobe. *'Djy's ytgevat, Shorty. Hoe change hulle dan daabyte?'* (You're all dressed up, Shorty. What's happening on the outside?)

'Die blok is benoud, Gimba, maa os het darem 'n paa lekke squares geslat.' (We're wanted by the cops, but we hit some big scores.)

I didn't care about their big scores. *'Gaan loer julle nog in daa by my tanie, Gif? Sien julle haa nog?'* (Do you still make a turn by my mother, Gif? Do you see her around?)

'Sy is olraait, Johnnie. Ons sien haar altyd op die stoep en Bybel lees.' (She's alright, Johnnie. We always see her on the porch reading the Bible.)

After the visit was over and they got up to leave, Gif dug a roll of money out his pocket. *'Ek gan 'n kroon op julle property sit.'* (I'm going to put some money on your property.)

'*Salute!*' said Gimba.

That evening while I lay on my bed reading a dog-eared magazine, Gums's lackey approached and told me Gums wanted to see me. I tucked the magazine under my blankets and followed him.

I stopped at Gums's high bed and I could not hide my disgust as I stared at Gimba, who was lying at the back of the bed, behind Gums.

'*Ek hoo djy kan lekke stories vi'tel*,' said Gums. '*Vi'tel 'n storie.*' (I believe you can tell good stories. Tell a story.)

I weighed my options. '*Wat's innit vi my?*' (What's in it for me?)

Gums jumped up snarling, '*Djy tief! Djy dala soes die nomme jou wys!*' (You bitch! You do as the number dictates!) He hit me with a flurry of blows and I covered my face but stood my ground. I looked at him deep down, looked beyond the bravado in his eyes, and I saw uncertainty there. All eyes in the cell were turned towards us. A murmur spread through the cell.

He threw another flurry of shots at me and Timer intervened. '*Daai's nou genoeg!*' (That's enough!)

Gums turned on Timer. '*Wat is djy boekant die nomme, Timer?*' (Are you above the number, Timer?)

'*Ek vondela net om te kan sê die laaitie het fokkol gemaakie*,' Timer replied. (I'm just saying that the kid did fuck-all wrong.)

The murmur became louder.

'*Ek seconds daai!*' said Ghost. (I second that!)

Gums looked to his henchmen, who looked back at him, waiting for him to respond, and he knew that he could lose control. '*Dan sal hy moet vol raak vannie nomme! Os moet ronne tafel sit en os gan nommers maak vanaand!*' (Then he must wise up about the number! We must sit around the table and we'll make numbers tonight!)

Timer agreed. '*Salute! Os maak soe.*' (We'll do that.)

Gums and Dog, the two 28s, and Ghost and Sampie, the two 26s, hooded their heads with blankets and sat in a circle around me. Timer acted as my 'lawyer'.

Gums spoke. '*Volgens my is die laaitie reg vi die agge!*' (According to me, this kid is right for the 28s!)

'*Djy jiegiejela nwatas, Gums*,' Ghost retorted. '*Die laaitie is 'n soldaat.*

Hy't hom klaa bewys as 'n maroebaan!' (You talking nonsense, Gums. This kid is a soldier. He's already proved himself as a robber!)

Timer intervened. *'Lat os hoo wat die laaitie te sê het.'* (Let's hear what the kid's got to say.)

I chose my words carefully. *'Ek wil net my tyd stoot sonne om an die nomme te vat, maa ek kan werk virrie nomme.'* (I just want to push my time without taking the number, but I can work for the number.)

Gums fumed. *'Wat het djy om te offer?'* (What have you got to offer?)

I gave the question some thought. *'Ek kan lies en skrywe en ek kan stories vi'tel.'* (I can read and write and I can tell stories.)

Gums was not convinced. *'Ek issie vol nie!'* (I'm not satisfied!)

'Kyk, Gums,' said Timer, *'djy wou hê dat die laaitie stories moet vi'tel. As hy kwaai stories vi'tel, kan hy os help om os tyd te stoot.'* (Look, Gums, you wanted the kid to tell stories. If he tells a good story he can help us to push our time.)

'Ek seconds daai,' Ghost agreed, *'maa ek gan hom bêre by die hek van maroebaan. As hy back speen, dan is hy 'n 26.'* (I second that, but I'm going to bury him at the gate of the robbers. If he returns to prison he will become a 26.)

They gave each other the finger salute and got up. Timer walked with me to my bed. *'Thanks, Timer,'* I said.

Timer lit a tobacco joint, tugged on it and bounced it to me. *'Maak net dêm vi'sieke djy vi'tel 'n kwaai storie of môre is djy 'n hoer!'* (Just make damn sure you tell a good story or tomorrow you will be a whore!)

12

The cinema

The inmates were going about their usual night-time games of chance. Some were playing dice for matchsticks; some were playing dominoes or snakes and ladders. In one corner, a group was playing cards for small amounts of money. Gums and I stepped into the middle of the cell. Gums had to shout to get their attention. '*Listen up! Vinaand gan os bioscope het. Die laaitie gan vi os 'n storie vi'tel! Julle betaal met kroon, ganja of gebryke!*' (Listen up! We're having bioscope tonight. The kid is going to tell us a story! You pay with money, dagga or tobacco!)

I sat down on my bundle of blankets as Gums continued, '*As hy 'n kak storie vi'tel, dan sa hy net moet vat an die nomme, want die nomme soek hom!*' (If he tells a shit story, he will have to take on the number, because the number wants him!)

The inmates gathered around me in a half circle, the Dog right in front. He leered at me. A convict at the back complained, '*Os kannie soe lekker sien nie, sit 'n bietjie hoër!*' (We can't see so well, sit a bit higher!) A convict tossed me another bundle of blankets and I occupied the high seat.

I scanned my captive audience. Gums and Dog were sitting right up front, their heads hooded with blankets. Timer stood at the back, sweeping in one place with a broom. Gimba and the other weaker convicts were sitting on the sides. There was excitement in the air as dagga joints were lit and everyone stared expectantly at me.

But the words wouldn't come. I was tongue-tied and the Dog glared at me. '*Die laaitie kan mossie stories vi'tel nie, lat hom aaire sing oor Gums se mic!*' (I don't think this kid can tell stories, let him rather give Gums a blow job!) The audience roared with laughter.

I searched my mind for a story to tell but nothing was forthcoming, so I decided to suck a story out of my thumb. '*Okay ... Os is op 'n aeroplane soes hy begin te sak en os sien die liggies vannie Kaap wat wink, dan hoo os die pilot sê: "Welcome to Cape Town at night."'* (Okay … We're on an airplane as it starts its descent and we see the flickering light of the Cape and we hear the pilot saying: 'Welcome to Cape Town at night.')

Dog interrupted. *'Watsie naam van die storie?'* (What's the name of the story?) I was thrown by the question as the story had no name, and Dog added, *'Djy moetie vi my vi 'n gat vattie.'* (Don't take me for an arsehole.)

Timer prodded Dog with the broom handle. *'Gie die laaitie 'n kans, Dog!'* (Give the kid a chance.)

I settled in and continued with my narrative. *'Die storie los os daa en os gaan af na die dubbeldeure by arrivals. Die deure swish oepe en os sien die bra daa staan. Die ou is geslat met 'n swart chalk-stripe suit, 'n breërant Stetson beaver, 'n wit silk scarf en 'n paa Ray-Bane. Hy hou 'n opgerolde koerant onder sy arm.'* (The story leaves us there and we go down to the double doors at arrivals. The doors swish open and we see this brother standing there. He is dressed in a black chalk-stripe suit, a wide-brimmed Stetson beaver, a white silk scarf and a pair of Ray-Bans. He has a rolled-up newspaper under his arm.)

Ghost could not contain his excitement and exclaimed, *'Roebana! Roebana!'* (Robber! Robber!)

I honed in on him. *'Hoeko sê die man dan soe?'* (Why does the man say that?)

'Hoe sien djy dan my tjappies?' Ghost said, taking the story forward. *'Hy's 'n pickpocket man, hy spring in 'n bus of 'n trein, dan maak hy net twee draaie met die koerant en oep is jou baadjie. Dan sluk hy jou pak en djy wiet van niks!'* (How do you see my tattoos? He's a pickpocket man, he jumps onto a train or bus, he makes two turns, opens your jacket with the newspaper and your wallet is gone. You don't feel a thing!)

I took over the narrative. *'Die bra lig sy hoed soe effens met die koerant en os sien 'n tjap voo sy kop, "Call Me Dog"!'* (The brother lifts his hat slightly with the newspaper and we see a tattoo on his forehead, 'Call Me Dog'!)

Gums spluttered, *'Dog! Waa kry Dog sulke nxa klere? Hy is 'n fokken bergie oppie vryes!'* (Dog! Where does Dog get such nice clothes? He's a fucking bergie on the outside!)

Dog smiled like a fat cat, lit a dagga zol and handed it to me. I accepted, tugged on it and scanned the faces through a haze of smoke as I gathered my thoughts. *'Die Dog is op 'n pos en sy oë deursoek die "new arrivals".'* (The Dog is on a mission and his eyes screen the new arrivals.)

My eyes picked up on Timer still sweeping in one place. *'Dan stiek daa 'n toppie yt met 'n besem in sy han en hy vee so op een plek. Hy watch die Dog wan die toppie is 'n undercover cop!'* (Then an old guy arrives on the scene with a broom in his hand and starts sweeping in one place. He watches the Dog because the old guy is an undercover cop!)

Timer chuckled, gripped the broom and danced a minstrel jig. *'Fuck me, Charlie!'*

Gums glared at Timer, who ignored him completely.

I tugged at the dying joint and Dog pulled his lighter like a gunfighter and lit it for me. Gimba sidled forward and Dog hit him with a bullet of profanity. *'Fokkof!'*

Gums intervened. *'Los hom, Dog!'* (Leave him, Dog!)

Dog grudgingly made a space for Gimba. *'Sit daa, moetie roer nie, moetie ees asemhaal nie.'* (Sit there, don't move, don't even breathe.)

Gimba stared at the joint enviously. I tugged again and bounced it to him.

Dog grabbed my hand in mid-air. *'Daai's jou joint, hy moet skarre vi sy eie bien.'* (That's your joint, he must hustle for his own bone.)

I continued my story. *'Dog se oë dwaal so deur die mense, dan sien os twie speurders gekoppel aan 'n ander gevangene. Die ou se oë flicker die-kant en daaikant. Hy is kak bang want hy is in "witness protection" en hy is biesig om te piemp op die ouens. As hy opkyk, sien os die 28 tjap in sy nek. Dit is Gums!'* (Dog scans the crowd and his eyes latch onto two detectives handcuffed to another prisoner. The guy's eyes flicker this way and that. He is shit scared as he is in witness protection and is informing on his fellow gangsters. When he looks up we see the 28 tattoo on his neck. It is Gums!)

Dog looked suspiciously at Gums, who snarled at him, *'Hoeko de fok kyk djy soe na my?'* (What the fuck are you looking at?)

I intervened. '*Dan sie os die gun innie Dog se koerant en hy beweeg vining op Gums af. Die toppie gan vi sy gun maa dis te laat, dan klap die skote. Een innie kop en twie innie bors en Gums slat neer ... dood voordat hy die grond vat!*' (Then we see the gun in the Dog's newspaper as he moves swiftly in Gums's direction. The old guy goes for his gun but he's too late. The Dog fires, one in the head and two in the chest, and Gums falls down ... dead before he hits the ground!)

Gums fumed. The bell rang for lights out and the inmates shuffled to their beds.

Timer stepped up to me and gave me a bankie of tobacco, saying, '*Djy loop op heilige grond ...*' (You walk on holy ground ...)

Gums barred my way. '*Djy! Tief! Moetie dink dat djy hoeg sit djy is iets nie! Djy is 'n fokkol! Die agge pasellie binne en byte die tronk!*' (You! Bitch! Don't think because you're sitting high you're somebody! You are a fuck-all! The 28s are in control inside and outside the prison!)

The next morning in the ablution block, Timer confronted me. '*Wat speel vanaand?*' (What's playing tonight?)

I hadn't worked it out yet, so I just shrugged my shoulders. Koegedam arrived swinging his baton but I was wiser now and fell in at the back of the line and avoided going to work on the building site.

Later that morning, another warder arrived and picked a gang to work on the bowling green. This was good as it was light labour. We sat in a row on our haunches and took out all the weeds with our eating spoons. The bowling green was situated near the only shop in the area. There were lots of civilians to be seen, and they were also a source of income as some of the prison visitors would drop us some money, which we would collect as soon as we got a gap.

That evening more prisoners were gathered. Number gangsters with tattooed faces were present. Crime and violence was their game, so I knew I needed to set some boundaries. Somebody had removed one light bulb and half the cell was in semi-darkness. They lit their joints and looked expectantly at me. After they were settled in, I started my narrative. '*Okay! Vi'dag vat ek vi julle op 'n boat trip, maa ees moet os boundaries maak. Niks gegwara nie. Moet oek nie skarrel nie. Hie is oek nie gangsters of nommers nie, os meet innie mind en os gaan dwarsdeur die dak!'* (Okay! Today I'm taking you on a boat trip, but first we've got to make some boundaries. No taunting of each other and no hustling. There are no gangsters or numbers here, we meet in the mind and we go through the roof!)

The convicts murmured among themselves. Timer handed me a burning joint. '*Vi jou, Johnnie.*' (For you, Johnnie.)

I needed to concentrate on the story, so I declined the offering. '*Dankie, Timer, maa nie vi'naand nie.*' (Thanks, Timer, but not tonight.)

Timer threw me a strange look. '*As djy soe sê...*' (If you say so ...)

I had made some notes and stuck them together with a pin. I paged through my notes to buy some time before beginning. This story, I told them, was about a guy with the name of Themba. Themba and 147 others were captured by slave dealers in Madagascar. They were then loaded onto a boat that set sail for the Cape.

A match flared in the dark as I continued.

The slave handlers were the sort of drunken, bored thugs who are found on any seedy wharfside. On their way to the Cape, Themba got a high fever and he was nursed by a slave girl, Rachel. To cut a long story short, they got together and made out in a secluded corner of the boat.

The audience stirred at the mention of sex.

On a warm day, I continued, the main slave handler decided that the slaves should clean the weapons. That's their slice! They unloaded the guns, except for one that a bored thug gave to a dopey slave, with the idea that Dopey would shoot himself.

A convict murmured, '*Hy's 'n fokken vuil hond ...*' (He's a fucking dirty dog ...)

The slaves started cleaning the guns. Then the Chinese overseer with a whip decided to have some fun and cracked the whip, and the dopey slave dropped the gun and a shot went off. Then the boere opened fire on the slaves.

I let the audience hang while I lit a tobacco joint and stared at them through the smoke. Their faces were animated as they hung in suspense. They were hooked.

Themba dived for cover as the guns fired, then he grabbed a spear and threw it underhand at the Chinese thug. The spear smashed through his throat and he tumbled overboard into the sea.

Suddenly Timer held up his hand for silence as he listened intently to the sound of keys rattling in a lock and the distant bang of a cell door. We dived under our blankets as Koegedam banged on our cell door with his baton. He looked through the eyehole and then moved on, banging on cell doors as he went along. We listened to the fading sound of his boots before scurrying back to our positions.

I checked my notes again and the pin slipped out and dropped to the floor. All eyes watched as the pin hit the ground. I continued.

The slaves overpowered the boere and took control of the ship. Now these slaves knew fuck-all about boats, so they threatened the Captain to drop them at the nearest island. The boat changed course but Themba did not trust the Captain.

As the boat reached a small tree-covered island, twenty slaves jumped into the water and enjoyed their freedom. But Themba watched the Captain closely, then he looked towards the jungle and saw guns. A long fucking row of guns poking out the bush.

There was absolute silence in the cell.

It was a trap, I explained. The farmers on the island were waiting for them and opened fire. Dopey tried to swim back to the ship and was blown out of the water and landed like a dead fish. Twenty slaves were killed. The slave handlers took control of the boat and the slaves were propped into the belly of the boat and they set sail for the Cape. In the cargo hold, the slaves spoke only in whispered syllables. They were soaking wet and kak scared.

'Fok, hulle herrit ampe gemaak...' Ghost said. (Fuck, they almost made it...) I had them in the palm of my hand.

When they reached the Cape, I continued, Rachel discovered that she was pregnant, and she was taken to the women's section of the slave house. Themba would have none of that and wanted them to stay together, but the boere beat him viciously until he lost consciousness.

A sigh swept through the audience.

Themba had to slave on the docks, he had to load and unload big fucking bags of rice and salt, but in the process he was building some muscle. One night, tired and covered in sweat, Themba decided to look in on Rachel and found a Boer busy raping her. Themba hit him with his fists, three shots to the head, and the Boer dropped! He was dead before he hit the ground!

The audience hung in suspense and I let them hang for a moment before saying, '*Themba kry toe die doodstraf.*' (Themba was sentenced to death.)

A convict sighed in disappointment and murmured, '*Fok …*'

They felt let down so I picked them up. '*Maa dis noggie klaa nie …*' (But it's not over yet …) Their eyes lit up and I continued.

Themba pleaded for mercy and the authorities cut him a deal in exchange for a life sentence. They knew he understood a smattering of the Chinese language, so they asked him to eavesdrop on four Chinese prisoners who were accused of murder and who claimed not to be able to speak English.

Themba was placed into the cell where the four Chinese were held. They were seated in a circle, their heads hooded with blankets, talking quietly to one another. Their eyes followed Themba as he took up a position in a corner. One of the Chinese, with a scarred face, looked at him suspiciously. He got up and grabbed hold of his penis and spoke in Chinese, saying he was going to rape Themba's wife after he was hanged. Themba's eyes flickered and they knew that he understood what they were saying.

Scarface produced a thin-bladed knife and advanced on Themba with deadly intent, with the others following, and Themba knew he was going to die there. He flung himself at Scarface in a low dive, taking his feet from under him and sending the knife flying. Then the Chinese were upon him, kicking at him viciously as he tried to roll away and avoid the attack. But there was nowhere to hide, so he staggered to his feet and slugged it out with them. Scarface got hold of his knife and stabbed him in the face. With blood flowing from the wound, Themba twisted and turned to allow himself some space, but to no avail. Scarface stabbed him in the chest and Themba hit the ground with his blood pooling around him.

I kept silent for a while and then added that later we see a pregnant Rachel and her son on Greenmarket Square, where they are bought by a slave owner.

I let my words sink in before concluding my story. *'En hie sit os nog altyd agter tralies na driehonderd jaar terwyl os mense daa buite nog steeds sukkel.'* (And here we languish behind bars after three hundred years while our people on the outside are still struggling.)

An eerie silence followed.

Suddenly the door burst open and Koegedam and four coloured warders rushed in with batons swinging. Koegedam shouted, *'Staan teen die muur!'* (Stand against the wall!) We scurried to the wall as the warders tossed our beds, searching for contraband.

Koegedam got hold of my notes. He scanned them once, tore them into tatters and scattered them over my head. *'Die'sie jou ma se huis nie!'* (This is not your mother's house!)

He turned towards the door and barked, *'Kap hulle toe vir drie maaltye!'* (Lock them up for three mealtimes!)

13

Riding the mare

One morning, Koegedam entered the cell with a medical orderly who was holding a list of names.

'*Folla twie-twie!*' Koegedam shouted.

The orderly waited until we were in line and then told us to listen for our names and to answer if called. Then he began. '*John Fredericks!*'

I stepped out of the line. '*Ja, baas!*' (Yes, boss!)

'*Richard Carelse!*'

Gimba stepped out too. '*Ja, baas!*'

Koegedam gave him a shot to the head with the baton to help him on his way.

We were escorted to the infirmatory, where a doctor ran some medical tests and found us fit to receive our lashes. I was sweating in trepidation as we entered a big cell where we found a group of convicts who had also been sentenced to lashes sitting on the cold cement floor on their naked butts. The cell smelt putrid with fear, sweat and smelly butts. In the middle of the cell, screwed to the floor, was an elongated wooden table with handholds and a splatter of blood drops. It was known as the mare, and we were about to ride the mare.

A big oaf, his lips grey with fear, gave me a grim smile and asked me, '*Hoeveel?*' (How many?)

I showed him six fingers. '*Ses latjies.*' (Six lashes.)

'*Kom vries jou gat, dan issit nie soe seer nie.*' (Come freeze your butt, then it won't hurt so much.)

I dropped my pants and followed suit.

Babba Jan entered the cell and displayed his smoke-yellowed teeth in a wolfish grin as he whipped the air with a thick cane. The big oaf was up first and he got nervously onto the mare and lay down on the contraption. Babba Jan whacked him and I watched as the lash across his butt became grey and droplets of blood popped up before the next blow fell. He screamed in agony and almost fell when he got off the mare. A trickle of blood ran down his thighs as he walked unsteadily towards the door. Babba Jan grinned sadistically. '*Hy't vrot vleis!*' (He's got rotten meat!) My blood ran cold.

'*Fok! Shit!*' Gimba whimpered.

I looked at him and saw the fear lurking in his eyes. '*Kyk vas, Gimba!*' (Look ahead, Gimba!)

Babba Jan wiped the cane with a wet cloth and grinned at me. It was my turn. '*Is djy bang, Sprinkaan?*' he asked. (Are you scared, Grasshopper?)

I got onto the mare. '*Ja, Babba Jan.*'

The Babba stroked my butt with the cane. '*Mooi.*' (Good.) Then he whacked me with the cane and the pain shot through my body but I refused to cry out. I closed my eyes and gritted my teeth as five more lashes followed.

I got off the mare unsteadily and almost stumbled, but the Babba steadied me and shoved two sticks of dagga into my shirt pocket. I was surprised by this action and thought it was a trap. I hovered uncertainly, struggling to pull my pants over my sore buttocks. The Babba looked at me deep down and murmured, '*Wies watchful, Sprinkaan ... ever watchful ...*' (Be watchful, Grasshopper ... ever watchful ...)

As I left the cell, I could hear Gimba screaming as he rode the mare.

Timer and three other convicts were pushing food trolleys when I strode down the corridor. They stopped and stared as I came marching on. Timer grinned and lit up a tobacco joint. '*Trek 'n skyf, Johnnie.*' (Pull a puff, Johnnie.)

I accepted the offering, took a few drags and handed it back to him. '*Thanks, Timer.*' I didn't want to linger or tell Timer about the sticks of dagga that were almost burning a hole in my shirt pocket, so I moved on.

Back in the cell, I hid the dagga in my bundle of blankets and lay down on my mat as the Dog approached me and asked me to sing a number. I didn't feel like singing but I sang anyway. I began an old melancholy prison song about slavery: '*Show me the river, take me across* …' It was a song about slaves working deep in the fields under a scorching sun, and each convict identified with the song. Soon Dog started harmonising with me and others joined in. There was a knock on the window and the Babba appeared and indicated for me to come nearer. I stepped up to the window and he gave me his wolfish grin. '*Hoe's daai deng, Sprinkaan?*' (How's that thing, Grasshopper?)

I put on my dumb convict face and asked him in all innocence, '*Watte deng, Babba …?*' (What thing, Babba …?)

A few other convicts gathered and hovered behind me in curiosity.

The Babba chuckled and pointed to my shirt pocket. '*Daai deng wat ek jou gegie het, man!*' (That thing that I gave you, man!)

I tried to read his intentions and the Babba continued, '*Djy moet daai deng enjoy, Sprinkaan, daa'sie pyn nie …*' (You must enjoy that thing, Grasshopper, there's no pain …)

I was flooded with relief when I realised he was sincere. As I moved away, the Babba made a request. '*Druk wee daai nomme vi my.*' (Sing that number for me again.) I sang and the others harmonised with me.

The Babba left and Gums pounced on me and mimicked the Babba. '*Waa's daai deng, Sprinkaan? En moetie met my kak praat van watte deng nie!*' (Where's that thing, Grasshopper? And don't talk shit to me about what thing!)

I had no choice, so I took out one stick of dagga and showed it to him. He grabbed the stick and walked off. I pleaded with him, '*Wat van my? Dis my score!*' (What about me? It's my score!)

Gums snarled at me. '*Djy's a fokken frans, djy dala soes die nomme jou wys!*' (You're a fucking lackey, you do as the number dictates!)

'*Gie my dan net 'n sandjie …*' (Just give me a small piece …)

Gums opened the stick of dagga and reluctantly gave me a small piece. '*Djy klop an vir 'n moerse klap!*' (You're begging for a fucking slap!)

I had him fooled, because now I had reason to smoke the other dagga stick and Gums would be none the wiser. It lasted for quite a while, as I only smoked one small joint of tobacco sprinkled with dagga.

I had earned some status in prison, so in the mornings when Koegedam arrived, I fell in almost right at the back of the line and avoided going out to do hard labour. Timer was in charge of a group that polished and shined the corridor every day. He approached me one morning and gave me some cloth for my knees and a hard brush that was covered with cloth too. '*Ko val in hie, Johnnie.*' (Come fall in here.)

We got onto our knees and polished the floor to the rhythm of Timer's beat. He walked in front of us with a broom, sweeping from side to side as if clearing the way and rhymed, '*Jou ma't gepraat, uh, uh. Jou pa't gepraat, uh, uh. Maa hoor was min, uh, uh. Nou sit djy in die maksimum, uh, uh.*' (Your mother spoke, uh, uh. Your father spoke, uh, uh. But you didn't listen, uh, uh. Now you're here in maximum, uh, uh.)

Timer and I got on well together, but I had a feeling that he was grooming me for something more sinister, so I was watchful, ever watchful, as the Babba had warned me. One day Timer put me in charge of the corridor boys. I took over the broom from him and sang the rhyme. It was a break from boredom and gave me lots of time to reflect. I had messed up my life and disgraced my parents, but I was determined to make good on the outside.

Then a draft of convicts came to Pollsmoor from Bellville prison, and among them was Kannie Worry, who had stolen our polonies and beaten us up years before. He had almost completed a corrective-training sentence of two to four years and only had a few months to go before his release. Now, if you had served time in the quarries of Bellville prison and survived, you got status in the prison community. Many hard-core convicts had cut their sinews to avoid the hard labour, but Kannie Worry was a survivor and also one of my enemies from my youth.

He was full of bravado as he swaggered into the cell and walked right up to Gums and his henchmen. He sabelaed the number with Gums and stated his credentials in the number and Gums welcomed him into their fold. Gimba was quite embarrassed as Kannie Worry leered at him and saw that he had made his bed with Gums. I still felt that Gimba and I owed Kannie Worry big time for what he did to us in the past, although I didn't want to commit any crimes in prison, because I had already made up my mind that I was going to change my life around.

I watched him closely all the time, and one Saturday evening, after Gimba went to the ablution block to take a shower, I saw Kannie Worry furtively entering the block a short while later. I gave it a few moments before heading in their direction.

I took off my clothes as I entered and saw Gimba butt naked under the shower. Kannie Worry, also naked, hovered behind him and moved closer. Gimba whirled around, his face full of soap. '*Fokkof hie yt! Ek gan vi Gums sê waamee djy bymekaa is!*' (Fuck off out of here! I'm going to tell Gums what you're up to!)

Kannie Worry cackled with laughter. '*Fok Gums!*'

I hit him with a 'two feet' from behind, sweeping his feet from under him, and he hit the ground with a thud. He scrambled up and I kicked him under the chin, sending him sliding across the wet floor and under the hand basins. Gimba went ballistic, kicking him in the face in a frenzy of fury, banging his head against the wall with every shot until he lost consciousness. We got under the shower, dried ourselves quickly, dressed hurriedly and exited the block, leaving a bleeding Kannie Worry behind.

A fellow inmate discovered the comatose Kannie Worry some time later and raised the alarm. Koegedam and the four coloured warders arrived in a rush and Koegedam commanded us to stand against the wall.

We did so and they checked all of us for blood spatters but found none. Although Koegedam couldn't care less about Kannie Worry, he still fumed, '*Wie het die bandiet aangerand!?*' (Who assaulted that convict!?)

There was no response.

Koegedam turned to the warders and pointed towards the showers. '*Vat die bandiet hier uit en kap die hele sel toe vir drie maaltye!*' (Take that convict out of here and lock down this cell for three mealtimes!)

The convicts murmured their displeasure as the cell door swung shut. The next day we had to stay in our cell without getting any food. Needless to say, the inmates were very grumpy and tensions ran high in the cell.

Two days later, Kannie Worry returned to the cell. He didn't squeal on us, partly because his broken jaw was wired shut. One of his eyes was swollen closed and the other glared at me as he passed on his way to Gums's ranch. I assume Gimba told Gums about the incident because Gums reacted violently, shouting at Kannie Worry, '*Op jou fokken knieë!*' (On your fucking knees!)

Kannie Worry's eyes were full of fear as he went down on his knees. Dog gave Gums a goemba and he twisted the belt around his wrist and hit him one shot against the head with the mug, snarling, '*Trug stof toe, bandiet!*' (Bite the dust, convict!)

Kannie Worry hit the ground moaning in pain. Dog picked him up and dumped him on the 'island' among the other lackeys. It seemed Dog didn't like him either.

Soon after that, Timer stopped at my bed with a wide grin on his face, carrying a tattoo kit in a small box. He gave me a tobacco joint and I lit up. Timer pointed to the tattoo kit. '*Ko, Johnnie, ek wil vi jou 'n tjap stiek!*' (Come, Johnnie, I want to give you a tattoo!)

I was wary of this whole move. '*Watse tjap, Timer?*' (What tattoo?)

He looked at me deep down. '*Kykie, my laaitie, djy's 'n asset vi os hie met jou stories en wat-wat. Soe djy moet vrylik kan beweeg hie tussen die nomme's en die tjap sal jou daai status gie.*' (Look here, kid, you're an asset for us with your storytelling and what-what. You should be able to walk freely here among the numbers and this tattoo will give you that status.)

I contemplated this for a moment, then I agreed. '*Okay, gan voort.*' (Okay, go ahead.)

He took out a ballpoint pen and on the back of my right hand he drew a sun rising, which depicted the code word of the 26s, *sonop* (sunrise). Below that he drew a handshake with the three-finger salute of the 28s. From the box he produced a needle inserted between two matchsticks that were tied together with cotton, with the point of the needle sticking out. Next he made a paste from torch-battery dust mixed with spit in a bottle top and proceeded to tattoo my hand. After he was done, he squeezed out the blood and left me with the words '*Kap safe!*' (Be safe!)

14

Regret and remember

One night I had a bad dream about my mom and I awoke with a start. I lay awake for a long time, staring at the droplets of dew gathering on the corrugated roof as I wracked my brain trying to remember what the dream was about but to no avail. Fear clutched at my heart and I murmured a Bible verse: '*For God so loved the world He gave his only begotten Son …*' I tried to fall asleep again but sleep would not come.

The next day, my name was called for a visit and my heart fluttered for a moment. The visiting room was a cacophony of sound as I entered. I scanned the visiting boxes for a familiar face and my eyes latched onto my dad. He waved to catch my attention. I sat down opposite him and I could see the strain in his eyes.

'*Hallo, Pa, dis goed om vi Pa wee te sien.*' (Hallo, Dad, it's good to see you again.)

He gave me a tight smile. '*Djy lyk goed, Johnnie.*' (You're looking good.)

I had a feeling that he was playing for time. '*Dis sieke maa die tronk-kos, Pa. Hoe gannit met Ma …?*' (It's probably the prison food, Dad. How's Mom …?)

Tears pooled in his eyes and he struggled for words. '*Jou ma … jou ma is innie hospital, Johnnie. Sy't geval.*' (Your mother is in hospital, Johnnie. She fell.)

Fear gripped my heart. '*Geval …? Het Pa haar weer geslaan!?*' (She fell …? Did you beat her again, Dad!?)

Tears were streaming down his face as he shook his head and explained what had happened. Two ouens had come looking for me and Dad threw them out. Then they attacked Dad, and Mom stepped in. The one guy pushed her and she fell, hitting her head.

My fear turned to anger. Why were these guys looking for me, I asked. Tears stung my eyes as I stared at him.

He shrugged his shoulders. '*Ek sal'ie wietie, Johnnie ...*' (I wouldn't know, Johnnie ...)

I was overwhelmed with a feeling of regret. '*Ken Pa vi hulle?*' (Did you recognise them?)

'*Nooit gesien nie, Johnnie, en hulle't balaclavas opgehet, dit lyk ampe of hulle gestier was.*' (Never saw them before, Johnnie, and their faces were covered with balaclavas. It looked as if they'd been sent on a mission.)

Gums's image jumped into my mind and I was filled with fury. I prepared to leave even though the visiting period was not yet over.

Dad pleaded, '*Wag nou, Johnnie, besoek is noggie klaa nie.*' (Hang on, Johnnie, the visit isn't over yet.)

I got up. '*Dis als reg, Pa. Sê groete vir Ma en die meisies ...*' (It's alright, Dad. Send my love to Mom and the girls ...)

He was still crying when I left the visiting room. I had made up my mind. I was going to find out who had attacked my family and Gums was number one on my list. My belly tightened in anticipation.

I returned to my cell and sat down on my bed, staring at my feet, and the concrete floor dissolved into a puddle of blood. I shook off the image as Timer approached me with a blank piece of writing paper in hand and asked me to write him a letter. I stared at him with unseeing eyes and he asked, '*Watte gwan, Johnnie? Hoe change hulle?*' (What's up, Johnnie? What's changed?)

I was hesitant to confide in him but I needed to talk to somebody. '*Iemand het my family gechice, Timer. My Tanie is innie hossie.*' (Somebody attacked my family, Timer. My mother is in hospital.)

Timer cursed softly. '*Fok!*' He lit a tobacco joint, tugged on it and handed it to me. I took a drag and pointed to where Gums and his crew were gathered.

'*Ek wonner wat wiet hulle daa'van ...?*' (I wonder what they know about it ...?)

Timer took a sneak peek towards Gums and his crew. '*Djy sal moet 'n besluit maak, Johnnie. Djy kannie heeltyd wandel in "no man's land" nie. Die agge ennie sesse gan jou tronk toe werk, Johnnie. Is bietere as djy 'n 27 word, dan kan djy bloed vat!*' (You will have to decide, Johnnie. You can't always wander in no man's land. The 26s and the 28s will work you deeper into prison. It's better to become a 27, then you can take blood!)

I looked him in the eye, read between the lines and replied, '*Same difference, Timer.*'

Timer gave me a tight grin, peeked at Gums again and furtively withdrew a sharpened spoon from his waistband. He pushed the spoon under my blankets. '*Salute! Makie nomme vol!*' (Salute! The number dictates!) Timer walked off again.

I fondled the sharpened spoon and immediately a droplet of blood appeared on my fingertip. I sucked at the blood and words jumped into my mind. '*The kid loves blood.*'

So I plotted and planned; I had a one-track mind, and my hatred almost burnt a hole in my heart. I learnt that hatred so deep could make my heart weak. Days and weeks passed and Timer promoted me to yard boy. I was in charge of a group of prisoners tasked to keep the yard clean. At night I would write letters for the inmates and read their letters from home. I was privy to most of their private lives and I earned their respect by writing soul-stirring letters for them.

Every Tuesday we got meat with our food, and Gums and his crew would buy the meat from other prisoners in exchange for tobacco. At night they would feast on meat pie, which a lackey would make over the fat lamp. They had a good thing going for them and prison was their home.

I kept a low profile as I bided my time until the moment arrived on a sunny Tuesday afternoon. Gums was seated next to the entrance of the yard, shouting his wares. '*Vleis vi twak, vleis vi twak!*' (Meat for tobacco!) The prisoners entered the yard with their plates of food in hand, and those in need of tobacco headed towards him. His crew stood around handling the trade. Gimba was leaning against the wall alongside them. Timer was sitting alone some distance away. I sat on the opposite side of the yard, directly across from Gums. I watched and waited for the right moment to put my plan into action. More inmates arrived and closed in on Gums and I made my move.

I held the knife under my plate and moved swiftly across the yard. I was halfway there when Gimba pushed himself off the wall and hurried towards me and grabbed my right wrist, stopping me in my tracks. '*Is djy befok!? Moetie jou liewe soe weggooi nie, my broer. Een vannie dae is os op die vryes.*' (Are you fucked up!? Don't throw your life away like this, my brother. One of these days we will be on the outside.)

I tried to wrench my hand loose, but he held on and I looked him in the eye. '*My broer ...? Djy's nie my fokken broer nie!*' (My brother ...? You're not my fucking brother!)

He looked at me for a long moment and let go of my arm. I aborted my mission and walked off, as we were already attracting attention.

Timer was unhappy that I didn't follow through on Gums, and he demoted me from my position as yard boy and I ended up working on the farmlands that produced the vegetables for the prison population. It was back-breaking labour if you couldn't handle a spade, and the warder, 'Lang Leer' (Long Ladder), a tall, morose Boer, had the reputation of a hard taskmaster. The convicts feared him. We had to stand two in a row, and the first convict had to dig a depth of one spade and the second in line had to dig a depth of another spade inside the first hole and move down the line. A tattooed, toothless old convict was my '*eeste stiek*' (first spade), and I had to follow in his footsteps.

The old con was an old hand at the game and he flew down the line. I struggled to keep up, and when I came to the end of the line he was well rested and smoking a tobacco joint. He grinned at me with purple gums and offered me a drag on his smoke, which I breathlessly declined. '*Ek's olraait, ek wil'ie nou roek nie.*' (I'm okay, I don't want to smoke now.)

He gave me another purple-gum smile. '*Ek kan jou help, wiet djy?*' (I can help you, you know?)

I bristled at him. '*Ek hettie jou help norig nie. Kom, os doen dit!*' (I don't need your help. Come, let's do this!)

Two days later I kept close on his heels, giving him no time to rest or take a smoke break. The warder acknowledged my prowess and gave me another convict to work with. I became first spade and I could rest at the end of the line until he caught up with me. As soon as he caught up, I would start another line. I became stronger and more confident as I turned the negatives into positives.

That night my body ached and I just wanted to sleep, but there was no rest for the wicked. I could not drop my guard. I was watchful, ever watchful, when Gums stopped at my bed. '*Storietyd vi'naan, Johnnie!*' (Story time tonight, Johnnie!)

I hated this guy so much that I wanted to spit in his face, but I stayed focused. It was almost time for our release and I knew anything could happen so I played along. '*Daa'sie fout'ie, Gums.*' (No problem, Gums.) I got up and prepared my seat as the convicts gathered, paid Gums and settled in.

My eyes panned the crowd and settled on Timer on his bed reading a comic book. He was still mad at me and he ignored me completely. I decided to suck a story out of my thumb. '*Okay, manne ... vi'naan gan ek julle 'n storie vi'tel van Johnny-Boy.*' (Okay, guys ... tonight I'm going to tell you a story about Johnny-Boy.)

A match flared as a convict lit a smoke.

Now Johnny-Boy loved the girls, I told them, but he loved himself more and only used them for his own pleasure. Then he met this girl and fell head over heels in love with her and she with him.

I didn't know where the story was going, but I plugged on.

Johnny-Boy had a good job and he decided to get married to the girl. They had a good life and soon they had two children ... but then he lost his job!

I let the story hang in the air as I did a quick scan, looking for inspiration before proceeding.

Johnny-Boy looked for a job for a long time but there was no work. Unemployed and with Christmas around the corner, he decided to rob another guy. He succeeded in his first attempt and then decided to make a habit of robbing people, until the cops arrested him.

My eyes flicked towards Timer and I could see that I had his attention.

Johnny-Boy was sentenced to three years in prison. He was shit scared when he arrived, so he decided to take on the number ... to hide behind the number ...

There was shifting and shuffling of feet as my words hit home.

He pushed his time without problems and after a while, once he'd got the hang of the rhythm of the prison, he became a tough guy and started klapping other convicts around ...

Timer had dropped his comic book and was listening to my story.

Just before Johnny-Boy was due to be released, the number gave him a blade and told him, 'Here's a blade, stab that warder soaking wet with blood!' Johnny-Boy stabbed the warder and his three-year sentence turned into fifteen years.

I watched Dog as I spoke, because this had happened to him: he had been sentenced to a short term in prison but had stabbed a warder and his sentence was increased. I knew I had his attention when he cursed and said. '*Fok! Hy was dom!*' (Fuck! He was stupid!)

Johnny-Boy served his time, and when he was released his wife was waiting for him. Her family forgave him and gave him money to set up a fruit stall.

For a long time his business flourished, until four of his number brothers arrived. The number was calling him and they wanted to involve him in a robbery but Johnny-Boy refused. He had made up his mind.

The men pulled out knives, and Johnny-Boy knew, it was now or never. He grabbed his pumpkin knife and stabbed blindly at his perpetrators. He killed one of them and then a knife plunged into his throat and Johnny-Boy hit the ground with a bloody knife in his hand!

A convict groaned in disappointment. Gums came out of his reverie, stood up and shouted loudly, '*Dis slaaptyd. Toe mettie kop en oep mettie hol!*' (It's bedtime. Close your heads and open your bums!) The convicts returned to their beds and for a long time silence reigned in the cell.

A week later, on a Saturday, our names were called: we were going home. We stood around waiting for the cell door to open when Timer approached me and gave me an intricate handshake. '*Djy moetie wee tronk toe ko nie, Johnnie. Die'sie 'n plek vi jou nie.*' (You mustn't come back to prison, Johnnie. This place is not for you.)

I smiled at him in relief. '*Nooit wee nie, Timer. Van nou af is ek die "wary transgressor".*' (Never again, Timer. From now on I'm the wary transgressor.)

Gums chortled and grabbed Gimba's head with both hands and kissed him full on his mouth. Gimba was embarrassed and spluttered to get out of Gums's embrace. Gums chuckled and patted him on his backside. *'Djy MOET trugkom, my bokkie ... Papa wag vi jou!'* (You MUST come back, my darling ... Papa is waiting for you!)

The key rattled in the lock, the cell door opened and I was out of there.

We first went to the reception where our bags of clothes were retrieved and we got dressed in our civvies. An orderly gave us our train tickets and we walked out of prison. It was a glorious day. I looked back at the prison windows above the barbed wire and the windows stared blindly back. I put on the amulet my mom gave me and set off at a fast pace for Retreat railway station. Gimba lagged behind.

We got onto the first train that arrived and entered an empty carriage. Gimba sat down beside me, but I ignored him and after a while he went to sit on the opposite side of the carriage and stared through the window. When we reached Athlone station, we got off and I split from him. I just wanted to get home and see my family.

Part Four

Once you're in, there's no way out

15

Once a thief

When I got home, Mrs Lubbe was standing at our communal gate, smiling her fake smile. '*Hallo, Johnnie, welkom tuis,*' she said. (Hallo, Johnnie, welcome home.)

I ignored her and brushed past her.

When I entered the house, Mom was sitting at the table paging through her Bible. Her long hair hung loose and covered her face like a shroud. Her eyes lit up and filled with tears when she saw me. Dad was sober and sitting on a new couch strumming his guitar. I was home. Mom got up and hugged me tight and murmured, '*Dankie, Here … Kom, laat ons bid.*' (Thank you, Lord … Come, let's pray.)

Dad stopped his strumming, we all gathered around and held hands, and Mom prayed. Afterwards Dad hugged me, followed by my sisters, and all of them wanted to speak at the same time.

I sat down and Gloria asked if I wanted coffee or tea. Francis was working at Bauman's Biscuits now, she told me, so they had lots of biscuits.

'*Dankie, Gloria. Tee, asseblief.*' (Thanks, Gloria. Tea please.)

I sipped my tea and looked at Mom over the rim of the cup. '*Ek het opgemors, Ma, maar ek belowe ek gaan verander en vir my 'n werk kry.*' (I messed up, Mom, but I promise I'm going to change and find myself a job.)

A tear rolled down her cheek. '*Dis goed so, Johnnie.*' (That's good, Johnnie.)

Francis slipped out of the room and came back carrying a round box, which she put down in front of me and opened with a flourish. '*Vir jou, Johnnie.*' (For you, Johnnie.)

Inside the box was a navy-blue Stetson hat. Tears stung my eyes as I stared at it. '*Jissie, maar jy's oppie ball, Francis.*' (Jeez but you're on the ball, Francis.)

Gloria was having none of that. *'Mama het dit gekoop, Johnnie, nie Francis nie!'* (Mom bought it, Johnnie, not Francis!)

Mom chuckled and said, *'Sit dit op, Johnnie, laat ons sien hoe jy lyk.'* (Put it on, Johnnie, let's see what you look like.)

I put it on at a jaunty angle and posed for them. The hat was a perfect fit.

I decided to take a bath before having supper, and from the bathroom I heard the continuous whistle of our call floating on the breeze. My friends were waiting for me to make my appearance. My parents gave me a strange look when I sat down to supper and the whistling continued. I felt uncomfortable and wanted to be out of there to face my fears.

Gloria said, *'Vertel ons van die tronk, Johnnie ...?'* (Tell us about prison, Johnnie ...?)

I looked at her deep down. *'Nee, Gloria, daarvan word nie gepraat nie.'* (No, Gloria, we don't talk about that.) I believed that prison stuff should stay in prison.

The whistling continued and I was restless, so Mom suggested that I go and meet with my friends, otherwise the whistling would go on all night. As I stepped to the door, she warned me again to be careful.

When I arrived at our corner, Gimba was at the word. Chip, Solly, Robbie and some other new faces were there. There was no sign of Gif or Shorty. Rumour had it they were on the run from the cops.

I noticed two unknown girls sitting on Boeta Mike's porch. Rodney, a new member of our group, was chatting to the older girl and they looked lovestruck. The other girl was listening to Gimba boasting about his prison exploits. Robbie's two sisters were also there, giggling, and I saw them pointing me out to the girl. A drink was put into my hand and I chilled for a while as Gimba carried on trying to impress everybody. I noticed that he had a big pair of tailor's scissors sticking out of his pocket and I was not impressed at all. Gimba turned on the charm as he spoke to the girl. Robbie stepped up to me and murmured, *'Ek hou nogal nie van Gimba se style nie. Daai kin is my cousin en sy's nog baie jonk.'* (I don't like Gimba's style. That girl is my cousin and she's still very young.)

Gimba's behaviour rubbed me the wrong way, so I stepped up to him. *'Ek sien djy het nogal 'n gevaalike wapen in jou sak, Gimba, wat gan an?'* (I see you've got a dangerous weapon in your pocket, Gimba, what's up?)

Gimba turned on me and snarled, *'Staan trug, bandiet! Kan djy nie sien ek is biesig om met die kin te praat'ie!?'* (Stand back, convict! Can't you see I'm busy talking to this girl!?)

I could see that he was spoiling for a fight, so I pulled his chain. *'Ek sê maa net, Gimba, ek is bang djy maak jou netnou seer ...'* (I'm just saying, Gimba, I'm scared that you might just hurt yourself ...)

The girl chuckled and Gimba lost it. He pulled out the scissors, took up a knife-fighter's stance and played to the crowd. *'Vi'naan gan ek jou bloed vat, Johnnie ...'* (Tonight I'm going to take your blood, Johnnie ...)

I danced back as he swiped at me with the weapon. I pulled out my clasp knife and whipped it open with a flick of my wrist. The crowd became still as I danced with him. I taunted him. *'Dala soes die nomme jou wys, Gimba ...'* (Do as the number dictates, Gimba ...)

Just then, Boeta Mike, who was Robbie's dad and the girl's uncle, appeared on the porch. He pointed at me and told her, *'Bly weg van hom af. Hy's bad news!'* (Stay away from him. He's bad news!)

I respected the old guy and I kept my mouth shut. I was labelled.

A dice game started in the opposite alley and Robbie went over to join it. Minutes later a squabble broke out and Robbie got smacked around, so Gimba shouted, *'Ko os dala, ouens!'* (Let's go, guys!)

Our cache of weapons was stashed further down the alley, so we rushed to arm ourselves. I grabbed a small axe and sped towards the scene. As I ran past the girl, she shouted at me, *'Jongetjie, jy kom net vandag uit die tronk uit.'* (Young man, you just came out of prison today.)

I swerved away from the fight and ran home with the axe in my hand. When I got there I went straight to bed and I heard Mom praying softly, thanking God for my safe return. I lay awake for a long time as I thought about the girl's words.

The next day, Francis introduced me to her boyfriend, Boy, who worked as a pipe fitter in the Cape Town dockyard. He was a bit wary of me at first, but as the day passed he became more relaxed and he offered to get me a job as a labourer on the docks. I jumped at the chance to get a job, and early the next day I found myself at the West Quay. I was eager to work.

I hung around waiting for the foreman to arrive, and everyone who came to work that morning stared at me, looking at my prison tattoos, and dismissed me in the blink of an eye. I was nobody. The foreman arrived and asked for my credentials and I gave him my ID card. I had nothing else except the tattoos that he kept staring at.

Boy, dressed in his overalls, approached the foreman and explained my situation to him. On his recommendation, the foreman decided to employ me for a three-month trial period. I had a job and I was going to make the most of it.

It was a fitter and turners' workshop and all the fitters and turners were white Englishmen who were hired to attend to the Irvin & Johnson deep-sea fishing trawlers when they came into dock to unload their catch. There were no South African white men and all the 'boys' were black or coloured and each one was assigned to a fitter.

Most of them worked on the docked trawlers to fix and repair whatever was needed to make sure the trawlers were seaworthy. I was assigned to Mr Moss, a seventy-year-old in-house fitter who chain-smoked Westminster 85 cigarettes. His job was to overhaul any piece of faulty machinery that the other fitters brought in for repairs. He disliked me from the word go and would only speak to me in irritated syllables. It was hard working in the workshop, cleaning and lifting all kinds of machinery and then delivering the repaired parts to the designated trawler. But it was a new beginning and I was prepared to take any snide remarks in my stride.

I liked the smell of the sea, and every day I had to go and fetch a box of freshly fried fish on the North Quay, which supplied all the workshops with fried fish. At lunchtime, I would enjoy my fish on the harbour among the huge tanks of unloaded fish. I would feed the seagulls and watch them dip and dive or catch the titbits of food in mid-air. I never ate in the cloakroom or spent time with the other workers.

I would rather spend my time reading a book, as I was always at the end of their crude jokes and I had promised myself that I wouldn't do crime again.

Mr Moss made it hard for me to stick to my promise. It was unbelievable how much hatred Englishmen had for coloured people. He made me carry a heavy loaded toolbox up a rickety gangplank and then he would only use one tool. The old man had a sadistic streak, but I sought his favour and would help him to his car every day after work. We worked late hours, but twice a week I would get a 'fry' of fish to take home and Mom was at her happiest.

One Thursday evening I got off the train at Athlone railway station with a James Hadley Chase book in hand and saw Robbie's two cousins waiting for a train. The younger girl was holding a couple of library books. I approached them and introduced myself. I said I'd seen them there at Boeta Mike's place and asked how they were doing.

The younger girl blushed and smiled at me. She told me her name was Una and the other girl was her sister Jenny and that they lived in Harfield Village.

'O, soe julle bly in die suburbs …?' (Oh, so you stay in the suburbs …?)

She blushed some more. Jenny turned her nose up and gave me a steely look.

I indicated towards Una's books and asked her if she liked reading.

She showed me her books. 'Ek hou graag van lees … Ek het my biblioteekboeke vergeet by Boeta Mike se huis, toe moes ek dit kom haal.' (I love reading … I left my library books at Boeta Mike's place so I had to come fetch them.)

I showed her my book. 'Miskien kan ons boeke ruil …' (Maybe we can exchange books …)

She grinned shyly and her eyes flickered towards Jenny, who was clearly not impressed. But Una was friendly and comfortable in my company, so I took a gamble. 'Don't you want to go to the cinema with me …?'

She contemplated for a moment, then shook her head. 'Ek dink nie so nie … my stiefpa …' (I don't think so … my stepfather …) Her words hung in the air.

I persisted. *'Wat van Saterdagmiddag? Ons kan 'n bietjie daar by Claremont Gardens gaan kuier…'* (What about Saturday afternoon? We can go visit the Claremont Gardens …)

She gave it some thought and then her face broke into a smile. *'Okay, ek kry vir jou op Claremont-stasie so om eenuur.'* (Okay, I'll meet you at Claremont station about one o'clock.)

Jenny glared at me as their train pulled into the station and she tugged at her sister's arm. *'Kom, Una, hier's die trein!'* (Come, Una, here's the train!)

They got onto the train and I watched her get settled in. She waved to me and I blew her a kiss. I had a swagger in my step as I set off for home.

The next day was Friday and I was eager to get my pay envelope. I stood in line outside the pay office with the other boys, who were already discussing what to drink on the train home. After giving Mom her share of my pay, I went to Athlone Main Road and bought myself a new shirt at Cape Flats Store.

On Saturday I arrived at Claremont station half an hour early as I was excited to see Una. Surprisingly enough, she was early too. We spent a glorious afternoon in the gardens, just chatting and no hanky-panky. She was good company and spoke freely about her home circumstances, mostly about her belligerent stepfather, Walter, who was many years younger than her mother. I also learnt that her father had died a few years earlier and that she had five brothers and two sisters. Not once did she ask me about my criminal past and I appreciated that very much.

The day flew by and soon it was dusk and I offered to walk her home. She was hesitant at first, but then she agreed. I walked her to their gate and waited for her to enter her house when this rotund guy came up behind me and rasped, *'Is djy 'n gangster!?'* (Are you a gangster!?)

I turned and looked into the brutal face of Walter, her stepfather. He had a big scarred forehead, mean green eyes, a small mouth with pink lips and he smelt of liquor. I sensed that Walter was looking for trouble but I stayed focused. *'Wat is 'n gangster, meneer?'* I said. *'Enige een kan 'n gangster wies, os amal trek dieselfde aan…'* (What is a gangster, sir? Anybody can be a gangster, we all dress the same …) Wrong answer, but there was no way I could respect him.

Una was standing at the open front door, and her mother appeared behind her, their eyes filled with trepidation.

Walter grabbed me by my shirt collar and spit-sprayed into my face, '*Djy lyk soes 'n fokken gangster en ek hou nie van gangsters nie!*' (You look like a fucking gangster and I don't like gangsters!)

Una's mom intervened. '*Los hom, Walter!*' (Leave him, Walter!)

Walter was on a roll and tugged at my collar, popping the buttons. He ripped my sleeve and snarled when he saw my prison tattoos. '*Djy was sieke 'n wyfie innie tronk!*' (You were probably a concubine in prison!)

I stepped back and whipped his feet from under him in a quick practised move and Walter hit the ground with a thud. He stared up at me with confused eyes as his wife came rushing to his aid. Una looked accusingly at me and my exposed tattoos, her eyes brimming with tears. '*Kyk wat het jy nou gedoen ...*' (Look what you've done now ...)

I was filled with regret as I turned on my heel and set off towards the railway station.

It was late and the township street was quiet. As I walked past our corner, Gimba suddenly stepped out of the shadows. He had a knife in his hand and he was looking for trouble. He walked up to me threateningly. '*Djy hijack nogal my kin!*' (You hijacked my girl!)

I was in a real bad mood and snapped at him, '*Watte kin, waa kry djy dan 'n kin ...?*' (What girl, where did you get a girl ...?)

Gimba gave a derogatory chuckle. '*Djy wiet mos watte kin. Djy het sieke al klaa die cream geëet!*' (You know which girl. You probably already ate the cream!)

That's when I hit him with a looping right into his throat, sending his knife flying to the ground. I kicked the knife away. '*Moetie met my fokkie, Gimba!*' (Don't fuck with me, Gimba!) I moved on home.

That night I lay awake for a long time going over the day's events. '*No rest for the wicked,*' I thought, before falling into a fitful sleep.

I returned to work on Monday to find a hung-over Mr Moss waiting for me. He pushed my buttons the whole day. After lunch we had to go and dismantle a water pump on one of the trawlers. I staggered up the rickety gangplank with the heavy toolbox. He pointed towards the water pump. '*Loosen that nut!*' I took a spanner from the toolbox and struggled with the salt-rusted nut. A lone sailor on standby was sitting a distance away working on a net.

The spanner kept on slipping and Moss screamed at me, '*Use some fucking elbow grease!*' I tried again and the spanner slipped and dropped into the sea. Moss went ballistic and came at me with the hammer, screaming, '*You fucking ignorant coloured bastard!*'

All my pent-up fury and hatred for white men exploded. I grabbed the hammer in mid-air as he swung, and for a moment the shadow of death loomed in his eyes as I whispered to him, '*It's a nice day for dying…*'

I was about to bash in his head when the lone deckhand spoke up and said, '*Ek sallie daai doen as ek djy was nie. Issie werd'it nie…*' (I wouldn't do that if I were you. It's not worth it …)

My anger subsided as I took in my surroundings: the mountains, the sea, the waves lapping gently against the keel of the boat. I lowered the hammer and told him, '*I will pay for the spanner…*' I took out another spanner from the toolbox and succeeded in getting the nut loose while Moss seethed and chain-smoked.

We returned to the workshop and Moss complained to the foreman, accusing me of trying to assault him. I could see in the foreman's eyes that I wouldn't be needed after my three-month trial period was up. Nonetheless, I still helped the old coot to his car every day after work. I was thinking that maybe the foreman would give me a reprieve, but then I did something that made this impossible.

On a windy Friday night in November, I helped Moss to his car and helped myself to his pay packet sticking out of his side pocket, which included his month's salary. He earned a lot of money, more than I had ever held in my hands before. I felt vindicated because of the way he had insulted me and treated me like a lesser human being. As soon as he drove off, I regretted what I had done. On the train home I tried to read but I couldn't concentrate; the pay packet in my pocket played on my conscience. When I got home I hid the money in the chicken coop and I didn't touch a cent.

I stayed at home all weekend. I was restless as I kept thinking about the stolen money. I kicked the idea around of taking it back on Monday and dropping it in the workshop. I weighed up my chances and in the end I decided to hang onto it.

I had butterflies in my stomach when I returned to work on Monday and found all the fitters in the workshop waiting for me. A well-built whitey grabbed my arms and frogmarched me towards a bolted-down vice. He put my right arm into the vice and tightened it, snarling, '*I'm going to cut off your fucking hand!*'

I put on my dumb convict face and gave a coloured boy whine. '*What did I do wrong…?*'

Moss, who had experienced my dark side, read the fakery in my voice and snarled at me, '*You stole my fucking money, you coloured son of a whore!*'

I stared at him, with hatred radiating from my being and enveloping the group of white men. Nobody calls my mother a whore and gets away with it. Code of conduct.

The foreman told them to let me go and called me into his office. He paid me two days' holiday pay and sent me on my way. They had no case, I had no job, but the feeling of regret for stealing money from the racist Moss had dissipated.

16

Caught up

Mom was unhappy about me losing my job and my weekly pay packet, so I spent the next few days puttering around the house. I cleaned the yard, weeded the garden and chopped firewood. While cleaning the chicken coop, I came across a dagger that I had stuck into the ground a few years back. I wiped the blade and placed it with my hidden money stash. Early one morning just before the festive season, I heard Mom praying, pleading with the Lord for some financial aid. I wasn't so sure if the Lord worked this way, but I decided to answer her prayer. After she left to go to the shop, I retrieved Mr Moss's money from the chicken coop and put most of the crispy notes into an envelope. I pocketed the rest before tearing up the pay packet.

I was restless, and the call of the gang floating on the breeze didn't make things any easier, so I pocketed the dagger and went looking for a dice or card game. Before I left, I popped the envelope in the letter box.

I hit the street and whistled the call. I got three replies in return and I headed in their direction and found Robbie, Solly, Chip and two others involved in a game of rummy at our hangout. There was a huge amount of money in the pot. Other players were hanging around, chugging on chalices of dagga while waiting for a chance to play.

A cigarette was hanging from Robbie's long lip. He was good at the game, as could be witnessed by the stack of notes in front of him. Two young identical-twin brothers, Ikey and Christy, who were both runners for the gang, were tasked to clean and refill the chalices from a parcel of dagga. Dagga smoke billowed in the air.

I'd never had dealings with the twins before, but I'd heard about their escapades. They were up-and-coming young wannabes who were looking to enhance their reputation. I was watchful when Ikey handed me a full chalice, saying, 'Roek 'n pyp, Johnnie ...' (Smoke a pipe, Johnnie ...)

I didn't want to smoke, as I wanted to be clear-headed when I got a chance to play, so I declined. '*Nei, ek sal aaire 'n slow boat roek.*' (No, I would rather smoke a slow boat.)

Ikey tried to chortle like an old gangster. ''*n Slow boat ...?*'

I looked him in the eye and I knew that violence was brewing when Chip snarled at him, '*Wat's jou molefisie, Ikey!? Djy hoo mos wat die man gesê het, maak hom 'n fokken slow boat!*' (What's your problem, Ikey!? You heard what the man said, roll him a fucking slow boat!)

That took the wind out of Ikey's sails and all he could offer was '*Aweh ...*'

Chip ranted some more. '*Nie aweh nie, respek. Gie die man respek!*' (Not aweh, respect. Give the man respect!)

The other twin, Christy, gave me some respect and volunteered to roll the joint. He passed it to me when he was done and I tugged leisurely on it as I watched the game.

Robbie was on a winning streak and he bet enormous sums against the other players. He made them squirm nervously until they lost the game. Robbie grinned from ear to ear as he hauled in his winnings. I pulled out some crisp new notes and took a seat opposite him. A nerve ticked under his right eye as he stared at my money. Even though Robbie was a bit wary of me, he loved gambling and winning. He was also zonked by now and I was not.

I lost the first game, and as he hauled the money towards him, I took out more notes and doubled the pot. '*Win or lose, Robbie ...*'

Robbie's eyes flickered nervously as he shuffled the pack of cards. I cut the cards and he dealt me three jokers and I knew I had him. He took a card, looked at it and dumped it. I picked it up, laid down all my cards, and hauled in my winnings. Robbie was pissed off, to say the least, so I gave him some money and bought the guys two cases of beer.

When I got home, my parents were sitting in the dining room celebrating Mom's gift from God, which she held up for me to see. Dad was all smiles and said, '*Die Here het jou ma geseën, Johnnie. Nou gan sy vi my 'n deposit gie vi 'n van!*' (The Lord has blessed your mom. Now she's going to give me a deposit for a van!)

I felt a bit guilty of my sham, but I played along. '*Daai's kwaai. Hoe het daai gebeur ...?*' (That's great. How did it happen ...?)

Gloria, all excited, piped up, '*Vyfduisend rand, Johnnie, ek het dit in die letter box gekry!*' (Five thousand rand, Johnnie, I found it in the letter box!)

I was happy for them, and I felt that Mr Moss had redeemed himself. Three days later, Dad drove home in an old Fargo van with two double doors at the back. The van became his pride and joy and he spent hours on end tinkering on it. He would wash and polish it and even the tyres had a high shine. The van created a lot of envy among the neighbours, especially Mrs Lubbe.

One morning, Dad discovered that all four tyres had been slashed and he could not hold back the tears. I was overwhelmed with hatred for the perpetrator, so I decided to find him and fix him. I asked around and soon found out that a guy called Georgie was the culprit and he was the eldest son of Ballie Honne-oor. I also found out that he worked as a boy on a cool-drink truck and the time he usually came home. So one misty night I got a hockey stick and lay in wait for him in the bush. I waited for a long time and my clothes were soaked by the wet grass, but my hatred was overpowering. Then Georgie came down the path through the bush. I let him pass and then I smashed him with the hockey stick and broke both his arms. He never knew what hit him and I left him there in the dark, moaning in pain.

One Friday night just before Christmas, I was roaming the streets looking for a dice game. Armed with my knife, I also had a half-jack of gin in my inside jacket pocket. I checked out the dice games and saw how much money was involved, and now and then I would join in, win some bucks and move on. I would sip from my gin, which made my hands a bit sticky. Then I came upon a dice game where the Road Devils gang hung out. This was quite a distance from my territory, but two members who were there were my cousins, Tolla from Aunt Lucky, and Arthur, the son of my mom's other sister Elsie. I figured they had my back as they were my blood relatives, but they proved me wrong.

I got into the game and won more than I lost. Then I got into a winning streak and accumulated a lot of cash. Tolla did not like it one little bit when I won all their money. I was on my haunches picking up my winnings when he kicked me in the face and I toppled over. Arthur threw a brick at my head, hitting me just above the eyes and shaving off both my eyebrows. Another brick hit me on the head and I ran off, half bowed in pain.

As I neared our corner, I whistled the call and I got a whole barrage in return. When I got to our hangout, there were a lot of guys hanging around. They saw my condition and Chip was the first to respond and asked, '*Watte gwan, Johnnie …?*' (What's up, Johnnie …?)

I gave them a quick rundown of events and we armed ourselves and I led the way to my house. I went inside and Mom was appalled when she saw my injuries. '*Wie het jou so geslaan, Johnnie?*' she wanted to know. (Who beat you like this, Johnnie?)

'*Tolla en Arthur, Mama, maar ek gan hulle kry!*' (Tolla and Arthur, Mom, but I'm going to get them!)

Mom was almost hysterical and cried, '*Maar hulle is familie …*' (But they are family …)

There was no love lost between Dad and Mom's relatives, so he grabbed the keys to his van.

Our whole crew jumped in the back of the van and Dad set off towards the Road Devils' hangout. They scattered as the van pulled up and we jumped out and laid into them. Tolla scampered down the road and I went after him. He dashed in by my Aunt Lucky's gate and I was hot on his heels, my knife drawn. For a moment he was obscured by a hedge, and as I came around it he was waiting for me and stabbed me in the neck.

When I came to in hospital, I had stitches in my neck and a bandage around my head, and I was discharged two days later. No charges were laid, as per the unwritten law of the gangs. Gangsters don't lay charges against other gangsters.

Recuperating at home, I seethed with anger and disbelief that my own blood had taken my blood. Knowing that they could have killed me, I vowed to take revenge. Gone was my resolve to change my life around. But, as the days passed and the pain and anger subsided, I took a hard look at my life and found that there was something missing.

Deep inside of me there was a yearning to be someone different, to walk away from gangsterism and crime.

To seek an escape, I took out my typewriter, slid in a page and painstakingly typed a heading: *Hulle Noem My Skollie* (They Call Me Gangster). I sat and stared at the words for a long time and my mind journeyed to far-off places of which I had read over the years. I closed the typewriter without typing another word and settled down with a book by James Hadley Chase: *The Things Men Do*.

In the next week or so, I read three more books as my wounds healed. Then one night, the air was shattered by the continuous call of the gang and I knew that something was amiss. I had to answer the call and my parents knew that, so they just stared at me as I stepped outside and whistled a reply. When I arrived at our hangout, the guys were sombre, so I asked the question, '*Hoe change hulle dan, ouens...?*' (What's changed, guys ...?)

Solly, cleaning his nails with the blade of his knife, answered for them. '*Wanie Road Devil het vi Ebie wit biene gemaak!*' (Wanie Road Devil killed Ebie!)

Ebie, or 'Smash', who'd had his head banged in while jumping a bus, was harmless and we saw this as an act of cowardice.

We decided to mourn our brother by celebrating his life before seeking revenge, so we pooled our money and sent Ikey and Christy to buy a few bottles of whisky, a parcel of dagga and two crates of beer. A fire was started in the brazier and we settled down to celebrate and plot our revenge. Robbie took out a roll of bills. '*Ekkit 'n kroon hie vi Smash se tanie, miskien kan sy 'n bus huur...*' (I've got some money here for Smash's mother, maybe she can hire a bus ...)

We all pooled our resources and added to the fund.

The funeral was on the following Saturday, and eight of us got onto the bus on our way to the cemetery. The mourners murmured among themselves as we gathered around the grave. Each of us plucked a flower from a wreath and chewed on it, and everyone knew that blood was going to be spilt. After the coffin was lowered into the grave, we grabbed the spades and filled the hole quickly, much to the disapproval of the other mourners. After paying our respects, we got back onto the bus.

When dusk fell that day, we armed ourselves and went hunting. I was high on fear and danger. We arrived at the Road Devils' hangout to find the place deserted, so we went searching for them. We searched for a long time, but to no avail. But it wasn't over yet. They had declared a gang war, and Wanie was on our hit list, along with anybody else who stood in our way.

In the following days we had daily skirmishes with the Road Devils as we tracked them down, but there was no sign of Wanie. We wanted him dead. Three weeks later, Chip, Solly and I were on our way home from Belgravia Estate when we spotted him. He was sitting alone on the stairway of a block of flats close to Main Road.

We converged on him, knives drawn. He saw us and fled by jumping through an opening in the wall. We followed hot on his heels. Wanie was quick and had worked out his escape route. He sprinted like an athlete, but this was our game and we kept pace with him. We crossed Main Road towards Athlone. Wanie looked back once and saw us coming as Chip screamed after him, '*The gallows is our destiny!*'

That spurred Wanie on, his brown jacket flying like a cloak behind him as he picked up his pace.

Wanie was frightened out of his wits, and as the Athlone police station loomed before him, he ran straight through the doors. We pitched our knives away and went after him. Inside the police station a frightened Wanie was jabbering to the cop behind the counter. The confused cop looked at us as we walked in and demanded, '*Wat gaan hier aan?*' (What's going on here?)

We closed in on Wanie, putting the fear of God into him, and he ran behind the counter screaming, '*Ek het iemand doodgemaak, ek wil myself opgie!*' (I killed someone, I want to give myself up!)

We waited while the cop took down his statement. When Wanie was led back to the cells, Chip shouted, '*Nog Young Ones!*' (More Young Ones!)

I felt almost relieved at the way things had turned out and that there was no blood on my hands. My status grew among the gang members, and when I spoke, they listened. So I decided to call off the gang war, and only Ikey questioned my decision. '*Wat van jou twie nefies,*

Tolla en Arthur, Johnnie?' (What about your two cousins Tolla and Arthur, Johnnie?)

Ikey was bloodthirsty and I did not want to play judge and jury on my cousins, so I let him down gently. *'Los hulle vi my, Ikey. Daai's family business ...'* (Leave them to me, Ikey. That's family business ...)

It was a wise decision, as my parents got together with Uncle Piet, Aunt Lucky and Aunt Elsie to discuss the situation. My decision also gave Tolla and Arthur protection from the Young Ones and they steered clear of our territory. The war was over and the community was happy. Once again, we took over our role as gatekeepers – or should I say toll-keepers – as more and more guys flocked to our chapel.

There was no shortage of liquor, dagga or money, as every member hustled to bring something to our hangout. We even had regular 'customers' who paid us for our friendship. Life was good, but deep in my heart I knew that was not what I really wanted. I got bored with the daily drinking and dagga smoking, the dice games and the tough-guy banter. Bored with the drudgery of township life. There was a yearning in me that I could not explain to my gang fellows. There were no dreams to share with them.

One evening when I came home, Francis was all excited and told me she had good news.

'Watse goeie nuus, Francis? Gaan jy trou?' (What's the good news, Francis? Are you getting married?)

She stifled a laugh and said, *'Jou meisie Una het vandag by ons begin werk!'* (Your girlfriend Una started work by us today!)

'My meisie ...? Dis die eerste keer wat ek daarvan hoor.' (My girlfriend ...? This is the first time I've heard about that.)

Francis kept going. *'Maar sy sê dan vir almal by die werk dat jy's haar boyfriend!'* (But she's telling everybody at work that you're her boyfriend!)

I was stupefied but left it at that.

17

My first real job

Two of the guys who had flocked to our group, Stretch and Muis, were members of the Jolly Pickers, a small gang from Block 8, and they actually worked shifts at the Lion Match factory. They were cool, well dressed and not into crime and violence at all. They just came to smoke dagga and gamble, be it cards or dice. I liked them, and when they spoke about their jobs, I envied them. But Ikey was heard to say, *'Perdewerk!'* (Horses' work!) Anyway, my curiosity was aroused.

The next Monday morning, I found myself in front of the gates of the Lion Match factory in Observatory, where a lot of job seekers were standing around. They were mostly gang bangers from various townships across the Cape Flats. We stood in line and we were called in one at a time by a supervisor and many were turned away. Some came out cursing and spitting profanities. I didn't give myself much chance of succeeding, but I hung out there in the slow-moving line under the burning sun.

A siren went off for tea break and the supervisor closed the office door. The workers came outside, all dressed in white overalls, including Stretch and Muis. When Stretch saw me, he came over with a big smile on his face and invited me into the grounds. *'Kom in, Johnnie, ek gan 'n way maak vi jou ...'* (Come inside, Johnnie, I'm going to make a way for you ...) Their eyes were bright from smoking dagga so I was a bit unsure, but I stepped inside anyway. I sat down with them and they shared their sandwiches with me and Stretch gave me the lowdown on the factory. *'Djy sien, Johnnie, die mense is baie confused, soe na die tea break gan ek jou wys hoe djy moet maak ...'* (You see, Johnnie, these people are very much confused, so after the tea break I will show you what you've got to do ...)

I looked at the long line of job seekers and I was a bit uncertain of Stretch's move. *'Is djy vi'sieke ...?'* (Are you sure ...?)

Stretch and Muis grinned at each other.

After the tea break, the workers went inside and I followed them. Just inside the door there was a long table scattered with broken boxes of matches and Stretch pointed me towards it. '*Kap vas hie by die tafel, dan sort djy amal die stukkende bokse yt.*' (Stand here by this table and sort out all the broken boxes.)

The factory floor was huge, with a lot of different machines scattered throughout the various departments. The operators started up their machines and the place became a cacophony of sound. Nobody bothered me or asked any questions until a top-heavy coloured supervisor in his fifties stopped at the table, looked at me in surprise and asked, '*Wie is jy dan? Waar kom jy vandaan en wie het jou aangevat?*' (Who are you then? Where do you come from and who employed you?)

I pointed to Stretch and Muis, who were standing and working next to each other. Stretch waved to the supervisor, who stomped over to them, and they conferred.

The supervisor came back to me and said, '*Okay, ek is oek van die Road en ek gaan vir jou 'n kans gee, maa as jy opfok, dan is dit uit met jou gat!*' (Okay, I'm also from the Road and I'm going to give you a chance, but if you fuck up you're out on your butt!) He took down my details and I was in. I had a job, a second chance.

He gave me white overalls and took me to a long conveyor belt sending full boxes of matches in my direction. I had to grab them with two hands and pop them into a huge wooden box. When the box was full, it was replaced with an empty one and the full one was wheeled to another machine where the boxes were neatly wrapped in packs of ten. You had to be quick and I struggled at first, as the matchboxes kept slipping through my fingers, but after a while I got the hang of it.

I earned twelve rand a week. I always loved nice clothes, so I opened lay-by accounts and bought myself some new shirts and wore tailor-made pants with my numerous pairs of shoes. I became a trendsetter, and each time I got something new, everybody else went to buy it. Our gang became a bunch of good-looking guys with bad ideas.

One Saturday night, Francis had a party and invited some of her co-workers. Most of them knew of my bad-guy reputation so I usually steered clear of these events, but this one was a surprise for me because she hadn't told me about it. I heard the music playing, so I stepped inside the house to find the lights down and a few couples dancing the blues. I turned to leave, but Francis gripped my hand and told me to hang on for a bit, because she had a surprise for me. The music stopped, the lights went on and there was Una standing there like a wallflower.

I found myself in a situation. Everybody present gave me knowing smiles as if they knew something that I did not. A Chubby Checker twist song turned on the deck and I played the game. I took Una's hand and we got onto the dance floor and did the twist. She was good at it so I showed them my moves, whirling and twirling her around in her above-the-knee red dress. We took centre stage and the others cheered us on.

Later I asked her the question, '*Hoekom sê jy dan vir die mense ek is jou boyfriend ...?*' (Why are you telling the people that I'm your boyfriend ...?)

She chuckled and replied, '*Jy sien, almal die ouens by die werk klop aan om my uit te vat, toe sê ek vir hulle jy is my boyfriend!*' (You see, all the guys at work hassle me to go out with them, so I tell them you're my boyfriend!)

I grinned at her. '*Jy's slim ... maar pla hulle nog altyd?*' (You're clever ... but are they still bothering you?)

'*Uh-uh, Francis maak seker dat hulle weet van jou reputasie.*' (Uh-uh, Francis makes sure that they know about your reputation.)

That was a sobering thought and I wasn't sure that I liked it.

A blues number started playing and we danced cheek to cheek and I whispered in her ear, '*Ons moet weer 'n keer uitgaan, Una. Miskien moet ek kom verskoning vra vir jou stiefpa ...*' (We must go out again, Una. Maybe I should ask your stepdad for forgiveness ...)

'*Ek dink nie so nie,*' she whispered back. '*My stiefpa is 'n haatdraende man!*' (I don't think so. My stepdad is an unforgiving man!)

We made a date to go to the cinema the following Saturday.

On Monday, I started working the afternoon shift, which finished at ten at night, and I met Una briefly twice that week at Mowbray train station. When I got off there, she got onto the same train on her way to Harfield after visiting her relatives in Kewtown. We confirmed our matinee cinema date for the Saturday. So my co-workers who were travelling onwards to the Southern Suburbs came to know her, which gave voice to a lot of banter at work the following day.

'Sout', an English-speaking older guy from Plumstead who fancied himself as a ladies' man, had a lot to say and he would needle me. *That girl is too young for you, Johnnie. You're not on her level, and with those sagging pants I don't think you're going to make it with her parents.* I took this in my stride, but I knew what he was saying was true.

Saturday came around and we went to the matinee show at the Orpheum Cinema in Claremont because she had to be home early. She was seriously interested in watching the film and not in any hanky-panky. She was younger than I was, and the fact that she liked me and was comfortable in my company brought new meaning into my life. I intended to keep it that way, but trouble always found me.

Walking her to the corner of her street at dusk that day, I was hustled by her homeboys, who didn't like the fact that I was from Athlone. They didn't like the way I walked or talked or dressed. Also, Una was seen as a poster girl in her community, who had hooked up with a gangster with sagging pants and a Stetson hat, and they weren't happy about that. I had a knife clasped tightly in my right hand inside my jacket pocket and I was prepared to defend myself. The message was clear. I was not welcome in their territory; they belonged to the Doolans and I was an outsider.

Two of those guys who I later learnt were called Arrie and Ta-Black approached us as we stopped at the corner of Harvey Road where she stayed. Arrie was at the word. *'Hallo, Una, wat soek djy dan met die boef, my meisie?'* (Hallo, Una, what are you doing with this thug, my girl?)

Una responded angrily. *'Jou meisie…? Van wanneer af is ek jou meisie, Arrie? Moetie jou luck kom try nie!'* (Your girl…? Since when am I your girl, Arrie? Don't come try your luck!)

Arrie and Ta-Black went into wannabe gangster mode, folding their arms across their chests, and Arrie taunted her in a sing-song voice. *'Moenie soe sê nie, my meisie, djy wiet dan…'* (Don't say things like that, my girl, you know that…)

I didn't have time for this and cut him off by taking out my knife and whipping it open with a flick of my wrist. I snarled at him, '*Fokkof! Djy hoo mos wat sy sê, moetie kom tyd stoot nie!*' (Fuck off! You heard what she said, don't push time!)

They stepped back at my action and tone of voice as I continued. '*En as julle wee die girlie pla, dan ruk ek julle fokken tjoepe yt! Fokkof!*' (And if you bother this girl again, I'll rip out your fucking tubes! Fuck off!)

Una held onto my jacket. '*Los hulle, Johnnie, hulle is dom!*' (Leave them, Johnnie, they're stupid!)

Arrie tapped on his watch with his finger and said, '*Met tyde saam …*' (Time will tell …)

I waited until Una's gate banged behind her before I left for the train station.

At the factory, about half of the coloured workforce smoked dagga during their lunch or tea breaks in the many hideaways on the factory grounds, but few had the pluck to bring dagga to work because they feared the railway police. I saw a gap and bought myself a parcel of dagga from Mr C and rolled it off into dagga sticks, which became a lucrative sideline. Life was good.

Then one lunch break, a white-coated supervisor walked in on us in our hideaway and I quickly hid my stash away. The place was thick with smoke and I knew we were in trouble. He sniffed the air and said, '*Ek ruik dagga …*' (I smell dagga …)

Nobody answered and he continued, '*Relax … ek soek 'n stop dagga …*' (Relax … I'm looking for a stick of dagga …)

I was relieved, but then I recognised him. It was Pock Marks, the thug who had smashed my bike so many years ago, but he didn't recognise me. He was older and the pockmarks had faded, but his image was burnt into my brain. He had got himself a good job as the supervisor in the packing department, which meant that he also earned a lot more money than any of us.

I sold him a stick of dagga and told him, '*Stretch kan somme die stop regmaak vi die lanie …*' (Stretch can clean the dagga for the boss …) He was a vain character who liked the accolade. He immediately took a liking to me and the fact that I could supply him with dagga. He responded with '*Djy's slim! Wiet jou ma djy's soe slim?*' (You're clever! Does your mother know you're so clever?)

We all chuckled at his silly joke; he liked that too and cracked some more jokes while Stretch prepared a pipe for him. I lit the chalice and he tugged at it and the dagga crackled and popped inside the bottle head. He exhaled through his nostrils like two exhaust pipes. He was greedy and held onto the chalice for two more drags instead of passing it on, which was the norm. His action was noted by Stretch and Muis by a flicker of their eyes.

We became great friends, but I was moulding him for my revenge. One day we were chilling with cold beers and dagga and everyone was boasting about their exploits and escapades when Pock Marks decided to tell a story to prove that he was also a tough guy.

This is how he narrated his story. '*Op 'n Vrydagaand stiek die groot boef yt op osse territory met 'n bike ... Die bra was heel sterk gevriet, toe vat ek sy bike af en gooi dit flenters teen die pad.*' (On a Friday night this big thug arrived in our territory on a bike ... This guy was a tough guy, so I took his bike and smashed it to smithereens.)

I was seething with anger, but I stayed focused and asked, '*Toe wat maak die bra?*' (Then what did the brother do?)

Pock Marks gave a derogatory chuckle and said, '*Ek vat mossie kak van kabouters nie ... Ek gie hom toe 'n paar klappe en toe vlug hy!*' (I don't take shit from dwarfs ... I smacked him a couple of times and he fled!)

The others chuckled inanely and I responded with '*Nei ... djy is daai ou, my bra.*' (No ... you're the man, my brother.) He basked in the hero worship and bought some more sticks of dagga for us to enjoy. Pock Marks didn't know it yet, but I was setting him up for a big fall.

One lazy Saturday afternoon I was sitting on our porch typing a few lines on my typewriter when Una came to visit Francis. They chuckled and chatted with each other as Gloria prepared tea and biscuits. Mom was sitting at the dining-room table knitting a jersey. Gloria came outside to serve me tea, with Una close behind. They watched me as I typed a few words with my one finger: *Drome Sterf Nooit.* Dreams Never Die. Una reckoned, '*Dit klink na 'n interessante storie ... Ek kan jou leer hoe om te tik, weet jy?'* (That sounds like an interesting story ... I can teach you how to type, you know?)

I closed the typewriter. *'Nie nou al nie ... ek sal regkom ...'* (Not now ... I'll get it right ...)

Suddenly Sampie, the 26 prison gangster with whom I had served time, appeared at our communal gate with two other thugs. Sampie was holding a small suitcase in his hand. My mouth went dry at the sight of them. I did not know what they wanted, but I certainly didn't want them around my home or family so I shoved the typewriter at Gloria and told her to take it inside and close the door.

Once they were inside, I stepped off the porch and went to meet with the three thugs. Sampie was all smiles and gave me the 26 thumbs-up salute. *'Salute, my ma se kin!'* (Salute, my mother's child!)

I summed the other two up as hard-core gangsters, so I was wary and watchful. I didn't return Sampie's finger salute and responded with *'Salute, ja!'* I wasn't a member of the 26 gang and I didn't want to give the wrong impression or pretend to be a number gangster.

Sampie indicated to the suitcase. *'Ek het 'n klom jewellery hie, Johnnie ... Os soek a buyer ...'* (I've got a lot of jewellery here, Johnnie ... We're looking for a buyer ...) Sampie was about to open the case when I saw Mrs Lubbe's curtain flicker ever so slightly in the window.

I stopped him. *'Nie hie nie, Sampie ... Kom os vat 'n walk.'* (Not here, Sampie ... Let's take a walk.)

We set off through Disa Court, passed Wilton's shop, and headed for an open field scattered with Port Jackson bushes towards Gleemoor. We stopped behind a clump of bushes and Sampie popped open the case. It was filled with stolen jewellery and I knew I was onto something big. Sampie enquired, *'Wat dink djy, Johnnie? Wiet djy van 'n buyer?'* (What do you think, Johnnie? Do you know of a buyer?)

I had a buyer in mind. *'Geen probleem nie ...'* (No problem ...) My words trailed off as Una appeared behind us.

Sampie swiftly shut the case and looked at her, saying in a sing-song voice, *'Hallooo ... kyk wie het os hie ...'* (Hallooo ... look who we've got here ...) The eyes of the three thugs licked over her body.

I stepped up to her. *'Wat maak jy hier? Gaan huis toe!'* (What are you doing here? Go home!)

She looked me in the eye and said, '*Jou ma het gesê ek moet saam met jou gaan!*' (Your mother told me to go with you!)

I spluttered, '*My ma …? Jy kan nie saam met ons gaan nie, ek is nou weer terug!*' (My mother …? You can't go with us, I'll be back shortly!)

She was adamant. '*Ek gaan saam met jou …*' (I'm going with you …)

'*Lat sy saam gaan, Johnnie,*' said Sampie. (Let her come along, Johnnie.)

I looked at that stubborn slip of a girl who had just lowered my status in front of those gang bangers and decided that there was no way that I could put her life at risk. I turned to Sampie. '*Ek vat haa gou trug, wag net hie!*' (I'll quickly take her back, wait here for me!)

Sampie and his crew murmured obscenities as I marched Una towards Wilton's shop.

I turned on her when we reached the shop. '*Wat gaan aan met jou, hoekom agtervolg jy my?*' (What's wrong with you, why are you following me around?)

She just kept on looking me in the eye. '*Jou ma het gesê …*' (Your mother said …)

I cut her off. '*Maar jy is nie eens my girlfriend nie!*' (But you're not even my girlfriend!) Tears filled her eyes and I felt immediate regret and apologised to her. '*Ek's jammer … kom ons gaan terug huis toe …*' (I'm sorry … let's go back home …)

She wiped her eyes. '*Dis okay, Johnnie … Ek gaan sommer nou die bus vat.*' (It's okay, Johnnie … I'm going to take the bus right now.)

I walked with her towards the bus shelter as dark clouds gathered overhead. We walked in silence and she did not utter another word. She got onto the bus and never looked back once. I hated myself and my stupid actions. Then the rain came pouring down and soaked me to my skin. It was winter in my life.

The following week I went to a tattoo artist and had Una's name tattooed on my right arm.

Back at work, Pock Marks became a pain in the neck at our 'joint' meetings, always taking centre stage with his stupid jokes and boastfulness. Every time he told a story, he would look at me to make sure he had my attention. I guess he really thought I was his best pal and that we'd become tight. But I didn't forget my grudge. On breaking-up day he took me out for lunch at a restaurant. We took off our jackets and hung them over our chairs. After a nice lunch and some draughts of beer, he became tipsy and excused himself to go to the bathroom.

When he left, I decided to play musical chairs with him and swopped seats. On his return, he sat down in my chair and continued with his boastfulness. I put my right hand on the table and leant over as if I was mesmerised by him. I slipped my left hand under the table and neatly lifted his holiday pay out of his inside jacket pocket. Pock Marks was none the wiser. Later I put him onto a bus and went home.

Early that Saturday morning, I was home alone when Pock Marks arrived at my house. With shock in his eyes, he looked accusingly at me and blurted out, '*Ek soek my kroon, Johnnie!*' (I'm looking for my money, Johnnie!)

I gave him my best dumb convict face. '*Djy soek jou kroon … wat bedoel djy …? Dink djy ekkit jou geld gesteel? Toe ek jou gisteraand gelos het, toe het djy dan jou kroon op jou!*' (You want your money … what do you mean …? Are you accusing me of stealing your money? When I left you last night you still had your money on you!) He was hung-over and confused. I continued my indignant diatribe. '*Ekkit gedink djy's my broe, nou kom vi'tel djy my die kak?*' (I thought you were my brother, now you come tell me this shit?)

Pock Marks was tongue-tied and looked uncertainly at me, so I tightened the screws and snarled at him, '*Fok van my jaart af!*' (Fuck off my yard!) He turned tail in the face of my fury and left.

I had the best time of my life that festive season. On the day that the factory reopened, I was late because I was busy rolling dagga sticks to take to work, so I missed the train. I couldn't afford to sit on the railway platform with my stash of dagga, so I decided to jog to work.

I was sweating when I arrived in the cloakroom to change into my overalls, and Pock Marks and two security guards walked in. Pock Marks snarled at the two guards, '*Skud hom yt!*' (Search him!)

I had nowhere to run in the confined space. The guards confiscated

my stash of dagga sticks and marched me to the office, where the foreman decided not to lay a charge but fired me on the spot.

As I left, I threw a last barb at Pock Marks. *'Daai groot boef wie se bike
djy gesmash het, was ek, jou fokken skororo!'* (That big thug whose bike
you smashed was me, you fucking cockroach!)

Only then did recognition dawn in his eyes. The blues kept knocking
on my door.

18

The gallows is my destiny

Unemployed and with no future prospects, I realised I was nothing but a thug who would probably never change. I wrestled with my conscience but could not see my way clear. I took out my typewriter and tried to put my story into words, but the words wouldn't come so I left it there and puttered around the house. That whole day I had a premonition that something bad was going to happen. I tried to read a book, but the words were just a blur and I couldn't connect with the story. I fell asleep with the book on my chest.

When I awoke, it was dusk and my sister Valerie was standing over me. With a concerned look in her eyes, she asked, '*Is jy olraait, Johnnie? Mama het weer siek geword ...*' (Are you alright, Johnnie? Mama has got sick again ...)

I looked at her for a long moment as her words registered and I swung my feet off the bed to go and check on Mom. I found her in bed with a bandage around her head, moaning in pain from a recurring headache. Dad gave her some tablets, and when the pain subsided she fell into a fitful sleep.

We all sat around the table while Cecelia dished us supper, and still the premonition did not fade and my stomach nerves were fluttering. I looked at my dad and said, '*Ek het opgefok, Pa. Vergewe my, asseblief...*' (I fucked up, Dad. Please forgive me ...)

Dad nodded solemnly and Francis answered for him. '*Ons het jou lankal vergewe, Johnnie.*' (We forgave you a long time ago, Johnnie.)

Gloria blurted out, '*Maar ek sal nooit daai boef vergewe wat vir Mama beseer het nie. Mag hy verstik aan sy vrot tande!*' (But I'll never forgive that thug that hurt Mom. I hope he chokes on his rotten teeth!)

Suddenly reality dawned. Miley was the guy with the rotten teeth who stopped us at the gate of Hippy's yard. A curse escaped from my lips. '*Fok!*'

I got up and Dad tugged at my arm. '*Wat nou, Johnnie, wraak?*' (What now, Johnnie, revenge?)

'*Dis okay, Pa, ek stap gou winkel toe ...*' (It's okay, Dad, I'm just going to the shop ...)

The southeaster howled and moaned through the eaves as I stepped outside and opened my knife. I stuck to the shadows as I moved swiftly through the courts and alleys towards my destination. I had a made-up mind and an open knife in my hand, the blade tucked inside the sleeve of my jacket. Vengeance would be mine.

When I arrived outside Hippy's house, the place was in darkness with not a soul in sight, so I hung in the shadows across the street. The corrugated-iron fences in the area rattled in the cutting wind. A mangy dog appeared and trotted down the street in search of food. After a while, I took a short run at the high fence and launched myself over and dropped to my haunches. My eyes pierced the gloom as I scanned my surroundings. Nothing! I hid behind a wall and settled down to wait. Minutes passed and I was about to abort my mission when a babble of voices reached my ears and grew louder. I peeped around the corner of the wall and froze. Hippy, wearing dark glasses at night, strode into the yard with six others, all heavily armed with handguns. Hippy spilt a bag onto a table and more guns fell out. I watched as they handled the guns. Hippy chuckled and barked an order. '*Kry die zoek, Miley, maak 'n paa pype!*' (Get the dagga, Miley, make some chalices!) Miley was my other target in addition to Hippy, but this was suicide. I waited until Miley disappeared inside the house before I jumped back over the fence and took off in a quick, wind-blown jog.

As I strode down the court towards the shop, a flurry of calls pierced the air from close by. On an impulse I returned the call. As I passed the alley, Gif stepped out of the shadows with Shorty and Gimba following close behind. All of them were dressed in coats with the hoods pulled over their heads. Gif grinned at me, showing his gold dentures. '*Heita, my broer, djy's skaars, my mieta ...*' (Greetings, my brother, you're scarce, my friend ...) Shorty also sported gold dentures. They looked haggard from their time on the run and they were edgy. My stomach nerves fluttered again as I replied, '*Nei ... ek help maa net my tanie met werk daa by die joint.'* (No … I'm just helping my mom with some job at home.)

Shorty took out a whiff of money, riffled it and said, *'Perdewerk … Why should we linger when nice times are calling …?'*

A sudden breeze tugged at Gif's coat and exposed a gun in his waistband. I addressed him. *'Ek sien djy's opgesaal, Gif!'* (I see you're all saddled up, Gif!)

Shorty chuckled. *'Os het 'n lekke square wat os kan slat, Johnnie. Gat saam, dan kan djy oek staan met 'n kroon.'* (We've got a big score that we can pull, Johnnie. Come with us and you can also earn some money.) His tone of voice sounded more like an order than a request.

I turned to Gimba, who was hanging in the shadows behind them. *'Djy sê niks, Gimba?'* (You got nothing to say, Gimba?) He opened his mouth to reply, but I cut him off. *'Djy het gewiet Hippy en sy 28-broers het my family gechice, maa djy sê niks!'* (You knew Hippy and his 28 brothers terrorised my family, but you said nothing!)

Gimba gave me a soft answer. *'Hoe moet ek wiet …?'* (How should I know …?)

I pushed on. *'Jou man innie tronk, Gums, moet gewiet het, en as hy gewiet het, dan het djy oek gewiet!'* (Your husband in prison, Gums, would have known, and if he knew, you would have known too!)

Gif and Shorty chuckled at the revelation and Gimba exploded. *'Djy wiet fokkol van my en Gums nie! Ek het vi Gums om my pinkie gedraai en djy was onner my protection!'* (You know fuck-all about me and Gums! I had him wrapped around my little finger and you were under my protection!)

I laughed in his face. *'Ek, onner jou protection …? Djy praat mos kak!'* (Me, under your protection …? You're talking shit!)

Gif intervened. *'Hippy …? Sy pet moet bars!'* (Hippy …? We should blow his head off!)

'Lossie lospraaitjies,' Shorty said. *'Is djy in, Johnnie?'* (Forget the loose talk. Are you in, Johnnie?)

His question hung in the air as we stood there as we had been standing since childhood. I had initiated the pact and there was no way I could refuse. I nodded my head. *'Ek's in maa ek gan ees joint toe, ek's nou trug!'*

(I'm in but I'm going home first, I'll be back now!) I left them there and set off.

When I got home, Una was standing on the porch and there was no one home. My heart skipped a beat at the sight of her. I quipped, '*Waar loop jy dan so laat rond, Una?*' (Where are you walking around so late at night, Una?)

A faint smile played around her mouth. '*Ek het vir Francis kom besoek, toe vind ek my by dooiemansdeur ...*' (I came to visit Francis and found nobody home ...)

I opened the door and she followed me inside. My arm brushed against her breasts as I turned to close the door and then she was in my arms. I gave her a long passionate kiss and she responded hungrily. I swear we were going to do it right there and then. As we came up for air, there was a knock on the door. I opened the door and there stood Mrs Lubbe.

Mrs Lubbe had a knowing glint in her eye as she asked, '*Is jou ma by die huis, Johnnie ...?*' (Is your mother at home, Johnnie ...?)

She knew damn well there was nobody at home, but I gave her a soft answer. '*Nee, Mrs Lubbe, daar's niemand hier nie. Wil u miskien inkom ...?*' (No, Mrs Lubbe, there's nobody here. Would you like to come inside ...?)

My invitation caught her unawares and she spluttered, '*Nee, Johnnie, ek wil graag met jou ma gepraat het. Ek sa weer 'n draai maak.*' (No, Johnnie, I wanted to speak to your mother. I'll come back later.)

Mrs Lubbe's intrusion had broken the spell, so we sat and chatted for a while until Una had to leave. One last kiss and she was gone. I decided to go back to my friends to tell them that I wasn't going with them.

When I arrived at our corner, they were gone. I whistled the call several times but got no replies. I hung around, smoked a cigarette, and after a while I came to the conclusion that they had left without me. I went home.

Early the next morning I heard a car screech to a stop outside our house. My eyes popped open at the ominous sound. Dad went to open the door and I heard him say, '*Goeiemôre, menere, waarmee kan ek help ...?*' (Good morning, gents, how can I help you ...?)

My blood ran cold when I heard the vaguely familiar voice answer Dad, '*Môre, mnr. Fredericks, ons soek jou seun, Johnnie. Is hy hier?*' (Good morning, Mr Fredericks, we're looking for your son, Johnnie. Is he here?)

Dad replied abrasively, '*Vi wat?*' (For what?)

The cop's answer sent a chill down my spine. '*Vir moord, mnr. Fredericks. Is hy hier?*' (For murder, Mr Fredericks. Is he here?) Without further ado, they pushed their way inside. I swung my feet to the floor and got dressed quickly while my sisters stared wild-eyed at the two detectives. I was surprised to see it was the same two cops who had arrested us in the furniture shop.

Noah handcuffed me and frogmarched me outside. I turned to my dad. '*Daar's nie 'n problem nie, Pa. Ek het niemand vermoor nie, ek is nou weer terug!*' (There's no problem, Dad. I didn't murder anybody, I'll be back in a jiffy!)

They loaded me into the back of the van and slammed the door. I looked back at my parents standing in the lighted doorway. They looked stunned and then I became really scared.

At their headquarters in Bishop Lavis, they handcuffed me to a high-backed chair and began to interrogate me. Whitey was at the word while he bounced a tennis ball on the floor. '*Ons is mos ou vriende, nè …?*' (We're old friends, aren't we …?) I didn't reply and he carried on. '*Vertel my wat het gebeur nadat julle in die taxi geklim het.*' (Tell me what happened after you got into the taxi.)

This caught me by surprise. '*Taxi, watte taxi? Ek wiet niks van 'n taxi af nie!*' (Taxi, what taxi? I don't know anything about a taxi!)

The two detectives looked at each other as if I was a dope. Noah put some pictures on the table of a man lying dead in a pool of blood next to a sedan taxi. A red fez lay close by. Noah leant into my face. '*Luister! Ons weet van jou en jou gang, die Young Ones, en al die kak wat julle aanvang! Wie van julle het die taxi driver vermoor?*' (Listen! We know all about you and your gang, the Young Ones, and all the shit you get up to! Which one of you killed the taxi driver?)

This was news to me and I did not recognise the person in the picture. '*Ek het my tyd gestoot,*' I said. '*Hoeko sal ek dan iemand vermoor wat ek nie eens ken nie …?'* (I've done my time. Why would I kill some-body that I don't even know …?)

Whitey was relentless and kept on bouncing the ball, bounce and catch, bounce and catch. *'Hoe moet ons weet, jy's mos die bad guy!'* (How would we know, you're the bad guy!)

I protested. *'Ek weet niks van 'n moord nie!'* (I don't know anything about a murder!)

Noah took a black bag out of a cupboard. *'Die jong praat 'n klomp kak. Laat ek sy kop in 'n sak druk!'* (This guy is talking a lot of shit. Let's put his head in this bag!)

I screamed at them in frustration, *'Ek's onskuldig!'* (I'm innocent!)

Whitey dropped the ball and slapped me so hard that the chair top-pled over. *'Fok onskuldig!'* (Fuck innocent!) I hit the ground and glared at them as blood seeped from my cut lip. I gathered the blood in my mouth and spat at Whitey and the bloody goo hit him in the face. He wiped at the goo and then he went ballistic. He kicked me in the belly, winding me, then Noah joined in and they kicked me senseless.

Noah ripped the amulet from my neck, threw it to the ground and crushed it underfoot. I moaned in pain as he pulled me up and uncuffed me. I vaguely remember Whitey saying, *'Kap hom toe, Noah! Ons hou hom aan totdat ons sy bendeboeties opgespoor het!'* (Lock him up, Noah! We'll hold him here until we track down his gang brothers!) Noah dragged me to the cell and shoved me inside.

I lay on the floor for a while and embraced the pain, trying to make sense of my situation. At the break of dawn, I pulled myself up and got onto the long bench under the barred window and stared at the long grass waving in the wind outside. I pressed my head against the bars as if trying to squeeze through and then I found myself crying silent tears.

Early the next day, I saw Dad for a fleeting moment as he passed my cell window and crossed the yard towards the detective's office. I watched as he returned from the office and stopped momentarily to stare up at my window. I was shattered by the sadness in his eyes.

Late that night as I was about to doze off, the key grated in the lock, the cell door swung open and Gif, Gimba and Shorty entered. They were butt naked and held their clothes in their hands. Apparently, the detectives had arrested them while they were taking a shower at the council sewage plant. A smile tugged at my swollen mouth as I stared at the trio. I figured that now that they'd been arrested, they would let me off the hook and I'd be on my way. They proved me wrong.

Shorty sat on the ground, his head hanging between his knees. Gimba stood at the back, struggling to get his pants on. His face was grey with fear. They avoided my gaze as I glared at them. '*Watte fok het julle aangevang?*' (What the fuck did you do?)

Gif told me they had waited for me and when I didn't arrive they decided to move on and hailed a taxi.

Shorty picked up the story. When they got into the taxi, they recognised the driver as one of a group of guys who had assaulted them when I was in prison. He paused for a moment. '*Hy't gesê my ma is 'n hoer!*' (He called my mother a whore!)

Gif chimed in. '*Os het hom toe gerob van sy kroon.*' (We robbed him of his money.) Then he pointed at Gimba. '*Die toppie wil toe yt die taxi spring en toe skiet Gimba hom.*' (The driver wanted to jump out of the taxi when Gimba shot him.)

I let his words sink in. '*Toe wat sê julle virrie boere?*' (So what did you tell the cops?)

Gif answered. '*Niks nie.*' (Nothing.)

I got up and faced him. '*Wat bedoel djy niks? Djy wiet dan ekkit fokkol met die saak te doen nie!*' (What do you mean nothing? You know I've got fuck-all to do with this case!)

Gif gave a derogatory chuckle and retorted, '*The gallows is our destiny, broer!*' (The gallows is our destiny, brother!)

I snarled at him, '*Moetie met my kom kak praat'ie!*' (Don't come talk shit to me!) I grabbed him by the shoulders and headbutted him in the face. His gold dentures deserted his mouth and shattered on the floor.

Gif, his eyes dark and menacing, wiped his bloody nose on his shirt sleeve and threatened, '*Same time, bra … os gan saam dood!*' (Same time, bro … we die together!)

They made their beds on the other side of the cell, away from me. A short while later, the key rattled in the door again and Noah appeared. '*Carelse, kom!*' (Carelse, come!)

Gimba got up and followed Noah, and the door slammed ominously behind them. We stared suspiciously at the closed door.

Thirty minutes later, Gimba was returned to the cell and Shorty asked him what was up.

Gimba had a packet of cigarettes in his hand and he looked slightly more confident. '*My toppie was hie ... Hy gan die ding stryt maak!*' (My dad was here ... He's going to sort it all out!)

I did not care a rat's arse about Mr C and raised my voice. '*Ek gie nie 'n fok om hoe jou pa dinge gan stryt makie, Gimba! Ek issie betrokke innie saak'ie en ek wil nou ytgan!*' (I don't give a fuck how your dad is going to sort this out, Gimba! I'm not involved in this case and I want to go out now!)

He responded with '*Aweh, broer ... met tyde saam!*' (Aweh, brother ... hang on!)

I seethed with fury and lay awake for a long time staring up at the ceiling. I felt caged in. Sometime during the night, I fell into a fitful sleep.

Early the next morning we were herded into a police truck and we set off for the magistrates' court for a preliminary hearing. The holding cells below the courthouse were packed with awaiting-trial prisoners from various townships across the Cape Flats. Fear was the key and the prisoners milled around in confusion as we entered. Gif took charge immediately and shouted, '*Listen up! My naam is Gif en ek soek julle kroon! Soe dop julle sakke om!*' (Listen up! My name is Gif and I want your money! So empty your pockets!)

Some of the prisoners complied; others who stood their ground were beaten and robbed of their valuables by my three erstwhile friends.

A court orderly called our names and we went up the steps and entered the courtroom. The court was empty except for the magistrate, the prosecutor and the two detectives, Whitey and Noah. The magistrate scanned us briefly before reading the document on his desk. Then he addressed us, explaining that this was a preliminary hearing and that we stood accused of murder and car hijacking, and asking if we had anything to say in our defence.

Gif declared, '*I always wanted to kill a man!*'

I stared at him in shock and blurted out, '*Is djy befok? Sê vi die hof ek was'ie saam met julle nie!*' (Are you fucked up? Tell the court I wasn't with you!)

Gif laughed in my face and I hit him. We tussled in the box and the magistrate banged his gavel several times until order was restored. He stared at us for a moment, then declared that we would be held at Pollsmoor prison to await trial. He banged his gavel once, got up and left the courtroom. My world caved in. I was being accused of a murder that I did not commit and Gif made the headlines of the daily newspaper for what he had said in court.

19

Committed for trial

In the truck to Pollsmoor, the trio continued their reign of terror and the prisoners cowered in the confined space. I stood in the corner of the truck and peered through the barred windows, watching the outside world go by. It was every man for himself and I had no intention of getting involved, although I was a known member of that crazy bunch.

The truck entered the prison grounds and drove past the huge sign that read: WELCOME TO POLLSMOOR. My heart sank.

We were all herded into an empty holding pen near the reception, where we would spend the night before being dispersed to different sections the following day. The holding pen was used to house incoming prisoners who arrived late from court. It looked like a warehouse, with broken windows and a stack of blankets and sleeping mats piled in a corner. I got myself a couple of blankets and a mat and made my bed in another corner.

When I awoke the next morning, I found that Gimba had selected himself a young thug from the group as his concubine. I was disgusted, to say the least. The cell door was unlocked but the bars were still closed, and I saw a sentenced convict sweeping the corridor outside. He had a spoon tied to his belt. Gif took out a bankie of tobacco, stepped up to the bars and bartered with him. '*Gie my daai liepel, broer, dan gie ek jou 'n bankie twak!*' (Give me the spoon, brother, and I'll give you a bankie of tobacco!)

The convict hesitated, his eyes flickering furtively around him, and Gif turned on the pressure, waving the bag of tobacco at him through the bars. '*Hesitate, you lose, broer!*'

The convict paused for a moment more, and then decided to take the deal. He took off his spoon and handed it to Gif, who grabbed it and then refused to give the guy the tobacco. The convict was stunned by this betrayal and uttered, '*Aweh ... soe djy's sterk gevriet? Djy gan nog vol raak vannie tronk!*' (Aweh ... so you're a tough guy? You're going to wise up about prison!)

Gif cackled. '*Djy't gehesitate ... daai's jou eie skuld!*' (You hesitated ... it's your own fault!)

The convict fumed at Gif's audacity and moved on, grumbling, '*Djy gan sien, ek gan jou wys!*' (You will see, I'm going to show you!)

Gif had lost it and now he was armed and dangerous.

Later that day, we were moved to the maximum-security section, but when we got there our reputation had gone before us and the prisoners showed us respect. Gif approached the 'Huis Baas', the guy in charge of the cell, and said abrasively, '*Ek is Gif en ek vat oor hie!*' (I'm Gif and I'm taking over here!)

The Huis Baas was an old con, wise in the ways of prison life, and he conceded his title without much ado. '*Daa'sie fout'ie, Gif, dala soes die nomme jou wys ...*' (No problems, Gif, you do as the number dictates ...)

Gif took charge and the three of them spread a wave of terror among the awaiting-trial prisoners. I slept apart from them and didn't partake in these activities, but I was running in the slipstream of my psychotic friends. They were over the edge and I watched them unravel.

Two days later I had a visitor. The visiting room was a buzz of sound when I entered, with visitors shouting to be heard by their loved ones behind bars. I looked around for familiar faces, but I saw none. Then a warder approached me and led me into an enclosed yard for a contact visit. There I found Mr C. I was surprised and I looked at him in suspicion. He must have bought the warders' services. He gave me a wide grin, his gold dentures flashing as he indicated for me to sit down. '*Wies rustig, my laaitie ...*' (At ease, my laaitie ...)

I was definitely not at ease when I sat down and almost immediately he slipped me a roll of money and a bag of dagga under the table. I had them in my hand and there was no way I could refuse or let them go without drawing attention. I'd been had and he looked at me for a long moment, nodding his head ever so slightly to confirm the situation. He continued in a conversational tone. '*Kykie, my laaitie, ek wil hê djy moet man staan vi die saak. Ek wil'ie nog he Richard moet wee tronk toe gan nie.*'

(Look here, my son, I want you to take the rap for this case. I don't want Richard to go back to prison again.)

I looked at him in stunned disbelief. *'Man staan …? Die ou maak seker 'n grap. Ek was dan nie ees daa nie, Mr C!'* (Take the rap …? You must be joking. I wasn't even there, Mr C!)

He wasn't joking; he was deadly serious. *'Djy het nou status innie tronk, Johnnie, en djy gan maa net 'n "three piece" kry vi die saak …'* (You've got status in prison now, Johnnie, and you'll only get about three years for this case …)

I was having none of that. *'No ways, Mr C!'* I blurted out.

Mr C's eyes turned deadly and his voice rasped when he spoke again. *'Djy kan my smokkelbiesagheid hanteer innie tronk en ek gan mooi kyk by jou family!'* (You can run my smuggling operation in prison and I'll take care of your family!) The last part sounded ominous and he watched me for a moment to see if I could read between the lines before he continued. *'Wanne djy ytkom wil ek hê djy moet oek my biesagheid oorvat!'* (When you are released I also want you to run my operation!)

I knew he was lying and I didn't trust him one little bit, but my curiosity was aroused. *'Richard kan mos ook jou biesagheid run, Mr C …'* (Richard can also run your business, Mr C …)

Mr C gave a derogatory chuckle. *'Richard is soe dom dat hy nie ees wiet hy's dom nie. Nee wat, ekkit geen vertroue in hom nie.'* (Richard is so stupid that he does not even know he's stupid. I've got no trust in him.) He got up to leave and told me to think it over.

When I came out of the visiting room, who should I see but Timer, with his small towel around his neck as usual. He was there with two other convicts to collect a share of the spoils from all those who'd had a visit and been brought something. His eyes lit up when he saw me, and he gave me the old familiar grin and said in a sing-song voice, *'Johnnie … Welcome to Pollsmoor, die's al familie wat djy ken …'* (Johnnie … Welcome to Pollsmoor, that's all the family you know …) Then his grin faded, his attitude became threatening, and the three of them boxed me in. *'Wat het djy gebring vi die ouens, Johnnie …?'* (What did you bring for the guys, Johnnie …?)

This was prison and I knew the rules: you give something or you get robbed of everything you've got. There was no way I was going to show them what I had, so I spoke their language. *'As die Ou daa by my seksie kan ytstiek, dan sal die Ou vol raak mettie hele waarheid.'* (If the Man can come around to my section, the Man will get his reward.)

Timer's sidekick, a pale-faced dude who was tattooed from head to toe, was not impressed. *'Os kan soema die move hie stryt maak!'* (We can sort out the move right now!)

Timer reprimanded him. *'Staan trug, roebana!'* (Back off, robber!)

The sidekick backed off and Timer turned to face me. *'Ek check jou later, Johnnie ...'*

I returned to my section and hurriedly took out my shipment and hid it in my bundle of blankets after taking out a share of the dagga for Timer. I had to pay my dues. My actions didn't escape the attention of Gif, Gimba and Shorty, and they swaggered over to my bed just as Timer and his cronies appeared at the barred door.

I went over to the door and the trio followed me. I slipped the dagga through the bars to Timer, and Gif demanded, *'Watte gwan, Johnnie?'* (What's going on, Johnnie?)

Timer stepped up close to the bars and snarled into Gif's face, *'Wie's djy!?'* (Who are you!?) Gif was taken aback by the abrasive tone of his voice. Timer slipped off the towel to reveal the '27' tattoo on his neck and spat, *'Ek vat bloed! Djy hou vi jou sterk gevriet hie oppie trial, maa ek wag vi jou. Daai is as julle dit gan maak, want die woord is julle is in lyn virrie galg!'* (I take blood! You think you're a tough guy here awaiting trial, but I'm waiting for you. That's if you're going to make it this far, because the word is you're in line for the gallows!) Timer cackled as he marched off.

Shorty was ashen-faced and Gif turned on Gimba. *'Is deur jou fokken daggakop-pa wat os hie is!'* (It's because of your fucking dagga-head dad that we're here!)

Gimba threw a punch at him and retorted, *'Fok jou!'* (Fuck you!)

They went into a scuffle and threw punches at each other at close range. I tried to separate them, but Gif held onto Gimba like a fox terrier and wouldn't let go. Gif spit-sprayed into my face, *'Dis jou skuld! As djy ytgestiek het daai aand, sal die nie gebeur het nie!'* (It's your fault! If you were there that night this would not have happened!)

There was no way I could reason with him and I managed to get Gimba away from him and said, '*Hoe kan dit my skuld wies? Djy was daa, djy het die pyp gehet!*' (How is it my fault? You were there, you had the gun!) I turned to Gimba and told him, '*Djy biete daa by my ko slaap, Gimba.*' (You'd better come and sleep by me, Gimba.)

'*Ja, fokkof!*' said Gif. Gimba followed me and made his bed next to mine. I turned my back on him.

After two weeks of high tension, we went to court for our trial date, which was set for six months later. The days passed slowly with no contact from the outside world until, after a week, my name was called for another visit. I entered the visiting room and immediately caught sight of Mom and sat down in front of her. We were divided by a thick glass window and we spoke through speakerphones. Mom gave me a smile and said, '*Hoe gaan dit met jou, Johnnie? Dit wil voorkom dat jy gewig verloor het…*' (How are you, Johnnie? It seems like you've lost weight …)

I gathered my thoughts. '*Dit gaan nie so goed nie, Ma, en ek bekommer my vrek oor die saak…*' (Not so good, Mom, and I'm worrying myself to death about this case …)

A tear rolled down her cheek and I made a request. I asked her to try to get me a lawyer, because things weren't looking so good.

She gave me another sad smile and held up her Bible, patted it and told me, '*Hier is jou advokaat, my kind. Onthou jy daai Bybelteks wat jy gelees het? Jy was gewaarsku, Johnnie, en ek glo daar is 'n rede daarvoor!*' (Here is your advocate, my child. Remember the Bible verse you read? You were warned, Johnnie, and I believe there is a reason for that!)

There was no arguing with her; she believed in her God and I felt much calmer. '*Aag, Ma…*'

She got up abruptly and told me she'd brought another visitor along. Then Una appeared behind her and she was a sight for sore eyes. The awaiting-trial prisoners whistled their appreciation and I suddenly realised how pretty she was and how lucky I was to have a girl like her. With that came the thought of my worthlessness. I was a thug with nothing to offer her but heartache and shattered dreams. I wasn't trying to fool myself.

She sat down and picked up the speakerphone and was all bubbly and excited as she said, '*Ek mis jou vreeslik, Johnnie, hoe gaan dit met jou...?*' (I miss you terribly, Johnnie, how are you ...?)

I shrugged my shoulders, gesturing to my surroundings, and avoided her question. I said I was glad to see her too and that I hadn't expected it and did her stepfather know she had come to visit me?

She shook her head. '*Te hel met hom. Hy's nie my pa nie en ek kan my eie vriende kies.*' (He can go to hell. He's not my father and I can choose my own friends.)

I was thrilled by her words and there was a stirring in my loins, but I felt I had to let her go. '*Miskien het jy verkeerd gekies, Una. Saam met my gaan jy net jou naam laat val. Ek dink jy moet aangaan met jou lewe...*' (Maybe you chose wrong, Una. With me you're only going to get a bad name. You must go on with your life ...) They were the most painful words that I ever had to utter. I cringed as her eyes brimmed with tears. '*Ek is jammer ... maar ek is seker jou familie sal my nooit aanvaar nie, Una. Ek is 'n boef en al die mense noem my skollie!*' (I'm sorry ... but I know for sure your family will never accept me, Una. I'm a thug and everyone calls me gangster!)

She wiped her eyes and stared at me intently, and her words caught me by surprise. '*Wat van jou drome, Johnnie...? Onthou, drome sterf nooit...*' (What about your dreams, Johnnie ...? Remember, dreams never die ...) She got up and walked away. I felt as if my soul was dying.

20

Cry me a river

Outside the visiting room, Timer and Ghost were lying in wait to 'tax' all those who had received a visit. Timer was in close conversation with a prisoner holding two bags of groceries.

Ghost gave me a wide grin. '*Salute, Johnnie, nou kan os mos die nomme vol maak!*' (Salute, Johnnie, now we can fulfil the number!)

According to Ghost, we had a deal that if I came back to prison I would become a 26. I hadn't been planning on coming back, but there I was and Ghost was adamant. I played for time. '*Salute, ja! Soe gou soes ek daa in die vooste linies kom.*' (Salute, yes! As soon as I get sentenced.) I slipped him some money and he said, '*Salute!*' and turned his attention to another prisoner.

I felt bad, I had no appetite and I sank into depression as the shadow of the gallows occupied my mind.

It seemed that our situation did not bother Gimba, Gif or Shorty much as they swaggered around and intimidated everybody in the cell. On an impulse I decided to sharpen the handle of my spoon on the cement floor.

I awoke one morning with a bad case of itching. I checked my blankets and found them crawling with white lice. I threw down the blankets and jumped out of bed in fright. Soon the other inmates tossed their beds too and we piled everything in the middle of the floor. Gif banged on the cell bars with his mug to get the warder's attention and we were moved to another cell.

One day Gums arrived at our cell door and shouted, '*Gimba! Kom bietjie back!*' (Gimba! Come here!) Gimba's eyes clouded over at the sight of Gums, who shouted again, '*Gimba!*' Gimba hesitated briefly before stepping up to the bars.

The two of them spoke. I couldn't hear what was being said, but I saw

Gimba blush in embarrassment. That visit became a turning point in Gimba's life, as he changed into a cruel and sadistic beast. I did not see Gums again.

The days dragged on and at night I cried silent tears of frustration. Although Mom had told me that the Bible would be my advocate, my parents could not afford a real lawyer.

I got a visit from a white court-appointed attorney, but he didn't show any compassion when I told him my story. It felt as if I was in no man's land.

One night while I was reading an old magazine, Gif, Gimba and Shorty swaggered over to my bed. I looked up and said, '*Watte gwan?*' (What's up?)

They were stoned on dagga and Shorty asked me with slurring words, '*Waa was djy dan daai aand, Johnnie?*' (Where were you that night?)

Maybe they came to make conversation, as I had been ignoring them the whole time, but the question sparked my fury and I got up to face them. '*Watte fok het dit met julle te doen?*' (What the fuck has that got to do with you?)

Shorty was taken aback and spluttered, '*Ek vra maa net.*' (I'm just asking.)

Gif, on the other hand, took a menacing stance, so I whipped out my sharpened spoon and snarled at him, '*Wat wil djy dala?*' (What do you want to do?) Gif backed down in the face of my fury.

After six months we went on trial. The gallery was packed with spectators when we arrived in court from the holding cells below. I took a quick scan and found my parents sitting close to the dock. Mom's eyes were closed in a silent prayer as she clutched her Bible to her bosom. Shorty's mom sat behind them next to Gif's aunt, and Mr C sat at the back.

The judge entered the courtroom and the orderly announced, '*All rise…*' The audience stood up until the judge took his seat. My heart was thumping in my throat.

The prosecutor called Detective Whitey to the stand to give his statement. According to his investigation, he said, accused number one, John Fredericks, stole the gun, planned the robbery and shot the victim.

A sob caught in my throat and my eyes flickered briefly towards my parents as if looking for help. Mom's eyes were closed in silent prayer.

The detective told the judge that he had taken statements from the three other accused, who all said that accused number one was under the influence of dagga. They had tried to stop him, but he pointed the gun at them. They were scared of him ...

I felt like a cornered rat, and before my attorney could object, I jumped up and screamed, '*Dis alles leuens, Ma, ek is onskuldig!*' (It's all lies, Mom, I'm innocent!) The court was in uproar as I turned towards my friends and told them, '*Julle het 'n nommer gedala, nou staan man vi julle eie nwatas!*' (You did the crime, now do as the number dictates and take the rap for your own shit!)

The judge banged his gavel angrily until order was restored. '*Ek waarsku jou, nommer een. As jy iets het om te sê, dan sê jy dit vir die hof!*' (I'm warning you, number one. If you've got something to say, say it to the court!)

Tears burned my eyes as I vaguely heard Mom speaking in tongues. An inexplicable silence descended on the courtroom. My attorney's eyes flashed at me in reprimand. I swiped at my tears and rolled the dice. '*U edele, as dit die hof behaag wil ek graag die hof toespreek ...*' (Your honour, if it pleases the court, I would like to address the court ...)

The judge gave me a long, piercing look then nodded his head. '*Gaan voort, mnr. Fredericks.*' (Go ahead, Mr Fredericks.)

I gathered my thoughts as Mrs Lubbe entered. Her hair was dyed red and huge earrings dangled from her ears. Her eyes searched for a seat, and her high heels clacked across the floor as she found one and sat down. Shorty fidgeted; Gif stared stoically ahead of him as I searched for words. I pointed to Mr C. '*Daai man het ons ingetrek by sy bende. Hy het vir ons opdragte gegee om verskeie kriminele dade te pleeg vir hom. Niemand kan met hom stry nie, u edele, want almal is bang vir hom, tot sy eie seun Richard ...*' (That man lured us into his gang and ordered us to commit various crimes for him. Nobody could argue with him, your honour, because everyone is scared of him, even his own son Richard ...)

A murmur ran through the courtroom, and the sound of shuffling feet, as I continued. I told the court that Mr Carelse had come to visit me in Pollsmoor and told me to take the rap for this crime so that I could run his gangster dealings in prison and then take over his dagga business on my release.

Gimba was shocked by this news as I turned to face him. *'Ja, jou pa het vir my gesê hy het geen vertroue in jou nie en dat jy so dom is dat jy nie eens weet jy is dom nie!'* (Yes, your dad told me that he had no trust in you and that you're so stupid that you don't even know you're stupid!)

Gimba stared at me in disbelief while Gif and Shorty looked sharply at me as the revelation dawned.

Gimba looked towards his father, who glared menacingly back at him, his face tight with anger. Gimba was close to tears, his lips trembled and he blurted out, *'Hy was nie saam ons daai aand nie, u edele. Hy's onskuldig!'* (He was never with us that night, your honour. He is innocent!)

The crowd murmured as the judge looked questioningly at Gif and Shorty. *'Stem julle saam met wat hy sê?'* (Do you agree with what he's saying?) They nodded affirmatively and the judge scribbled in his file before continuing. *'Mnr. Fredericks, jy kan maar afstaan.'* (Mr Fredericks, you may stand down.) He banged his gavel again and said that court was adjourned until next Wednesday at nine o'clock. I opened the gate of the dock and headed for the door and I was out of there.

21

Back on the street

Back home, after I had scrubbed and cleaned myself, I burnt the clothes that I'd worn in prison. The mood was sombre as I sat down to eat with my parents. I was fidgety and my mind was in turmoil at the thought of what the future held in store for me and my family. I had brought shame on them and I was so disgusted with my life that I did not even like myself. I saw the pitying look in their eyes and I knew that I had to pick myself up. My thoughts turned to Una, but I cut them off. There was no way I could go there. Although I had been acquitted, I knew that it was not over yet. Mr C was uppermost in my mind.

The ceaseless call of the gang rattled me, so I decided to go out and face my fears. When I arrived on our corner, with an open knife gripped in my right hand inside my jacket pocket, Chip, Robbie, Boere and Solly were there waiting for me. Boere, an old homeboy fresh from prison, had a concerned look on his face as he tried to read me. '*Johnnie, djy's in groot kak. Volgens die woord oppie strate het Hippy en Mr C 'n hit op jou gesit!*' (Johnnie, you're in big shit. The word on the streets is that Hippy and Mr C have both put a hit on you!)

Fear! I was overwhelmed by mind-bending fear. I took out my knife and challenged them. '*Soe wat wil julle vi my sê!?*' (So what are you trying to tell me!?)

Chip declined the challenge. '*Issie nog soe nie, Johnnie. Djy hou gevaar in vi 'n klom mense. Is bietere as djy vi jou yt die kol yt vat …*' (It's not like that, Johnnie. You are a danger to a bunch of people. It will be better if you leave the area …)

I understood their reasoning. I had to disappear to keep other people out of danger, especially my family. '*Is met 'n korrek, ouens, julle kan maa gly…*' (It's all good, guys, you can go …)

They gave me our intricate handshake and left me standing there.

I smoked a cigarette and hung on the corner for a while and the words came to mind, '*When days are dark, friends are few.*' I was jerked out of my reverie as Mr C's car came screaming round the corner. Hobo was hanging out of the back window and over the roof with a shotgun. The windows slid down and more guns appeared. I fled down the alley as the guns blasted at me. They were moving too fast and the car overshot the alley; the driver slammed on the brakes and reversed back. The guns started blasting again and I flew over high walls and sagging fences as I ran for my life.

Late that night I jumped over the school fence into our yard and slipped into the chicken coop. The rooster squawked once before settling down again. I turned the water bucket upside-down and sat on it. Listening to the sound of silence, my mind was racing as I tried to figure out my next move. I must have dozed off and awoke with a start to find Dad standing over me. It was the break of dawn. He gave me a sad smile and said, '*Kom, Johnnie, ek vat jou na Lenie toe innie Factreton Estate.*' (Come, Johnnie, I'm taking you to Lenie in Factreton Estate.)

I followed him into the house. My mom and siblings stared wordlessly at me as I hurriedly threw some clothes into a bag. Death hung in the air and I sensed that they were reluctant to see me leave, but they knew that I had to go. As I went out the door, a thought crossed my mind: '*Maybe I'm going to die today.*' I felt sick to my stomach. I got into Dad's van and we set off for Kensington, where my eldest sister Magdalene, or 'Lenie', had moved into a recently completed housing scheme called Factreton Estate. They stayed in the last street and the place was still raw, with no ceilings and a cement floor. The scheme was surrounded by bush and crawling with snakes and huge lizards. My heart felt heavy.

Lenie and her husband both worked, and I watched over their two small children during the day. I tried reading a book to occupy my mind, but the words became a blur. After a lot of soul-searching, I made up my mind: if I was going to die, I might as well die with my colours flying. I wasn't prepared to sit in that godforsaken place and just fade away. And like a storybook character, I decided to go after my perpetrators. So I plotted and planned. But first there was the trial verdict.

On the morning of the verdict, I was up early and I took a taxi to the High Court in the city. I entered the packed courtroom and took a seat in the back row. My eyes searched for Mr C and found him seated close to the dock, with other gang members sitting in the row behind him. I went unnoticed as Gif, Gimba and Shorty appeared in the dock from the holding cells below. Each of them had a rosary around their necks. They did a quick scan of the gallery, looking for familiar faces. Shorty fidgeted with his rosary. They were nervous and terrified as the judge entered. The judge tugged at his robe and sat down; a murmur swept through the courtroom.

The judge read their sentence. '*Richard Carelse, Martin Jacobs en Tyrone Felix, nadat ek al die feite negegaan het, vind ek julle skuldig aan moord en roof. Ek vonnis julle tot die dood. Al drie van julle sal hiervandaan vervoer word na 'n plek waar julle aan die nek opgehang sal word totdat julle dood is.*' (Richard Carelse, Martin Jacobs and Tyrone Felix, after due deliberation of the facts before me, I find you guilty of murder and robbery. I sentence you to death. All three of you will be transported from here to be hanged by the neck until you are dead.)

Their bodies whipped with shock, their knuckles white as they clung to the rail of the dock. The judge continued, '*Is daar enige iets wat julle vir die hof wil sê ...?*' (Is there anything that you want to tell the court ...?)

Gif grinned at the judge. '*Kan my antie vi my 'n pie en 'n koffie koep ...?*' (Can my aunt buy me a pie and a coffee ...?)

Gimba slumped in the dock as pandemonium broke loose in the courtroom, with screams, cheers, shock and tears. Mr C was catatonic. Gif turned to a news reporter in the court. '*Gie 'n man 'n magazine?*' (Give a man a magazine?) The reporter declined and Gif turned to the gang members in the gallery, pulled his finger across his throat and said, '*Maak die ding swak!*' (Make this guy weak!) As they were led down to the holding cells, Gif started singing loudly, '*My heart is pleased!*' He had lost it completely.

I returned to my sister's place in Factreton, and on Friday evening I got onto a train at Maitland station to Athlone. Main Road was teeming with people, so I stuck to the shadows and used the back streets on my way home. The house was in darkness when I got there. Mrs Lubbe's curtains moved slightly as I knocked softly on the door. It took a while before Dad opened the door. He had a cut across his upper lip and a bruise on his cheek. Mom and my sisters stepped into the dining room and looked at me in quiet terror.

'*Wat het gebeur, Pa ...?*' (What happened, Dad ...?)

Dad said nothing. He was at the end of his tether.

Valerie piped up, '*Die skollies het hom so geslaan, Johnnie!*' (The gangsters beat him up, Johnnie!)

My heart ached with hatred as I turned on my heel and headed towards the door as Mom started praying. As the door closed behind me, I heard her speaking in a babble of tongues. I wished I was dead because of all the pain and heartache that I had brought upon my family. I was going to talk to Mr C. It was time to pay the piper or die with flying colours.

When I arrived at Mr C's yard, he and his gang members were chilling around a wine-wet table littered with glasses and expensive bottles of liquor. Mr C grunted in surprise at the sight of me and a sadistic grin spread across his face. I stepped up to him and said, '*Ek het 'n request, my lanie. Ek wil hê die ou moet my family ytlos, want hulle het niks vi jou gemaak nie ...*' (I've got a request, my boss. I want you to leave my family alone because they did nothing to you ...)

Mr C growled as he came around the table, '*'n Request ...? Djy het sieke 'n fokken death wish!*' (A request ...? You've got a fucking death wish!)

He swung a looping right and I ducked under it and hit him with two headbutts in quick succession, then danced out. Hobo pushed me violently from behind and Mr C slammed me in my face. I went down. I was stunned by the blow but got up again and ducked and dived as Mr C threw wild punches at me. I gave as good as I got and landed a few punches on his face and drew blood. He went ballistic and came after me in the tight circle and knocked me down again.

I breathed raggedly, spat blood and taunted him. '*Is daai al wat die ou het ...?*' (Is that all you got ...?)

I got up and Mr C came in, swinging wild punches that missed as I danced around him. I danced in and hit him with a 'two feet', whipping his feet from under him, and he hit the ground hard. Mr C growled as he got up and swung a punch that exploded through my defences and followed up with a barrage of blows to my face. I tottered on wobbly legs and he grabbed me by the throat. Hobo gave him a gun, which he pointed at my head.

The gate banged open and Hippy entered with a gun in hand. Miley and Frizzy Hair were close behind him. Hippy's right eye was milky white from the wound I had inflicted on him with the hot chalice years before. His long hair was damp and hung over his sweaty face. His good eye flickered once when he saw me, as he did not expect to see me there.

He fired at Mr C but missed, and I dropped to the ground as Mr C turned his gun towards Hippy. Hippy's gun blasted again and the bullet caught Mr C in the spine on the turn. Mr C flopped like a fish out of water, overturning the table on his way down. Hippy continued firing, and I slid on my belly and took cover behind the table as Hobo returned fire. Hippy went down as a bullet caught him in the head, and Miley stood straddle-legged over his body. He screamed in defiance as he fired wildly at Hobo with two guns. The two men shot at each other, and as Miley went down, his last bullet smashed into Hobo's face and Hobo's body plopped down next to me. It was unreal, and it was all over in a matter of seconds. I could not believe that I had escaped with my life.

I peered around the table and surveyed the carnage. The air was heavy with the smell of cordite. Dead bodies were sprawled across the ground. Mr C was still alive; he tried to lift himself up but found himself paralysed. He looked at me with a pleading expression in his eyes but I ignored him. Miley was dead; a bullet had torn through his mouth, shattering his rotten teeth. I stepped over to Hippy, whose milky white eye was open, so I closed it. Then I sneaked out of the yard.

I hit the road and ran as fast as I could on my wobbly legs. I stuck to the shadows and ran until my lungs were on fire. When I reached home, I couldn't make it inside and I collapsed on the porch.

When I came to, I found myself in the back of Dad's van. My face and head were swollen like a balloon. I was confused when Una and her mom appeared at the back door of the van. Her mother, Farieda, gasped when she saw my injuries. I vaguely heard Dad telling Una, 'Ek het nie gewiet wat om te doen met hom nie, toe vat ek maar 'n kans…' (I didn't know what to do with him, so I took a chance …) Her answer got lost on me.

Dad helped me out of the van and I found that we were parked in front of Una's house in Harfield Village. We entered their gate and I jerked in shock as it banged shut behind me. Dad led me to a couch on their vine-covered porch. I sat down and immediately toppled over and moaned in pain. Dad was unsure of himself and Farieda told him, 'Dis okay, mnr. Fredericks, los hom maar hier…' (It's okay, Mr Fredericks, you can leave him here …)

Dad left and I heard the van start up.

Una's six siblings – her four younger brothers, Jenny and her eldest sister – came out of the house and stared at me. I felt self-conscious and tried to sit up, but I was running on empty. I slumped back, just wanting to sleep, when Walter arrived and demanded, 'Wat gaan hier aan…?' (What's happening here …?)

Una spoke up and told Walter that I was hurt.

Walter laughed at my strife and said, 'Hy's gelukkig, hulle moet hom doodgemoer het!' (He's lucky, they should have killed him!)

Una reprimanded him, 'Hoe kan jy so harteloos wees? Hy is beseer!' (How can you be so heartless? He's hurt!)

Walter was taken aback by Una's fury and backed down, muttering to himself as he stepped inside the house. Farieda gave me some tablets and Una covered me with blankets and I fell asleep almost immediately.

The next morning I awoke with a splitting headache. My body was weak, but I was too embarrassed to lie there on the porch. The family was still asleep when I got up and shuffled into their yard and sat there under their plum trees that were heavy with red plums. I embraced the pain and made it my own as I contemplated the way forward. I searched my soul and found myself wanting. I desperately wanted to change my life around, to find a job, but the future looked bleak.

Later, Una brought me some breakfast, but I couldn't eat and only drank the coffee. I couldn't even speak to her, as my mouth was too swollen to utter a clear word. I could not look her in the eye either. A deep depression came over me and I slumped into my body. Walter came into the yard to use the outside toilet. He glared at me and said, '*Ek sien djy's nog altyd hie!*' (I see you're still here!) I was not wanted there. I was labelled a skollie.

I stayed there until Monday evening just before Walter came home from work, and then I took the train to Athlone. I used the back streets as I sneaked home. When I arrived, none of my sisters were there and for days I never saw them at home. (It was only in later years that I discovered that every time I came in by the front door, they would slip out the back.)

During the day I would go to our corner, but I never found anybody there. I whistled the call but there were no replies. Late one night I took a walk to our corner again and found Boere, Robbie and Solly there dressed in council overalls, smoking chalices of dagga. I was glad to see them and asked, '*Hoe change hulle, ouens ...?*' (What's changed, guys ...?)

Boere chortled, tugged at his council overalls and said, '*Dis soe wat dit change, Johnnie, os werk nou virrie City Council. Die gangster-gangster biesagheid issie worth'it nie!*' (This is how it changes, Johnnie, we're working for the City Council now. This gangster, gangster stuff is not worth it!)

Robbie lit a chalice and spoke through the swirling smoke. '*Hulle vat manne an by die council, Johnnie, hoeko doen djy nie aansoek vi 'n job nie?*' (They're employing men at the council, Johnnie, why don't you apply for a job?)

I lingered for a while as they discussed their job descriptions, and the next morning I presented myself at the City Council's roads and drainage department in Maitland, and I was accepted for a job. At first I worked in Observatory, sealing the cracked pavements with a gooey tar mix called slurry. It was dirty work, but I was just happy I had a job with a pension fund and medical aid. Later I was sent to another work gang that repaired roads in the Salt River area. I was always telling stories during tea and lunch breaks and the workers would gather around me. The white foreman didn't like it and decided that I was distracting them, so I was transferred to Paarden Island. The council camp there stood in a scrubby field and we worked in the area and seldom moved elsewhere.

There were no houses around, only factories, and we ripped up the roads with picks and shovels so they could be re-tarred again. I excelled in the hard work and built some muscle. I volunteered once a week to be nightwatchman in the godforsaken camp to earn overtime money and to get the next day off. I loved the solitude at night and my mind could fly free.

Then Una sent a message with Francis that I must come see her at work during her lunch break on my day off. When I arrived at the factory, most of her fellow workers were sitting outside, so I waited for her at the corner of the building. When we met, she had a frightened look in her eyes. I was concerned and asked her what was wrong.

'*Ek is verwagtend, Johnnie ... Ek is te bang om vir my ma te sê.*' (I'm pregnant, Johnnie ... I'm too scared to tell my mom.)

I was filled with dearness as I held her in my arms. A sob escaped from her lips and tears filled her eyes. I loved her and I knew that I had to make this right. I whispered in her ear, '*Sal jy met my trou, Una?*' (Will you marry me, Una?)

She wiped her tears and looked into my eyes. '*Is jy seker, Johnnie?*' (Are you sure?)

I was sure. '*As dit 'n ja is, dan gaan ek sommer nou jou ma sien.*' (If that's a yes, I'm going to speak to your mother right now.)

It was a yes, so I got onto the train and went to go visit her mother at home. Farieda was hanging curtains when I arrived, and fortunately she was alone. I told her of our marriage plans and she gave me a long searching look before nodding her head.

22

The wedding

My parents and siblings were all excited about the wedding. Valerie and Cecelia were chosen as bridesmaids, and my cousin David and Lesley, a friend from the Lion Match factory, were to be the best men. Again, it would be years later before I realised that my family's excitement about the wedding was because they wanted me out of the house. I volunteered to work weekends to earn more money, I scrimped and saved, and I bought Una a wedding band. On my off day after my nightwatchman's duties, we went to look for furniture and I put down a deposit.

Then I went house-hunting and an old couple offered us two rooms to rent in Second Avenue in Harfield, around the corner from where Una's family lived. I paid a deposit and all was well and good. I had a second chance in life and my future was in my hands.

We didn't want a lot of fanfare, so we decided to tie the knot at Wynberg Magistrates' Court on a Friday and hold the reception the following day. The first hitch came on the Wednesday before. I was at the place in Second Avenue when the truck with the furniture arrived. I knocked on the door, but the old couple did not want to open up. My heart sank but I had nowhere else to go, so I kept on knocking on their door until they had to open it. The old man peered at me through the slightly open door and said, '*We changed our minds ... you can't stay here, you're bad news ...*'

I almost flipped. '*Wat bedoel die ou dan nou ...? Die ou was dan die heeltyd olraait?*' (What do you mean by that ...? You were alright with the arrangement?)

The old guy's eyes softened and he murmured, '*I'm sorry ... but people warned me not to rent the space to you ...*'

A curse escaped from my lips. '*Fuck! What people!?*'

The old man closed the door in my face as a crowd started to gather. The furniture delivery guys seemed to enjoy my predicament too and looked at me to solve the problem. My anger started to build as I didn't know what to do.

Then Farieda came down the avenue with shopping bags in hand and stopped at the gathered crowd. She looked questioningly at me and enquired, '*What's the problem, Johnnie …?*'

'*I don't know, Mums, the old guy says he was warned not to rent the place to us …*'

Her eyes tightened for a moment as she looked at the crowd of locals. She addressed the delivery guys. '*Bring the furniture to my house!*'

It was never my intention to move into their already crowded house, but I figured I was going to find another place to rent as soon as possible. We cleared a room and moved my bedroom suite in there. It was a tight squeeze and Walter was fuming all the time.

When the day came, we got married in court with only two witnesses. I was quietly excited when our wedding entourage arrived at the reception the following day. The guests stood up as we entered and I spotted Walter and his seven brothers lounging at the bar imbibing the liquor that I had bought. I reprimanded Walter. '*Die aand is nog jonk …*' (The night is still young …)

Walter swallowed a shot, banged the glass down and swore at me, '*Fok jou!*'

I slumped in my new suit. '*Wat is jou probleem?*' (What's your problem?)

He gave a derogatory chuckle and played the tough guy to his brothers. '*Djy is my probleem, djy's 'n gangster en ek haat gangsters!*' (You're my problem, you're a gangster and I hate gangsters!)

Uncle Piet, who had accompanied Dad to the reception, intervened. '*Jy's 'n groot man, jy kan mos nie so met hom praat op jou stiefdogter se troudag nie!*' (You're a grown man, you can't talk to him like that on your stepdaughter's wedding day!)

Emboldened by the liquor and the presence of his brothers, Walter grabbed a hammer from under the bar and swung at Uncle Piet. Big mistake. Uncle Piet went to his car and came back armed with a wheel brace and hit Walter twice on the head. Blood spurted and all hell broke loose. A bottle of mineral water came flying through the air and smashed against the opposite wall. We hurried outside as a free-for-all started. Lesley my best man gave me a knife and I was prepared to use it. Una pleaded and Dad forced me into the van and we sped off towards the police station as more bottles of minerals banged against the van and exploded in the street.

A large woman, unknown to us, took up the front passenger seat and Dad asked who she was.

She replied, *'Ek is die wedding singer...'* (I'm the wedding singer ...)

Dad replied drily, *'Niks singery vi jou vanaand nie...'* (No singing for you tonight ...)

We arrived at the police station and the whole wedding entourage marched into the charge office and we laid a complaint. A fat coloured cop was assigned to escort us back to the reception but he refused. He said he knew about Walter Swain – that his nickname was 'Thick Potato' and he was troublesome when drunk.

I could not believe my ears. For most of my life I had been in conflict with the law and this was my wedding day. I exploded. *'Djy's 'n fokken lafaard, jou vet tief!'* (You're a fucking coward, you fat bitch!)

Uncle Piet grabbed my arm. *'Los'it, Johnnie, ko os gan trug!'* (Let it go, Johnnie, let's go back!)

When we arrived back at the reception, most of the guests were gone and so was all the food and liquor. I screamed bloody murder and Dad and Uncle Piet bundled me back into the van and we drove back to Kewtown. Walter had made me a laughing stock of the Harfield community. I figured he was also the one who warned the old couple about me. My heart burned with hatred and I could not wait for daybreak. Vengeance would be mine.

Early on Sunday morning, Una, my cousin David and I arrived in Harfield Village. Una's aunt was sitting on a couch having a cup of tea. Farieda, her eyes downcast in shame, was roasting a chicken in the kitchen. I was too angry to greet her, so I just nodded to her in passing. I went into our bedroom and found that somebody had urinated on our new bed. A drumbeat started in my head and the urge to kill was almost overpowering. I looked through the window and saw Walter and his brothers sitting under the plum trees, drinking liquor that *I* had bought.

I opened the back door and stood in the doorway with an open knife in my hand. I did not say a word as I scanned their faces. Somebody was going to die there on that Sunday morning and they could feel the evil intent emanating from my mind. A hush fell over the gathering as Una tugged at my jacket from behind and pleaded softly, '*Johnnie ... hulle is dit nie werd nie ...*' (Johnnie ... they're not worth it ...)

I wasn't listening and only had eyes for Walter, who cringed under my stare. His mouth opened and closed and then he said in a squeaky voice, '*Kan ons nie die ding ytpraat nie ...?*' (Can't we talk this over ...?) He was scared; all of them were scared. They got the message.

Slowly my anger dissipated. I went inside and David helped me to take the mattress off the bed and into the yard, where we scrubbed it and left it to dry. I heard Una's aunt saying, '*Die huwelik gaan dit nie maak nie ...*' (This marriage is not going to make it ...)

It was a rocky start. I was uncomfortable staying there and soon my nice shirts began disappearing from the washing line. For weeks I searched for a place to rent, but society was not on my side. One day I got the early edition of the daily newspaper and saw an ad for a house to rent. I phoned the number and made an appointment for an hour later as I had to catch a train. When I arrived, the woman scanned me once and dismissed me in the blink of an eye. She sputtered, '*Ek is jammer ... die plek is al klaar uitverhuur al ...*' (I'm sorry ... the place has been rented out already ...) I knew she was lying and cursed her under my breath as she closed the door in my face.

I continued to work as a nightwatchman once a week, and sometimes I would sleep at the council camp to avoid contact with Walter and the rest of Una's family. I felt like an intruder. As Una got heavier with child, I would come home, eat in our room then go out in the backyard and wash myself under the tap. Later that year, 1967, a son was born to us and we named him Eugene. When I held him for the first time, I vowed that I would always watch over him.

23

Hounded by my past

Six months after Eugene was born, we were tarring a road in Paarden Island when a police van pulled up and a cop spoke to the foreman. A chill ran down my spine but I carried on working with the knowledge that I had paid my debt to society. I was proven wrong when the foreman called me over and said that the police wanted to talk to me. I put down my rake and went to meet with them.

They told me that they had found my fingerprints and matched them to a long-forgotten crime. The prints were in a cupboard in a house that we had burgled many years before. We had got away with it then, but now the house had been burgled again and mine were the only prints they found. I was placed under arrest. My heart sank and my throat constricted as I got into the back of the van. I broke out in a cold sweat at the thought of going back to prison, and Una and Eugene were uppermost in my mind.

I was charged and fingerprinted and led back to the cells. Later that night, Una brought me some food but I was unable to speak to her.

I went to court the next day and was released on free bail. The case would be heard three weeks later. Walter rejoiced, throwing snide remarks my way every time he caught sight of me. The court was in Athlone, so when the trial date came, we dropped Eugene off with my Mom as children were not allowed inside the courtroom. During the tea break, Mom appeared and handed the baby back to Una, saying that she couldn't watch over him, as she had to go to Gracie in Heideveld.

Mom left with Una holding the baby as my name was called for me to appear in court. She had to wait outside. Inside the court I pleaded guilty and begged the magistrate for leniency. I explained my situation – that I was married, was working and we had a baby – but to no avail. The magistrate read out all my previous cases and sentenced me to four months in prison. As I turned to go down the well of the court, Una appeared in the doorway holding the baby. She was crying and it felt as if my heart was going to break. I took off my jacket and threw it towards her. She did not know what my sentence was and looked questioningly at me so I showed her four fingers, indicating the number of months.

Down in the holding cells, a gangster with a prominent '26' tattoo on his neck and dark rings under his eyes was busy shaking down the other prisoners, shouting, *'Ek is Doralingo! Wat het julle gebring vi die ouens? Dop julle sakke om!'* (I'm Doralingo! What did you bring for the guys? Empty your pockets!)

I watched him as he went around the cell collecting people's valuables. Some gave willingly; others were smacked around and robbed. He stopped in front of me and demanded, *'Waar's jou ding!?'* (Where's your money!?)

I was in a vile mood and snarled at him, *'Watte ding ...? Fokkof!'* (What money ...? Fuck off!)

He was caught flat-footed by my response and replied, *'Aweh ... djy's nogal sterk gevriet, djy sal vol raak vannie nommer!'* (Aweh ... you're a tough guy, you must wise up about the number!)

I knew I had to prove myself right then and put him down. *'Fokkie nommer, fok jou en fokkof!'* (Fuck the number, fuck you and fuck off!)

Doralingo backed down under my venom and the prisoners gave me a thumbs-up.

We were taken to Westlake prison, an old prison on the outskirts of Pollsmoor, and put into a cell that looked exactly like the one in the old Pollsmoor where I had served my time. In a far corner Doralingo conferred with his fellow 26 gang members, their heads hooded with blankets. I watched and waited because I knew what was coming; it was almost as if I had a death wish. I had tried to change my life around and failed, so I figured Una would be better off without me. The four hooded gangsters got up and headed my way with goembas in hand. I braced myself as the leader stopped in front of my bed. Tattooed on his throat was a 26 and the name Chico. Chico's face broke into a wide smile when he recognised me. It was my homeboy Chip.

He grabbed my hand, gave me the intricate handshake and said excitedly, '*Homeboy ... Hoe change hulle, my ma se kin? Ko slaap innie hoek, daar's koek!*' (Homeboy ... What's changed, my mother's child? Come sleep in the corner, there's cake!)

I took my meagre belongings and moved to Chip's ranch in the corner. Doralingo was not too happy about it, but Chip was in charge of the section and he had to do as the number dictated.

Chip's footlocker was well stocked with tobacco, dagga, sugar, coffee and other foodstuff, including a sealed bottle of whisky. We celebrated until late into the night as we took a walk down memory lane. I learnt that he was serving his time by working at the Athlone police station, cleaning the cells, washing police cars and smuggling contraband. He concluded his narrative by saying, '*Ek gan jou insmokkel by osse poliess-pan, Johnnie ...*' (I'm going to make a gap for you in our police gang, Johnnie ...)

The next morning, after having a breakfast of porridge and coffee with a dash of bluestone to keep the hormones down, the prisoners lined up into their work gangs. I was waiting for instructions when Chip, dressed in a civilian cap and tackies, hauled me into his work gang. A prison monitor with a writing pad checked the number of prisoners in the gang and hauled me out again. Chip took offence. '*Los hom innie span, roebana, ek gan latere jou biene sterk maak!*' (Leave him in the gang, robber, I will strengthen your legs later!)

The monitor showed us the writing pad. '*Sy naam is hie op die lys, Chico, hy moet die dokter gan sien ...*' (His name is on this list, Chico, he must go for a medical ...)

As it turned out, after the medical I was selected as a house monitor to work as a houseboy at a warder's house. The warder turned out to be Spy Thirteen, under whom I had served time before, but he did not recognise me. It also turned out that Spy Thirteen was a very disgusting person. I had to clean and polish everything in his house. I did his washing and found that his underwear was always dirty, streaked with skid marks. I had no respect for him, but I played him, seeking favour by doing more work than he had bargained for. I washed the walls without him asking me to do it. He was impressed and he took me with him to the shop down the road. I followed him like a lapdog and he rewarded me with cigarettes, tobacco and books to read.

The best part of the job was that I had a green monitor's badge on my jacket and I could move freely in and out of prison because of my job description. I also slept with other house monitors and prison chefs in a section apart from the main prison population. The chefs supplied the food while those of us working outside prison supplied the contraband. It was luxury living and we had some good times.

Another perk was that Una could come and visit me without signing in at the prison. The Spy's house was opposite the bus stop where the prison visitors disembarked, so I pretended to work in the garden when she arrived and we could spend time conversing to our hearts' content. But there was no contentment there. She had put our furniture in storage and gone back to work. The future looked bleak.

Two months later I was released on parole. I arrived in Harfield at dusk and caught Una by surprise, as she was unaware of my release. She was sitting on the porch, cutting a forlorn picture when I arrived at her gate. She jumped up and flung her arms around my neck and kissed me in full view of the passers-by. Love bloomed again and I held her tight.

I was unemployed with no place of my own, and Walter made my life a living hell. I was staying in his house and I had to humble myself. Una and the baby slept on a settee in the dining room, and I would sit around a fire brazier in the yard until everybody went to sleep, when I would slip in beside her and try to sleep on the wooden edge.

My parole conditions were that I should get a job as soon as possible, stay out of trouble and be home at a certain time. Walter offered to get me a job at his workplace. I had to give my parole papers to the boss to sign and send back to the correctional services. It was agreed that the information about my parole would only be shared by the boss and me, but soon everybody on the factory floor knew about me thanks to Walter. He was a vindictive brute and it all came to a head one Friday night.

I was barefoot and needed to use the outside toilet but found two of Una's younger brothers and their friends playing dice in front of the toilet door and they didn't want to give way. I stepped over them and one of the brothers lost the dice down the drain. He screamed obscenities at me and Walter came rushing out. He saw a chance to teach me a lesson and swung at me. I evaded the blow, grabbed a metal stool and hit him across his belly. The guy was a bleeder and he bled profusely. I ducked out of the yard as he came after me, but he was fat and I evaded him easily. I knew I was in big trouble if Walter reported me to the cops: my parole would be revoked. I hid in a neighbour's yard for a long time, contemplating my next move. After midnight I sneaked back to the house, retrieved my shoes, socks and a long kitchen knife and went to sleep on the couch on the porch. Just before dawn I awoke with Walter looming over me. I showed him the knife and he whispered, 'Djy moet maak dat jy wegkom. Ek wil jou nie hie hê nie.' (You must get out of here. I don't want you here.)

Later that week I went to the council offices and collected my pension payout. I sorted Farieda out with a few weeks' rent and went job-hunting in Kenilworth's industrial area and struck it lucky at Charmore Knitting Mills, which produced pantyhose. They offered me twelve rand a week working three shifts, which wasn't much, but I did not need transport and could walk to work. I was employed as an examiner and I felt like a twit walking around with a trolley with a metal model of a woman's leg mounted on top. I had to examine the pantyhose by pulling them over the leg to check for any dropped stitches the whole day long. My operator, Ferguson Ricketts, was a drunk so I intimidated him and then befriended him so he would teach me how to operate the huge circular knitting machines.

One day I got a phone call from Mom, who informed me that Shorty's mother, Mrs Jacobs, had offered her a train ticket to accompany her to Pretoria to visit the boys on death row. The trio had lost an appeal and were due to face the hangman's noose. They went there for a week, and after Mom's return my parents came to visit. My dad looked different: he had stopped drinking and had turned his life around. He was a regular churchgoer and had used his musical skills to start a youth choir in church.

Walter was chilling on the porch with his buddies, so I sat with my parents in the van. Mom handed me a letter from Gimba. '*Richard het die vir jou gestuur, Johnnie. Hulle word môreoggend gehang.*' (Richard sent you this letter, Johnnie. They are being hanged tomorrow.)

I sucked at oxygen. '*Hoe is hulle, Ma ...?*' (How are they, Mom ...?)

Tears pooled in her eyes. '*Hulle het hulle bekeer, Johnnie, en hulle het vir ons so 'n mooi lied gesing. Ons het hulle elke dag gesien vir 'n volle week, en elke dag ná die besoek het hulle agterstevoor terug na hulle selle toe gestap ...*' (They have repented, Johnnie, and they sang such a beautiful song for us. We saw them every day for a whole week and after each visit they walked backwards when they returned to their cells ...)

I wiped my tears away as Mom continued. '*Hulle het na ons gekyk totdat hulle in hul selle verdwyn het. Hulle wil niks mis nie!*' (They kept looking at us until they disappeared into their cells. They didn't want to miss a thing!)

I sat there and let my tears flow freely. Tears of repentance, regret and remembrance of what we had become. I wiped my tears, pocketed the letter and got out of the van.

As I passed Walter and his buddies to go around the back, I heard him say, '*Daai's die gangster wat ek julle van vertel het!*' (That's the gangster that I told you about!) His buddies chuckled inanely.

I was working a morning shift, so I got ready for work bright and early. It was a beautiful day with not a breath of wind in the air. I made a cup of coffee and settled down on the couch on the porch and opened the letter. It was written on an A4 sheet of paper. On each corner of the page was a drawing of a tagged bunch of flowers. The tags in the two top corners read 'Good Bye'. The bottom tags gave Gimba's date of birth and the date he was going to die, which was that very same day. I read the letter:

'*Beste Johnnie, by die tyd wat jy hierdie brief lees wat Shorty geskryf het, sal ek sterk op pad wees om my Maker te ontmoet. Ek was 'n dwaas, maar as ek terugkyk oor die jare, besef ek jy het altyd verskil van ons.*' (Dear Johnnie, by the time you read this letter which Shorty wrote, I'll be well on my way to meet my Maker. I was a fool but looking back over the years I realise that you were always different from us.)

I wiped away the tears that were stinging my eyes and continued reading. *'Ek het gedink ek is 'n groot gangster, maar ek verlang vir die dae toe ons langs die vuur gesit en stories vertel het ...'* (I thought I was this big gangster but I long for the days when we sat around the fire telling stories ...)

I lit a cigarette before reading the rest. *'Ek kan nie glo dat ons jou by hierdie saak in wou trek nie. My hart bloei vir die familie van die taxi driver. Johnnie, ek het vrede gemaak met God en ek aanvaar dat ons die doodstraf verdien het. Niks meer gesanik vir die klong nie. Nietemin, jy het nog altyd die beste stories vertel. Vertel onse storie. Van jou vriend Richard.'* (I can't believe that we tried to involve you in this case. My heart bleeds for the family of the taxi driver. Johnnie, I have made my peace with God and I know we deserved the death sentence. No more screaming and beefing from this boy. Anyway, you always told the best stories. Tell our story. From your friend Richard.)

A dust devil gathered, whirled onto the porch and whipped the letter out of my hand. Then the muezzin began to wail from the mosque down the road, calling Muslims to prayer. And I knew that my friends had passed on. I sat there for a long while before setting off for work.

Part Five

Telling our story

24

Me against the world

Six months after starting work in the mills, I mastered the circular knitting machines that spun eight pairs of pantyhose at a time. I got my own set of machines to operate, and a promotion, with a six-rand raise in salary. I now earned eighteen rand a week and I was on a roll.

Una's mom, Farieda, who had been taking care of Eugene, started a new job and Una had to quit her job to stay at home. Making love to Una was difficult in the crowded house, and we were still sleeping on the settee. So we mostly took our chances on days when I worked the afternoon shift and there was nobody around. Una got pregnant again, and in 1969 our second son, Clint, was born. He came into the world screaming and as I picked him up he immediately became quiet. I held him close to my heart and I was so proud. I was happy that I had two boys who could grow up together, as my only brother, Ivan, was twelve years younger than me and we never had a chance to bond.

One Sunday morning, soon after Clint was born, Farieda called me into her bedroom, where I found Walter sitting on his bed with a vacant expression in his eyes. He had just had a stroke. He was trying to take a leak and Farieda asked me to point his withered penis into the pisspot. I was disgusted by the request but I held his penis and looked into his pleading eyes but I felt no pity for him. The ambulance arrived to take him to hospital, and he died of a blood clot in his brain the same day. A year later, my daughter Sonia was born.

We stayed in Harfield for a year after Walter's death until I found us a place to stay in Kensington and we became backyard dwellers. We took our furniture out of storage and moved in. Una was unhappy with the place, with its sagging ceiling, but I needed to be on my own.

The downside was that now I had to travel long distances, and working the afternoon shift was the worst as I only got home at eleven at night. It was a dark and dangerous place so I had to be alert all the time, but I walked boldly.

Three months later, on a stormy night, I came home soaking wet to find that Una and the children were gone. The ceiling had caved in and big rats were scurrying around the rain-lashed room. I went looking for my family and found them sheltering in the landlady's house.

The next day we packed up and moved back to Harfield Village. I felt like a fool, because I was unable to provide a home for my family. I kept to myself for most of the time. It was me against the world!

Four months later, a white man from the Group Areas depart-ment came to the house and told Farieda that Harfield Village had been declared a white area and that everyone had to move to various townships across the Cape Flats, effectively splitting up the close-knit community. Farieda was offered a council dwelling in Parktown, and her married children were allocated dwellings in different places, one in Manenberg, two in Mitchells Plain, and Jenny in Lavender Hill. We were allocated a council flat in a newly developed three-storey block in Ottery. It was a one-bedroomed flat with hot water and an en-suite bathroom, and our second daughter, Melanie, was born there in 1972. To me, the place was a luxury.

Most of the inhabitants came from District Six, Constantia and other areas earmarked for white people. Suspicion was rife, as every-body thought they were better than the other because of their origins, which was exactly what the apartheid regime had in mind for people of colour. I worked shifts and stayed out of sight, happy to have a place of my own. I vowed never to beg, borrow or bow down to any man.

I seldom visited my parents, as I felt like the black sheep of the family. Then I got the idea to write a play based on the Bible story of the prodigal son set in a modern-day township. I hauled out my typewriter and started to write. I called the play *Johnny Loskop*.

One Sunday morning, I came outside and had a chat with one of my neighbours, Boeta Gammie, who was sitting on a patch of grass between the three blocks of flats, drinking from a bottle of semi-sweet white wine. Gammie was a tattooed ex-convict who had served fifteen years in prison. I liked the old guy because he had interesting stories to tell. He swallowed the last of the wine in one long gulp and put down the empty bottle. As we chuckled and chatted, another neighbour, Cecil, came down the stairs and joined us. Cecil was a brutal-faced crayfish poacher who owned the only car in the area, a big shiny DeSoto car with flaring wings. Cecil was the Man.

As we stood there, Clint, my four-year-old second son, came to me, grabbed me by the waist and held me tight. To my surprise, Cecil snarled at him, saying that he was going to give him a bloody good hiding if he caught him throwing stones again.

My son cringed behind my back and I spat at Cecil, '*Wiede fok is djy om soe met my laaitie te praat ...?*' (Who the fuck are you to speak to my kid like that ...?)

The inhabitants of the flats started gathering on their landings, and Cecil played to the crowd, shouting loudly at me, '*Ek sal vi jou oek opfok!*' (I'll fuck you up too!)

I had a sudden urge to kill him for lowering my status in front of my son and the community. My anger rose up and I tasted blood in my throat. The people on the landings were my witnesses, so I said loudly, '*Moetie soe wies'ie, man, dis Sondag ...*' (Don't be like that, man, it's Sunday ...) Then I lowered my voice and taunted him, '*Doen'it, jou tief! Ek sal jou kar en jou hele huis opfok!*' (Do it, you bitch! I'll fuck up your car and your whole house!)

He was taken aback by my fury; he scanned me for any weapons but I was unarmed. He gave a derogatory chuckle. '*Vi jou klap ek yt die grond yt!*' (I'll hit you out of the ground!)

I pleaded again, saying that I didn't want to fight with him. The crowd chuckled at my cowardice and I lowered my voice again. '*Doen'it, tief!*' (Do it, bitch!)

That got to him and he turned on his heel, threatening, '*Ek sal jou wys!*' (I'll show you!) He ran up the steps, went to his house and came back out and stood on his landing with a big fisherman's knife.

The guy was playing into my hands and I pleaded loudly again, '*Jislaaik, my broer, djy gan haal nogal 'n mes ...*' (Jeez, brother, you actually went to get a knife ...) I had made a vow to watch over my children and Cecil had pulled the wrong strings. The bloodlust was like bile in my throat.

The crowd became quiet as he came down the stairs with the knife in his hand and faced me. I taunted him, '*You've got a long knife, do it bitch!*'

His eyes flickered with fear. I wanted him to stab at me so that I could stumble and fall onto Gammie's empty bottle, smash it and stab Cecil in the throat. Death hung in the air as Una approached. She read the signs and murmured, '*Los'it, Johnnie ... dis nie die moeite werd nie.*' (Let it go, Johnnie ... it's not worth it.)

Cecil got the message. He returned to his house and came back with a sealed bottle of whisky as a peace offering and said, '*Lat os aaire 'n dop drink ...*' (Let's rather have a drink ...)

I snatched the bottle out of his hand and snarled at him, '*Fokkof! Djy kannie same os drink nie, djy's 'n tief! En nog iets ... djy raak nie aan my familie nie!*' (Fuck off! You can't drink with us, you're a bitch! And another thing ... you don't touch my family!)

Una reprimanded me. '*Gee sy bottel terug, Johnnie.*' (Give him back his bottle.)

I reluctantly returned Cecil's bottle to him and he showed some respect.

A year later, Dad died of thrombosis. He wasn't feeling well, with pains in his legs, so he drove himself to Groote Schuur hospital. Mom waited in the van, as she thought he was just going to pick up some tablets. After two hours she went inside to see why he was taking so long. She couldn't find him and started to panic, and when she asked about him she was told that he had passed away. Mom was devastated.

At the graveside, I stood under a tree a short distance away and the mourners kept on staring at me. I had to listen to people who had only recently met Dad sing his praises. Nobody asked me as the eldest son to say anything, so I just put on my hard face and cried inside.

At the funeral, my younger brother, Ivan, came over to me. He was twelve years younger than me, born when I was already involved in crime and violence, so we never had a close relationship.

Ivan was in charge of a youth band, so I told him about my play *Johnny Loskop* and said that maybe his group could perform it. My request caught him by surprise and he gave me a strange look. He said he would talk to the group and hear what they had to say. I did not hear from him again for a long time.

With my newfound skills as a knitting-machine operator, I applied for and got an operator's job at Towles Edgar Jacobs (TEJ), a knitting mill in Steenberg. The factory was huge and made quality garments, mostly for Woolworths. Every operator wore a blue dust coat, each department had its own soccer team, and the company had its own private sports field, where most of the workers would gather during lunch break. I earned forty rand a week with plenty of overtime as they only worked twelve-hour shifts. It was 1976, and in June of that year the Soweto schools uprising began and the people went on strike. There was rioting across the country and most of the factory workers stayed at home because of the crisis. I figured that I had been in a crisis for most of my life and I went to work.

I worked in the Bentley department, knitting sleeves, fronts and backs for sweaters and jerseys. The long Bentley machine I worked had sixteen heads, so it knitted sixteen garments at a time, using eight rolls of yarn per head. Once my yarn was loaded and the machine was running, I would sit down and read a book. Once in a while, I would check the garments for dropped stitches and replace the broken needles, and then go back to reading. I would finish three books in a twelve-hour shift. I was productive and always on time, so I was rewarded with an increase in pay. I was happy, but something was missing.

When I got home in the morning after a night shift, I would open my typewriter and work on a story with the title 'One for the Road' for two hours before I went to bed. It was about a reformed gangster who is coerced by his former gang buddies to pull off one more robbery, which goes horribly wrong. I was starting to explore telling our story, as Gimba had asked me to do, but I used fictional characters, as I wasn't ready to truly face my memories.

My two sisters Valerie and Gloria had emigrated to the Netherlands many years before, and in 1979 when my third daughter, Janine, was born, Gloria came to pay us a visit. We hadn't seen each other for ages and she asked me about my stories. She had done well for herself and she was very different from the girl born in the backstreets of our township. She encouraged me to find a publisher for my stories, but I had no idea where to go.

At work during our lunch breaks, my fellow workers would gather around my table and I would tell them the story I was writing in 'One for the Road'. They loved my storytelling, especially during the night. Then one day one of the older guys showed me a clipping from a newspaper about a publishing company called Vantage Press in the United Kingdom that was looking for writers.

Now, my story was typed on different-coloured sheets of paper, in capital letters and with no punctuation. I posted it to Vantage Press and three weeks later they wrote back to me, saying that they just loved my story and that it had great potential. They painted a picture of international book tours and lucrative royalties. The downside was that I had to pay them four thousand pounds up front! I was earning seventy rand a week, so that was a bummer.

Back at work, the guys poked fun at me. Telling stories to them was one thing, they said, but trying to publish it was another. I had a reputation as a thug, and thugs don't publish stories. But I had been bitten by the bug. So on a sunny day, after much contemplating, I plucked up my courage and walked into the boss's office and gave him my manuscript to read, with the Vantage Press letter attached. He scanned the first page, gave me a strange look and said that he would give it to the personnel officer to read and that he'd come back to me. I had a swagger in my step when I returned to the knitting gallery.

Three weeks later the boss called me into his office and gave me my story back and said, '*You tell a good story, John, but you must never pay anybody any money; they must pay you.*' I really don't know what I expected from him, but his words were enough to pick up my spirit.

A week after my third son, Quinton, was born in 1983, I came across a newspaper clipping about a gathering for writers in Elsies River that Saturday. My curiosity was aroused. I arrived at the workshop dressed in my hat and gangster apparel. A stocky coloured writer could not contain his mirth and exclaimed, '*The last of the gunfighters.*' My anger bubbled up, but I stayed focused. I introduced myself and presented them with a short story called 'The Creep', about a gangster who is sentenced to death and then reprieved and who seeks vengeance after his release. The other participants were all established writers, playwrights, poets and teachers. They had education and ignored me the whole time. I was a thug and I did not fit in.

I was determined to succeed, and one Wednesday night I went to visit my brother Ivan and his group, the Gospel Crusaders, and laid my cards on the table. They were sceptical and listened to me with only half an ear. A week later I returned to them and they looked at me with empty eyes as if I hadn't been there the previous week. So it went week after week. But I kept badgering them, and six months later they performed my play *Johnny Loskop*, at the Joseph Stone Auditorium in Athlone. The place was packed to the rafters and my heart was filled with pride.

Then the choir group decided to take the play on their annual gospel crusade and I was asked to accompany them. I bought an old VHS camera and tripod that I found in the classifieds and I filmed them on their tours of small towns across the country. I also typed up their stories and testimonies, one A4 sheet for each story, and bound them into a book, which I sold to them and the public for five rand a copy. It was tiring work putting it together, but I enjoyed the challenge. I was a published writer, even though I published it myself.

Francis and my youngest sister, Dianne, were also singers in the band, and I came to love the group and the feeling was mutual. I trusted them because they never referred to my criminal past and accepted me just as I was. Sometimes gangsters would accost us, but with my prison status and my knowledge of gang life, I could easily talk our way out of a tight corner.

One icy-cold night, they were performing in East London when a group of ten thugs entered the hall. I was filming at the side of the stage and they crossed the floor and stopped in front of me. The music also stopped as fear swept through the hall. The leader of the group had a tattoo across his forehead that read *'Mongrel! Bungalow 13! Pay or die!'* I knew that he was the real thing, because the Mongrels gang was started in Koeberg near Cape Town in a row of bungalows, and they occupied Bungalow 13. The thought that my past had caught up with me crossed my mind until the leader said, *'Bid vi os!'* (Pray for us!) I looked to the stage for help, as praying was not part of my job description, but the prayer warriors were scared stiff. The guy followed my eyes and insisted, *'Nei, ek wil hê djy moet vi os bid!'* (No, I want you to pray for us!) I had no choice, so I prayed for them and they left peacefully after much gang talk. The congregation was relieved.

Later that year at the writers' workshop, the editor of the *Metro Burger*, Melvin Whiteboy, came to visit and asked us for any short stories that we had written. I gave him my story 'The Creep', which he translated into Afrikaans as 'Hulle Noem My Skollie' (They Call Me Gangster), a title I had used for a story I'd started years before but never completed. The story was published in 1984, to the chagrin of the other members with their high education, whose stories failed to make the cut. They had education, but I had the revelation of how to tell a story. My mom was proud of me again and would stand at the communal gate with the publication in hand and show it to everybody who cared to listen. I waited patiently for the postman to bring my royalty cheque, and in the end I earned forty rand for my story. I was over the moon: I was a writer. In the same year, another two of my stories were published in *Die Burger*. 'One for the Road' became a thirteen-part series, translated into Afrikaans as 'Die Pad na Glorie'. The other was a four-part series, 'Two for the Money', which became 'Twee teen die Noodlot'. I had a small bit of recognition.

The kids were growing older and we decided we needed a bigger house, so we applied to the council and moved to a two-roomed maisonette in Lotus River situated between two schools, Lotus River and Zeekoevlei High. I scrimped and saved and put down R200 as a deposit on a third- or fourth-hand Toyota bakkie, and in my spare time I would collect scrap in the area and sell it at the scrapyard. Old habits died hard, and I paid off the bakkie in no time.

In 1985 the riots started again, and burning and looting became the order of the day. Soon the schools were targeted and the government's coloured House of Representatives began hiring security guards to watch over schools. My stage play *Johnny Loskop* was being performed at Lotus River High School, which Clint, Sonia and Melanie attended. When a security guard's car was set alight at Zeekoevlei High School, I decided to try my luck and apply for a job. I figured that if my application to get a job in government was successful, I would be able to get a housing subsidy to buy a house of my own.

25

Security guard

I arrived in the city early the next morning to find a long line of unemployed men waiting to be interviewed for work as security guards. The line moved slowly and I was only called in after ten o'clock. A coloured guy gave me a form to fill in my details. I read through it and got stuck on the question *'Do you have a criminal record?'* I pondered the question for a while then wrote 'Yes'. He took the form, read it and a slow grin spread over his face. He asked me what made me think I could get a job as a security guard with my criminal record.

I looked him in the eye and told him I was looking for a second chance in life.

He pointed to the tattoo on my wrist and asked me to tell him more about it.

I gathered my thoughts and took him on a short journey of my past. I mesmerised him with my storytelling abilities and concluded my story by telling him about my play *Johnny Loskop*, which was currently being performed by learners at Lotus River High School. That got his attention, as they were looking for men to guard the schools against vandalism. He fiddled with my form and said that he couldn't decide what to do about me. My heart sank. He suggested I go with him to hear what his colleague had to say. I followed him into the office of another coloured guy.

I sat down with him and repeated my story. He found me interesting, but he too could not decide because of my criminal record. He passed me on to another office, and after that seven more people with higher rank interviewed me. I suppose they should have sent me on my way already, but I had them spellbound with my gift of the gab. In the tenth office I was confronted by an old white guy, Mr Friedman. I had no fond memories of white people and I knew my chances were slim. He listened to my story and when I was done he looked at me for a long time. I had a feeling that he was going to send me packing.

Mr Friedman spoke in a measured tone and asked me if I thought that my past would never catch up with me.

I humbled myself and told him that I was looking for a second chance in life and that I wasn't afraid to go work at the schools.

He looked at me deep down before replying. 'Ek gaan my vertroue in jou sit, mnr. Fredericks. Ek gee vir jou 'n tweede kans.' (I'm going to put my trust in you, Mr Fredericks. I'm giving you a second chance.) With that, he picked up his pen and signed my documents. I was in and it felt as if I was walking on holy ground. Mr Friedman was the first white man ever to show any trust in me.

The next day, I reported for duty at the Coloured Affairs offices in Broad Road, Wynberg, to find most of the new workforce hanging around, too afraid to go to their designated school sites. Most of them had a daily newspaper in hand to check at which schools the learners were rioting. Even the senior security officers coerced them not to go to their schools, as they too were scared to go into the township schools. After a week of idling at the offices, and afraid that the government might fire all of us, I decided to approach my senior and told him that if he sent three men with me, I'd go work at Zeekoevlei.

He looked at me sceptically and asked if I had a death wish. Didn't I know that the previous guard's car was set alight? He was reluctant at first, but he was ambitious and knew that if he placed guards at the school it would be a feather in his cap. He agreed, and the two of us set out to find three more guards with spunk who also lived near the school. I chose to work the day shift with my partner Graham Hill, and the other two worked the night shift.

We had no uniforms yet and arrived at the school in our civvies. The learners looked at us with suspicion. During their first break they gathered in the courtyard. I wandered in and saw what they were look-ing at. There were posters on the walls that read 'Botha's dogs must go!' and 'Botha's dogs must die!' We were dogs and we weren't wanted there. So for the next few days we watched their every move. They would gather during their break periods, and when they went back to their classrooms we breathed a sigh of relief. The situation was volatile. Janine and Quinton were still very young and there was no way that I was going to leave my post.

One day, after the learners gathered, Graham Hill murmured, '*Hier kom hulle, mnr. Fredericks ...*' (Here they come, Mr Fredericks ...) And they came marching towards us where we were doing access control outside our security hut. The leader of the pack was a Grade 8 learner who told us in a squeaky voice that we had five minutes to get lost. I stood my ground and looked at him deep down before replying. I asked him what he was going to do if we were still there after five minutes.

He wasn't expecting this reaction and he was stumped for an answer. '*Sorg net dat julle weg is ná skool,*' he mumbled. (Just see that you're gone after school.)

They left and I phoned the office to inform them about the incident. Time passed slowly. The bell rang and the learners came barrelling out of their classrooms towards us. There was no way that I was going to run from a bunch of kids. Squeaky Voice was in the forefront and screamed that they were going to burn our hut down.

I had no problem with that and told him to let me get my bag and then they could go ahead. I retrieved the bag and we stood a short distance away as they threw rocks at the hut, but they bounced off the toughened plastic material. They tried to set it alight, but it would not burn.

Then a security car with three armed officers arrived on the premises and the learners swarmed around the car. The officers got out and walked towards the administration block, the learners close on their heels. They found themselves trapped inside the principal's office. They had no way out and they drew their guns. Wrong move! The learners went ballistic and the officers were too afraid to shoot.

Gangsters jumped over the fence and chaos reigned until two trucks loaded with armed cops arrived on the scene. The learners and gangsters stoned the cops, who responded by firing rubber bullets. They arrested three gangsters and the learners fled helter-skelter. I could have left the site with the three other guards, but I chose to stay.

I only had to work eight hours a day, and because I lived within walking distance of the school I decided to split my shift. I worked from four to eight in the morning, went home, and went back to work at two in the afternoon, when school closed, until six o'clock. The learners had no time to plan on me, because when they arrived at school in the morning I left, and I returned only when school was out. I patrolled the school and checked for broken windows and other signs of vandalism. I started a garden on the school grounds out of sheer boredom. I planted trees and the garden bloomed. Soon my roster was adopted by all the schools in the province.

One day early in 1986, while I was watering the school garden, a car with a Joburg number plate pulled up at the gate. I hurried over to do access control. A bearded white man was behind the wheel and he signed his name Johan Blignaut.

Johan was a filmmaker and his company's name was Everis Films. He explained to me that he was visiting every school in the province to promote his film *Mamza*, which he had shot in nine days in Coronationville. He told me that he had got tired of yes-men who wanted to drink all day long, so he took out a second bond on his house to make the film. I thought he had pluck, so I got all excited and told him about my life and my stories. He listened to me and invited me to come to his flat in a block called Serengeti in Observatory.

I went to visit him that evening, and the meeting became a major turning point in my life, as he told me about scriptwriting. Before I left, he said that he liked my stories and my voice, and that he would contact me as soon as he got back to his office. I was elated and I had a swagger in my step when I hit the street.

The first batch of security guards were selected for training and I was included in the group. We were transported to the firing range in Faure for firearm training with handguns and shotguns. I excelled in this, and I became a good bad guy. Soon after the training, I was summoned to Mr Friedman's office, where he presented me with a 9-mil pistol, four walkie-talkie radios and two sets of uniforms. He said he was going to transfer me to A.J. Stals hospital in Tokai, where I would have to take charge. I was honoured but said nothing. He added that there had never been any security guards on that site and that he'd had many complaints about corruption.

A.J. Stals was a psychiatric hospital complex which included Westlake and D.P. Marais hospitals. When I arrived there, the main gate was open, the security hut was empty, and there wasn't a guard in sight. I drove through and stopped at another small security office, where I found four security guards having a lunch of fried chicken, supplied by the kitchen staff. They scrambled to attention when I entered and asked them who was in charge.

A guy with a long chin and thick blue-tinted glasses sputtered that he was. His name was John Wayne Scheepers. I checked their books and told him to go and do access control at the gate. Then I went out on patrol with another guard, Andre Coulson, a short, slovenly dude who seemed easily intimidated. The leafy, tree-lined complex was huge, with many hideaways. I discovered a hangout littered with broken glass, dirty chalices and evidence of people smoking Mandrax tablets. We moved on and stopped at a row of derelict garages. A red messenger's bike was parked outside one of them. A flicker of Coulson's eyes told me that he knew the owner of the bike. He said nothing and stood back as I opened the door and found the superintendent's personal messenger and a nurse with their pants down, having stand-up sex. They were shocked into immobility. I told them to get finished, that I would wait for them outside.

There was no more lust between them and they came out very quickly. I took out my notebook and wrote down their particulars. The messenger, a muscular guy, pleaded with me, but I was not interested. Coulson told me afterwards that he'd been doing this with the nurses for a long time.

Mr Friedman had put his trust in me and I was determined to live up to that trust. Apparently the married messenger was a well-known womaniser on the complex and word of the incident spread like wild-fire through the hospital. I had made a lot more enemies and a few more friends. I kept the guards on their toes. I worked staggered shifts so they were never sure when I would be arriving on site.

Down the road was Pollsmoor prison's training centre for warders, many of whom came to visit the nurses and stayed in their quarters until late at night. I spoke to the hospital superintendent about this, and she gave me a glimmer of a smile and told me, '*You must put a stop to this, Mr Fredericks. They must book in at the gate and everybody must be out at eleven!*' So every night we had problems getting those trainee warders off the premises. We had to go and find them, but some would hide away in closets or under the beds. One Friday night I got into an altercation with a high-ranking warder who didn't want to leave and he pulled a gun on me. I was armed too, but I did not dare pull my gun as the guy was drunk. I reported him to the police and the Pollsmoor authorities, and he was transferred to another prison.

Scheepers also pulled up his socks and he stopped every police vehicle at the gate, asked the cops which ward they were going to, and phoned the ward to confirm. If the cop hadn't been called, he would refuse them entry, because they were probably there to hobnob with the nurses. He became such a character that the station commander at Kirstenhof police station arrived in his green Uno and told me, '*Mr Fredericks, my officers tell me that the security here is tight, but when the guy with the blue Coke-bans is on duty, it is tight-tight!*' That was a great accolade for Scheepers. A man had come to town.

As the days passed, I got several anonymous phone calls giving information that certain staff were involved in stealing. Two weeks later I put up a roadblock at the main gate with all the guards on duty and started a seizure operation. We searched cars and bags and found fried chickens, pots of jam and peanut butter, and rolls of toilet paper. A whole grocery list of stolen stuff that was meant for the patients was piled high on the table in the security office. Later I sent the guards on patrol and they returned with more stolen foodstuff that had been abandoned in the forks of trees.

My work did not go unnoticed and a blond haired administrative officer came to inspect the site. He scanned me once, took in my tattoo and my ghetto walk that I couldn't shake off, and I got the sense that he was judging me. The old familiar feeling of hatred tasted like bile in my throat. I stayed focused as he lowered my status, and so began a journey of persecution that would dog me for many years to come.

Soon the news of my tough stance against corruption and my story-writing abilities reached the ears of the media who published the annual government magazine. A reporter came to our site to do enquiries. After he interviewed me, I gave him a short story titled ''n Pa vir Kersfees' (A Father for Christmas). The story was published and suddenly I became a person of interest. The blond-haired officer didn't like this, especially when he came to do inspection one day and found a reporter on site who had come to take pictures of me. I warned him that the officer wasn't going to be happy, but he couldn't care less; he took his pics and published them.

A few months later, I got a call from Johan Blignaut to inform me that he had secured a place for me and Melvin Whiteboy of the *Metro Burger* at a film workshop with the Afrikaans Language and Culture Association, the ATKV, in Joburg and that we had to pick up our flight tickets at the airport. I was gobsmacked. It was my first flight ever and we stayed at the Johannesburger Hotel, which was another first for me. I was walking on air. The lecturers were mostly directors and producers. I learnt a lot about scriptwriting and filmmaking from them.

Then one day I got a call from Grace, who told me that Mom was in hospital. She had got dizzy from the old recurring headaches, and she fell down and hit her head. I went to the hospital and stood outside the ICU until they wheeled Mom out. She smiled at me and held my hand for a moment before being taken to another ward. She died a week later. Again I was not asked to say anything at her graveside while strangers sang her praises. I took it in my stride. My sister Francis got the house and Grace divided all Mom's worldly goods among my other siblings and relatives. When I arrived at the house, the only thing that was left was a portrait of my dad. Nobody else wanted it, so I took it.

I took out my typewriter and wrote a story in her honour, ''n Kerskaart vir Mamma' (A Christmas Card for Mama). The story was published in the December issue of the government magazine, much to the chagrin of the administrative officer. In the next two years I wrote two more Christmas stories: 'Nog Rose vir Sally' (More Roses for Sally) and 'Nog 'n Kersfees vir Martha' (Another Christmas for Martha).

I never got paid for these stories but it wasn't about the money: I just wanted to write.

I knew all the tricks about thuggery and I excelled in my duties to combat corruption and theft at the hospital. I was not easily fooled by the huge nursing staff or groundsmen there. Acting on information, I took a few security guards with me and went to a general worker's house in Steenberg. We found that his entire home was furnished with hospital chairs and tables, as well as bed sheets, curtains and crockery. The hospital had to send a truck to collect the stuff. My team got some respect. The staff didn't want us there, but we were there to stay.

Soon after that, the hospital superintendent offered me a five-roomed house at the hospital to be closer to work. I sold my maisonette in Lotus River and moved to Westlake, much to the envy of high-ranking security officers from the head office in Cape Town. And slowly the poisonous head of jealousy stuck its head out. My team grew, as more guards were transferred to Westlake. Many of them were tough guys and troublemakers who did not want to abide by the rules. So they were sent to work under the 'skollie'.

I had a different style of management. I would first gather their trust, then sit down with them individually and discuss their problems with the security hierarchy. I solved most of their problems easily, sometimes with just a change of working hours. We became a force to be reckoned with.

In 1990 the hospital closed down and all the patients were moved to a newly built mental hospital in Lentegeur, Mitchells Plain. The empty wards and offices became storage spaces for broken or old school benches and other furniture. The place became deserted, run-down and quite scary at night. We still had to guard the premises and I was promoted to a senior security officer, with an increase in salary, so I decided it was time for me to buy a house of my own. I applied for a housing subsidy and bought a three-roomed house in Strandfontein Village, a five-minute drive from the False Bay coast.

Over the years, Una had attended each and every school event of our children, and all of them had excelled at school – except for Clint, who I caught bunking school in Grade 9. I was angry and wanted to take the belt to him, when he sombrely told me, '*Daddy, ek kan sien ons kry swaar. Ek sal aaire gaan werk, dan kan die ander maar verder studeer ...*' (Daddy, I can see we're having a tough time. I'll rather go and work, then the others can further their studies ...)

Una and I gave it some thought and agreed. He started work as a bakery assistant at Grand Bazaars in Wynberg. He was good at his job and he got paid even more than I did. His salary meant a great deal to the family.

Eugene had finished college and was working as an apprentice motor mechanic, and Sonia and Melanie were both at UCT. Sonia was in her fourth year studying to be a social worker and Melanie was a first-year law student. Janine and Quinton were still at school. Life was good. I had a job, a house, a car and a bakkie. Everything was just hunky-dory. But that was soon to change.

One day, the education department brought a truckload of old unwanted typewriters and school furniture to be stored in the empty wards of the hospital before being destroyed or buried at a later stage. I approached the clerk in charge and asked him if I could take a typewriter for my own use, as the ribbon on mine wasn't working. He agreed on condition that I check out thirteen more to see if they still worked, as he wanted to give them to a school in a black township.

I was excited to own a modern typewriter and I diligently checked the other ones. I wrote down the serial numbers and stacked them neatly in a corner. I secured the ward by making sure all the windows were closed tight, except for one that I had to tie with a wire. When I left work that Friday, I handed the keys to the guard in charge of the night shift, also a Mr Fredericks.

On Monday I was summoned to the security administrative offices in Broad Road, Wynberg, at noon. When I arrived I found most of my team there and I asked them who was on site then if they were all there.

Christopher Marco, one of my men who I trusted, spoke up. '*Ons het 'n oproep ontvang dat ons hier moet rapporteer, mnr. Fredericks ...*' (We received a call that we had to report here, Mr Fredericks ...)

On further questioning, Marco told me that the blond officer had made the call. I felt disturbed by the news, and by the fact that our site was left unguarded, so I decided to confront the officer. It was almost lunchtime when I reached his first-floor office with its huge windows facing the main gate. As I looked through the window I saw the green Uno from Kirstenhof police station enter the gate and a cold fear clutched at my heart.

I sensed trouble and ducked into a friend's office to make a call. As I picked up the phone, the blond officer entered and disconnected the call. '*Los maar die oproep vir later, mnr. Fredericks …*' (Leave the call for later, Mr Fredericks …)

When two detectives entered the office, I asked the officer, '*Waaroor gaan dié dan nou, meneer …?*' (What's all this about, sir …?)

A devil danced in his eyes as he replied, '*Die speurders wil met jou gesels, mnr. Fredericks.*' (The detectives want to talk to you, Mr Fredericks.)

I was arrested for the theft of thirteen typewriters. I was totally confused, but when a detective wanted to handcuff me I told him, '*Dis nie nodig nie, ek stap saam met julle …*' (You don't need that, I'll walk with you …)

As we approached the police car in the parking lot, all the people working in the building, including my team of security guards, stood watching. I was embarrassed and humiliated. For a moment I stepped back into my past and gave the crowd a double salute before getting into the car.

26

Answering the call

There was nobody at home when the detectives brought me to my house to search the place. They confiscated the typewriter that had been presented to me, and I tried to explain but they didn't want to listen to my story. I put on a change of clothing before getting back into the car. Although I knew that I was innocent of any criminal deed, I was ice cold and a silent scream emanated from my mind.

At the Kirstenhof police station the detectives interrogated me about the theft of the thirteen typewriters. According to their case, on Friday night they had come across a white man with the typewriters in his possession. On questioning, the man said he had bought them from a Mr Fredericks three weeks earlier and that Mr Fredericks was a security guard at Westlake hospital. I was confused and tried to clear my head. I asked the detective if I could see the typewriters.

He took me to a room and showed them to me. They were the same machines I had checked out the previous Friday. I told him I didn't understand: I had looked at these machines on Friday, but someone was saying he had bought them three weeks ago … I was talking sense and they went into a scrum.

They decided that I still had to appear in court and I was put into an empty cell. The walls seemed to close in on me. I banged on the cell door and screamed in frustration. The door jerked open and I asked the cop not to close the door, only the grill. He gave me a long, hard look but complied. Long after the night took over, I was still awake. I got up and jumped continuously from my bed of blankets to the wall in frustration.

Early the next morning, a cop gave me a katkop, a mug of black coffee and a bucket of cold water to wash myself. A sergeant arrived to start his day shift, and when he caught sight of me through the cell bars he stopped in his tracks. He knew me. His name was Theodore Mathys, a school buddy of Eugene's who had been in and out of our house when we lived in Ottery. He wanted to know why I was locked up. I explained my situation to him and he told the cop on duty to open the cell so that I could take a shower. Then he gave me his lunch box, his flask of coffee and his copy of the *Cape Times* to read.

Later, the detective arrived and brought me to his office. The first question he asked was which of the guards at Westlake owned a blue Ford Escort.

The penny dropped and I blurted, '*Mnr. Fredericks besit een!*' (Mr Fredericks owns one!) It was the security guard who had the same surname as me.

He tossed the file into a slot and I looked at him questioningly. '*Wat ...?*' (What ...?)

He gave me a lingering look before replying, '*Jy het my nou net gesê wie die skuldige is ... Laat ek jou baas inlig.*' (You've just told me who the guilty party is ... Let me inform your boss.) He picked up the phone and called the blond officer, giving him the status of the case. He also told him about the typewriter they had found at my home and the circumstances surrounding it. I clearly heard the officer saying, '*Dit is diefstal, u moet hom aankla!*' (That is theft, you must charge him!) My heart sank.

My namesake Fredericks and another guard were also arrested, and we appeared in court on separate charges. The blond officer and a few other security guards who I identified as my detractors were also in court. I was found guilty and the court orderly read out all my previous convictions and I had to sign the document. The other guards stared at me in disbelief when they discovered they had a bad guy in their midst. I was sentenced to a fine of R800.

Two days later I arrived at the Broad Road offices dressed in my gangster apparel. Black chalk-stripe suit and a wide-brimmed Stetson beaver on my head. I was angry as I walked through the building, my eyes daring anyone to say something. None of them did. The officer asked me to resign, but I showed him no respect and refused. We were in his office on the first floor facing the main gate and I had a sudden urge to grab him around the waist and dive with him through the big window. He must have sensed my intentions and changed his tune. Seeing that I did not want to resign, he said, he was transferring me to the Ottery School of Industries, an industrial school for juvenile offenders.

The school was an exact replica of the old Pollsmoor prison where I had served my first sentence, as it was built in the same era. The inmates were boys from across the province who were sentenced by the court to learn a trade there, such as bricklaying, carpentry, welding, tailoring, shoemaking or motor mechanics.

I reported for duty and found six very slack guards on duty in a small office next to the open access-control booms. The office, meant for two guards to do access control, was cramped with the six guards lounging around. They came to attention when I closed the booms before entering the office. They had been there for a long time, and they were in a comfort zone and on friendly terms with everybody on the site, including the inmates. They were also well fed by the kitchen staff and this raised my hackles, because I knew there was always a price tag for this. I immediately split them up and changed their shifts. They were angry and grumbled among each other, but I couldn't care less. I was no more Mr Nice Guy.

At the time I arrived at the industrial school, the inmates were rioting every morning at breakfast. They would complain about their food and throw their plates around, smashing them. The caregivers were powerless against the onslaught and the security guards were clueless. I studied the situation and decided to tell them a story. It had worked for me in prison, so it would surely work here. I asked the night-shift guards not to go off duty but to take up posts behind the dining hall and to stay out of sight. They moaned and groaned but they complied. The next morning, as the boys were starting their shenanigans, I walked into the dining hall with two other guards close behind. The youth shouted obscenities at us, thinking that we were alone, and then the night-shift guards entered by the back door. It took them by surprise. I could iden-tify with these gangsters, and the moment I had their attention, I took them on a journey, telling them stories about gangs and prison life. My voice got through to them, and I held their attention for a long time. Afterwards, they settled down and ate their breakfast. The guards and caregivers looked at me with respect. I was thrilled, and surprised at what I had just pulled off. As the days passed, many of the youth at the school would pop into my office asking for advice. I would motivate and inspire them to rise above the gang life. I also inspired the guards to be more motivated.

The principal of the school was impressed with my work and gave me a nice big office under a stand of bluegum trees, close to the administrative offices. In my spare time I sold detergents, meat, clothes and shoes. I made good money and my skills as a hawker stood me in good stead. With my gift of the gab I could sell anything to anybody so I began to chase the dime. But my dream of becoming a writer had faded.

Over the years, Eugene and Clint had got married; Sonia had graduated and started work as a social worker in Durban; while Melanie, Janine and Quinton were still living in the house. During this period I had rewritten 'One for the Road' as a feature-film script and retitled it as *A Gangster's Glory*. I wrote to Johan Blignaut telling him about the script but got no reply.

I had also written short stories and even poetry. Early one morning before I went to work, I tossed all my writings into the dustbin. I had decided that it was over, the end of a dream. When I got home that day I found that Melanie had retrieved all my work from the bin and put it on my writing table. I asked her why she had done this. She gave me an impish grin and replied, '*Daddy kan mos nie al die skryfwerk net so weggooi nie ...*' (You can't just throw all your writing away like that, Daddy ...) I looked at her deep down and gathered my stuff.

The very next day, I got a call from Johan. He had lost track of me, as I had moved twice since our last correspondence. He had moved to Cape Town and was staying in the Bo-Kaap. He organised for me to attend a two-day professional scriptwriting workshop with Jurgen Wolff at the Cape Town Film and Television School, where I listened and absorbed what was taught about scriptwriting, and as the hours passed, my dream of becoming a writer stirred and slowly came back to life.

Then Johan was commissioned by the SABC to make a four-part

TV series based on a book by Adam Small, *Krismis van Map Jacobs*, about the trials and tribulations of a gangster. Johan needed me to co-write the script.

He was paid script-development funding, from which I earned a per diem. For me it was not about the money; it was the thrill to be able to write the script. We did well and I was convinced that we were going to make the film as we held auditions, checked locations and gathered the wardrobe. Then Nelson Mandela became president and the SABC put our project on hold as a new guard took charge, and the correspondence with our commissioning editor dried up. It was another dead end. I also realised that it was a big blow for Johan. Like me, he had a lot of bills to pay, but I had a job and was earning cash money from buying and selling stuff.

In 1996 Johan gave me an old IBM computer, and my daughter Janine had the task of teaching me how to operate it. Then Janine left for Switzerland to go and work as an au pair. Before she left, she wrote down all the instructions on how to work the PC. Her notes covered a whole wall of my room. Some visitors found it funny, but I didn't care.

Soon after she left, Johan signed me up for a one-day Hollywood Film Institute course presented by American film teacher Dov S-S Simens. The course was memorable and taught me not to limit myself but to dream bigger.

Johan contacted me again with a new idea for a script, which we had to write from scratch. Called *Fiona*, it was about a female radio presenter who takes a tough stance against gangsterism. She lambasts them over the airwaves until her only son is assaulted and badly hurt by gangsters. I dug deep and we wrote a brilliant script. Again we held auditions and checked locations and Johan even went into more debt and filmed a pilot. He was convinced that M-Net was going to give him production funding. The cast had workshopped over months and we were ready to roll. Sadly, it was not to be.

On a Thursday morning I gave him a call to enquire about the promised production funding and I got his voicemail, so I left a message for him to call me back. At five o'clock I got a call from his wife Lynette to inform me that Johan had committed suicide and that he had left a note for me. The note read, '*Jy moet aangaan, my broer, jy is groter as wat ek ooit was.*' (You must go ahead, my brother, you are bigger than I ever was.) I was shocked and deeply saddened, because I had held him in high esteem.

A short while later, I was invited to speak at a seminar in the District Six Museum. After the proceedings I was approached by a strangely dressed Italian guy. He introduced himself as Davide Tosco. He wore a wrinkled shirt and a frayed leather jacket and his boots were held together with masking tape. He was an Italian youth activist, just arrived from Berlin, and he was on a mission to start a project of creative education with juvenile awaiting-trial prisoners in Pollsmoor prison. He invited me to accompany him to his first presentation and also to say a few words. I accepted the invitation and the next day he came to pick me up at work.

My heart fluttered when I entered Pollsmoor after almost thirty years. It was strange walking down the corridors as a civilian and not a prisoner. The place was overcrowded and sentenced prisoners now wore tracksuits. A senior warder escorted us to a huge courtyard where young prisoners were milling about. Among them were a group of schoolboy inmates still in their school uniforms. Some walked around hustling for smokes while others just lounged around. Something stirred deep inside my soul, as I saw myself in their situation and I could identify with them. The warder brought them to attention and introduced Davide and me. Davide introduced his programme of what he would like to do in prison and handed the mic to me. I scanned the crowd as I gathered my thoughts, then I took them on a journey. I spoke from the heart as I told them about my experiences, and my story had them spellbound; even the warders were paying attention. When I was done, I could see some tears flowing. They were moved by my eloquence and my Mom's words flashed through my mind. '*Be watchful, Johnnie ... you've got a higher calling ...*' I had found my calling.

Back in my office I did some soul-searching. I stared at the big blue-gum tree outside the door for a long time and decided, *If I have to stare at that tree for one more month, I'm going to run head first into it and kill myself.* I was tired of doing nothing. I was going to quit my day job.

At home that evening, I discussed my plans with Una and the kids. It was not an easy decision to make, but I figured that my business was flourishing and I was earning much more money from it than my salary. I convinced them that the time had come for me to chase my dream. I had watched over the kids since they were born and there was a strong bond between us. They trusted my decisions and they gave me their silent approval.

The next day, I went to the regional office in Wynberg and handed in my resignation to the chief security officer. A few other pot-bellied officers were lounging behind their desks when I entered. The chief was a vain guy who dyed his hair black and shaved his legs. There was no love lost between us. He read the letter, chuckled and said, '*Jy is vyftig jaar oud, Fredericks, wat gaan jy nou doen ...?*' (You're fifty years old, Fredericks, what are you going to do now ...?)

I looked around the office, stared at their fat bellies and told him, '*Ek gaan films maak!*' (I'm going to make films!)

Their cackling laughter followed me as I left the premises. I was tired of sitting around while our youth were dying for nothing. I wanted to make a difference.

In 1998 I was invited to participate in the first Scrawl film laboratory, held in Monkey Valley in Noordhoek. I learnt that Johan Blignaut had filed an application on my behalf before he died and had attached my script *A Gangster's Glory*. I was elated and I learnt a lot about script-writing from top South African and international filmmakers. At night a group of them would gather in my cabin and I would tell stories to them in Afrikaans, although many of them did not understand one word of the language. And this I did on their request. They loved my style of storytelling and did not need to understand the words.

Davide got funding to do a pilot project in the B4 juvenile section in Pollsmoor. We interviewed a lot of youth activists with various skills and disciplines and set up an NGO called CRED (Creative Education with Children and Youth at Risk). We did the pilot project, and Janine, who had just passed matric, accompanied me there. It was a great experience for her to know what prison life was all about.

Valda Lucas, a fiery youth activist, became the coordinator. Although I was coming in on the ground floor, I was elected as a director and creative-writing facilitator in prison. I was paid R1 500 per month, which just covered my bond repayments, but I had my mind set on making a difference among the youth. In my workshop I taught them to read, write and tell their stories. I coaxed them into writing their stories and I was amazed by their harrowing tales of crime and violence. Working with those youngsters was very inspiring, so one day during the school holidays I took Quinton with me, and he was shocked to see some neighbourhood guys there. At the end of our session the warders locked the boys in their cells and Quinton was locked up by mistake. A few minutes later the warder opened up the cell to let him out. It was a lesson to steer clear of crime.

We did roadshows in gang-infested townships across the Cape Flats. We also worked at Hawequa and Brandvlei prisons and at various places of safety. Then Davide, another writer Michael Wentworth and I were commissioned by the law department at UCT to do a radio play at Brandvlei prison's youth centre in Worcester with sentenced juveniles.

When we entered the prison, the first high-ranking warder I met was the very same guy from Pollsmoor who had pointed a gun at me. The first thing he said to me was, 'Fredericks, *don't tell anybody about what happened at Pollsmoor.*' I agreed.

We were supposed to bring only sound equipment, but I convinced him that we also wanted to film the workshop. He was a bit sceptical at first, but I had him over a barrel and he even allowed us to leave some sound equipment behind for the youth to capture the sounds of prison at night. We came across some very talented youth who had joined the number gangs. An idea for my first documentary, *Tomorrow's Heroes*, was born. The idea was to try to demystify the myth that if you don't belong to a gang, you are nothing. The documentary later became a co-production with Zenit Arti Audiovisive from Italy, where it was titled *HLK (Hard Living Kids)*. We worked with ten different youth gangs in ten townships across the Cape Flats.

Eugene was the driver on the shoot and also played a drug merchant in the film.

One night, we arrived in Manenberg to film the Hard Living Kids in their gang stronghold. When we entered the long shack, the place was humming. The senior members were on one side and the juniors in a smaller section cordoned off by a curtain. In the junior section, the French soundman Fred Salles from Marseille set up his equipment in a corner. Davide Tosco the Italian was behind the camera, while I sat on a wooden bench doing the interviews. A single naked light bulb hung from the rafters in the centre of the room.

As the youth started loosening up talking about their escapades, the curtain opened and a young gangster entered and pulled a gun on us. For a split second, time stood still as he brought his gun to bear. I said to him, '*Daai's 'n kwaai move, broertjie … kan djy trug gan en'it wee doen …?*' (That's a smart move, brother … can you go back and do it again …?)

Strangely enough he stepped back behind the curtain and did it again, pulling the gun with a flourish. He stood like that for a moment and asked me, '*Moet ek'it wee doen …?*' (Must I do it again …?)

I replied, '*Nei, daai's genoeg, kry vi jou 'n sitplek.*' (No, that's enough, get yourself a seat.) I pushed a paraffin tin in his direction; he sat down and started to boast about how he had killed people.

For a while he got lost in the telling and then realised that I was sitting higher than him and a worried look appeared in his eyes. He looked at me and said, '*Jaai … Wat praat ek dan nou …?*' (Yikes … What am I talking about …?)

I placated him. '*Moetie worrie nie, die film is vi oorsee.*' (Don't worry, this film is for overseas.)

Then the curtain opened again and a skinny youth entered. He did not see us at first as he stood under the naked bulb and gave them the bad news, saying, '*Een van os manne lê daa op die skoolgrond, hy's wit bene!*' (One of our members is lying dead on the school grounds!)

The group rose in frightened unison. They had pledged allegiance to the gang and one of them was heard to say, '*Kry die guns …*' (Get the guns …)

We moved outside with them. Fred was standing by our van dismantling his sound equipment. I bundled him and his equipment into the van and we set off.

I wanted the soundtrack for *HLK* to be hip hop, so I went looking for a rapper and the name Mario 'Mr Devious' van Rooy came up. I got his address in Beacon Valley, Mitchells Plain, so I went to visit him. When I arrived there, I found him sitting among a huge group of rappers, Rastafarians and gangsters. I didn't know him then, but he was easily identifiable because when he spoke everybody listened. He rapped for me and we decided to record him, Loit Sôls, Churchil Naudé, the all-female hip-hop crew Godessa, and a few other artists at Black Beach studios in Muizenberg. Devious was very good and he blew us away with his lyrics. He was also well travelled and had performed in many African and European countries. We became close friends although he was many years younger than I was.

In the same year, I met and worked with the film company Dark Continent from Durban and we filmed a mockumentary titled *Shooting Bokkie*, a story about juvenile assassins on the Cape Flats. The story was taken from a script that I'd written called *Coons*. All three of my sons acted in it. Utilising my ghetto skills, we entered the belly of the beast and filmed most of the film at night and on weekends. It was a low-budget film and Una was unhappy with me for putting my life and our sons' lives on the line for little money. The white crew were all professionals, so I watched and learned. I had never travelled abroad, but I was so confident that I got myself a passport, which lay on my bedside table for two years. I believed I could fly.

In the year 2000, I got a chance to go to Italy to edit *HLK*. I stayed with the producer, Massimo Arvat, in his apartment in the Balôn in Torino for four months and travelled to many other towns. I met a lot of people who had never heard about a coloured person from South Africa, and I mesmerised them with my stories and culture. All the guys in the production company wore their hair long, and they coerced me not to cut mine because they reckoned I looked like an Apache with my hair long. After a while, they gave me the nickname 'the Big Spirit'. What surprised me most was that in Italy nobody judged me, and I wrote a poem titled 'Mr Nobody', about a guy who wants to rise above the stigma of prison, poverty and gangsterism that is his heritage to become 'Somebody'.

We moved the editing suite to Davide's parents' place in Refrancore outside Torino. While I was there, I started writing a trilogy of scripts. I would listen to the Italian guys speaking among each other and I suddenly realised that I must tell my stories in my dialect. I always wrote in Afrikaans and English but never in Kaaps.

The first script, *The Second Son*, was based on the historical story of the *Meermin*, a two-masted schooner that had set sail from Madagascar in 1766 with 148 captured slaves on board. There was a mutiny on the ship and it disappeared at sea. The second story, *Call Me Dog*, was set in 1865 in the Tulbagh mountains of South Africa during British rule. The third story was *This Boy*, set in the 1960s in Kewtown, Athlone. I was eventually returning to my own experiences, and telling our story, as Gimba had asked me to do.

The main characters in all these stories had the same surname, after Themba Lonzi, a creative artist who worked with me at CRED and who was a facilitator in the female section of Pollsmoor. He also made ghoema drums and played them. I liked him and needed a character that I could identify with in the first story. So Themba Lonzi became that character. The protagonist in *Call Me Dog* was named Titus Lonzi, and my character in *This Boy* became Abraham Lonzi. *This Boy* would later change to *Noem My Skollie*.

HLK premiered in Torino and people were so impressed with it that the production company decided to do a short film about me and my adventures in their country titled *Broertjie in Italy* (Brother in Italy).

On my return to South Africa, both *HLK* and *Shooting Bokkie* had their premieres in Cape Town. I had some recognition and I had a batch of business cards printed with the slogan 'A room full of scripts'. I would hand out the cards to filmmakers who I met. Some would take it and others would refuse, looking at me suspiciously or just walking away. I would follow them and pop the card into their pockets when they weren't looking.

27

Screenwriting

In 2001 I returned to CRED, where Devious had started working in the meantime. He used hip hop to change the mindset of the youth. My group would write poetry and his group would turn the words into lyrics. We worked well together and we identified the need to catch the youth before they came to prison. So, together with Charlton George, an actor who used drama as a discipline in prison, we started running a voluntary workshop in the gangland of Heideveld.

Bold with the knowledge that we were making a difference, we approached a gang leader in the area and told him what we wanted to do. He found it funny at first, but when he realised we were serious, he agreed that we could run our workshop on an open field on a school ground. The youth gathered and they enjoyed themselves immensely and the community took note. A filmmaker, Kali van der Merwe, sponsored us with some 36-shot throwaway cameras, so we also ran a photography workshop.

The youth did so well with their photography that Kali had their pictures blown up and displayed at an arts centre in the city, and they were sold for up to R400 each. Devious had facilitated a hip-hop song with them, 'Shut it down man, shut it down ...', and they performed it at the photography exhibition. The whole event was then filmed for kykNET. A job well done and the song 'Shut it down' echoed through the streets of the township.

Our work in prisons flourished and some of the outcomes were radio plays and we had a book of prison stories published with the title *Groundfloor*.

Later that year, I was approached by the director of a film company to do a documentary about girl gangsters for e.tv. The title of the documentary was *Girlhood*. The director of the documentary, Tracey Collis, was commissioned to make the film on condition that she worked with me, as she knew nothing about girl gangsters. I had no problem with that, as I had a vast network of youth at risk. The three girls who were selected for the lead roles all came from a place of safety in Faure where we had held workshops before. We worked in various townships and I hired a 28 gangster, Rashaad Swain, to watch my back. Rashaad had a high rank in the gang hierarchy and had spent more than twenty years in various prisons across the country for armed robbery. He was a good-looking guy with almost no prison tattoos visible.

We filmed a night shoot one Friday in a square in Woodstock. It was a place where wanted gangsters from across the Cape Flats came to hide out. It was an evil place with lots of derelict cars parked around, their windows blocked by curtains. The sweet, sour smell of Mandrax hung in the air. When we arrived, a group of gangsters were warming themselves at a huge fire brazier. They looked at us with avarice. Rashaad got out of the van and mingled with the crowd. He was one of them and could participate in their conversations.

We were using a ladder pod that lay on the ground and we needed to put it up. A group of youth came barrelling towards us. As I bent down to lift the pod, they stopped next to me and I asked them, '*Can you guys help me lift this pole?*' They obliged and helped us to put up the ladder pod and then they hung around as if they were part of the crew. The film crew and actors definitely got their thrill of fear.

Early in 2002, on a public holiday, I took my car to my son Eugene, who was by now a fully fledged motor mechanic, to do some minor repairs on it. I was lounging in the yard with another local customer when a guy walked in by the gate. He wore tattered black denims, a flat cap and a patched leather jacket. I scanned him once, registered and dismissed him in a blink of an eye. He was nobody. The other customer reckoned to me, '*Die's Grumpies, hy sê hy't gesing met die Rockets, maa hy lieg. Hy's 'n droster...*' (That's Grumpies, he says he sang with the Rockets but he's lying. He's a drifter ...)

Eugene came around the corner and told him, '*Druk 'n nommer vir my pa, Grumpies!*' (Sing a number for my dad, Grumpies!)

I wasn't much interested in Grumpies until he began to sing. He sang the most beautiful ballads and the melodies soothed my mind. I had an idea and told Grumpies that I was going to make a documentary about him. He replied, '*Yes, Daddy* ...' Everybody was his Mommy or Daddy. As soon as I got home, I wrote a synopsis and treatment and mailed it to Rainbow Circle Films to have it included in the Ikon short documentary series. My pitch was successful and I was funded to make a ten-minute short documentary.

I did my research and tracked down Molly Baron, the former leader of the Rockets. Grumpies, real name Graham Wren, cleaned himself up and I gave him a new wardrobe. We went to go see Molly, who recognised Grumpies instantly and agreed to record a song with him in his studio. We filmed Grumpies behind the mic, but most of the time it was more about tracking him down, as he seldom stayed in one location for long periods of time. We had posters and flyers made – 'Grumpies in Concert' – and got the youth to hand them out. The event was at the Cameo Lounge in Heideveld, so I roped Devious in as the supporting event. The concert was filmed by a Swedish crew, and the crowd had great fun as Grumpies performed for them until the interval, when he disappeared.

Mr Devious took to the stage while I went looking for Grumpies and the cameras kept on rolling, capturing him on film at his best as he moved the crowd with his lyrics.

I found Grumpies in his darkened kitchen reading the classifieds of the newspaper and took him back to the concert. A few months later, *Grumpies* and *Shooting Bokkie* were both screened by the SABC and at a film festival in Rotterdam.

Later in 2002 I attended the Sithengi film market and met up with Kali van der Merwe again, who introduced me to a filmmaker named David Max Brown. I was a bit wary of him at first as he gave me his hand in friendship. But David was easy to talk to and soon I told him about myself and my writings. He asked me if I had written a script and I reached into my backpack and took out a hard copy of my trilogy: *The Second Son, Call Me Dog* and *This Boy*.

The next day when I dropped him at the airport on his way home to Joburg, David had my trilogy in hand. When he landed two hours later, he phoned me and said, 'John, this script is gold.' I was on cloud nine. The two of us started working the script, writing and rewriting draft after draft. It was a long process.

In 2003, David told me there was a call for scripts from M-Net, so I pitched a new script titled *Call Me Dog* to them. This was a different story than the one in the original trilogy. It was based on the story of a youth I had met when I was driving through the back streets of Grassy Park on a stormy night. As I came around a corner, my car splashing through a big pool of water, my headlights picked up a bedraggled youth sheltering against a wall. I stopped and asked him for his name and he slurred, '*Call me Dog.*' I asked him why, and he said. '*If you drive off now, you will forget my name, so Dog is fine.*' I offered him a lift and dropped him off at my brother Ivan's place, where they were holding band practice, and left him there. A few months later I was filming the group at the Athlone Civic, when 'Dog' walked confidently onto the stage, picked up a mic and began to sing. That was a poignant moment for me. I learnt that his name was Raymond. I wrote the story and it was later published in the book of prison stories, *Groundfloor*.

My application was successful. I had the opportunity to either direct or produce the film and I opted to co-produce the film with David and it was directed by Akiedah Mohammed. The title of the film changed to *Freedom Is a Personal Journey*. It was set in the female section of Pollsmoor prison. We did night shoots and at one point I found myself being chased by an old female prisoner dressed in only a flimsy nightie. She was having some fun, so I played along and ran like hell down the corridor.

I returned to CRED and found that new American funders had come on board. They checked our résumés and our tertiary education, of which I had none. I was told that I had to study further. I was also told that we must implement more life-skills programmes like teaching the youth how to build paper castles. To my mind, none of the youth that I worked with would build paper castles on their release. If they are hungry and broke, they will find a way to eat, as a hungry stomach knows no laws. Sometimes just a whiff of Mandrax is the decider. I quit CRED but still had close contact with Devious in our township workshops.

On Friday 24 January 2004, I was waiting for transport from Main Road Wynberg to Sea Point, where we were editing the *Freedom* doccie. The noonday gun sounded and my phone rang at exactly the same time. It was Devious, to remind me of an appointment we had for the next day to shoot a music video of him. I told him, '*Ek gaan wag vir jou …*' (I'll wait for you …)

Early on the Saturday morning, my phone rang and a voice told me, '*Devious is dood …*' (Devious is dead …)

I was totally blown away and blurted, '*Moetie saam my kak praat nie, ek wag vir hom!*' (Don't talk shit to me, I'm waiting for him!)

The voice on the other end said, '*Hy's dood, hulle het hom gisteraand doodgesteek …*' (He's dead, he was stabbed to death last night …)

I informed Una, got dressed and drove down to Beacon Valley, where I was met by Devious's pregnant wife Natalie and their two little daughters. I didn't know what to say to her, but she looked me in the eye and told me, '*Ek weet mnr. Fredericks sal 'n music video van hom gemaak het … maar nou verander dit na 'n dokumenterie …*' (I know Mr Fredericks was going to make a music video of him … but now it must change to a documentary …)

I nodded my agreement.

The following Saturday, Devious had a huge funeral that was attended by ex-inmates, male and female, who we had worked with. Youth at risk came in their droves and marched through the streets of Beacon Valley. They were dressed in yellow sweaters with the slogan 'Drumming for Justice', the name of a drumming programme that Devious had organised in Pollsmoor prison. His death was a great loss to the world.

I gathered all the footage of Devious, including the Grumpies concert. I wrote a proposal and pitched it to a panel of white people. When I was done, they looked at me with empty eyes that showed they did not understand what I was talking about and weren't interested in it. I leant over the lectern and stared at them and told them, '*I'm going to show you!*'

With the aid of Rainbow Circle Films we put together an eighteen-minute film. When the Sithengi Festival came around, we went to the film market and invited the filmmakers to a cinema in the Promenade in Mitchells Plain to come and watch the film. The cinema was packed with local and global filmmakers. The next day at the film market, the naysayers showed me some respect. The SABC commissioned us to make a forty-eight-minute version, and with that money Natalie and I went to Amsterdam to scout for Devious's music and footage of his performances. We then made a seventy-three-minute version of the film and a music CD. In 2005 I screened the film in New Jersey and it was selected to screen at the fifth Hip-Hop Odyssey in New York, where *Mr Devious, My Life* won the award for best feature documentary.

In 2006 David pitched the trilogy to the National Film and Video Foundation (NFVF), which is an agency of the Department of Arts and Culture. We were told that the script was not well written, that it didn't conform to the three-act structure, that it lacked a clear through-line for the protagonist, and that the film would have no commercial appeal. David was advised to find an experienced writer, because John Fredericks was not seen as one. David was adamant that I was the writer, so they chose *This Boy* and decided to send me on a six-month screen-writing course which would start the following year. I was sixty-three years old and under huge pressure to succeed.

On a Saturday morning early in 2007, I arrived at the NFVF offices in Joburg. I entered a huge hall where the other participants were already seated at a long, round table. There were writers, script editors and mentors. They were all young lions, educated people who had studied film, and I was the only coloured person present. I was also the oldest and the only participant from the Western Cape. I had passed Grade 8 in 1960. I hesitated in the doorway as they laid their eyes upon me, and I felt uncomfortable under their stares. I felt like a thug in their company but I nodded, found myself a seat and settled down.

They knew everything and I knew nothing, but we were on the same level as the course we were about to do was a new scriptwriting format. The teachings were way above my head and I struggled to stay focused.

That evening at our guest house, a tipsy black writer from the North West Province reckoned to me, '*You know, John, this morning when you stepped into the room I thought to myself, here is a Cape Town gangster. I just wanted to cut a small hole in your head to see what makes you tick.*' He cackled with laughter.

I was tired and my anger flared. I was holding a ballpoint pen and for a split second I wanted to stab him in the eye. He read my deadly intent, took a step back and spluttered, '*Hey ... John ... that's a joke ...*'

Sanity prevailed and I told him, '*I think you're a little brat ... You make shit jokes, but if you want to see a gangster, I'll show you what gangster is!*'

He got the message.

I dug deep, sacrificed and set out to fulfil my impossible dream. It was hectic. One weekend a month we had to go to Joburg, and I had assignments 24/7 with no money coming in. My business went down-hill as I spent most of my waking hours doing assignments, which we had to present at the following workshop. We received a small per diem, but I used the money to buy books that I needed for the course. My mentor was Thandi Brewer and we met in the mind. She knew that I was out of my depth, and one day she sent me an email telling me that she liked my story. That was a great pick-me-up, but every Monday when I returned from Joburg I wanted to quit the course as I had to find a way to put food on the table.

I made it through the first six-month course. Back home, I tried to catch up on my bond repayments. So I did some painting and gardening jobs and collected old furniture to repair and sell, but I refused to beg, borrow or bow down to any person. I hustled for my own bone. I was always neat and tidy, I had a swagger in my step and I looked successful, so nobody knew how broke I was.

28

Struggle and strive

Times were hard, but then my youngest son, Quinton, stepped up to the plate and offered to take over my bond repayments. I was lifted, but things were getting desperate. Writing was getting me nowhere and the thought of making a quick score jumped into my mind as I travelled back to my roots. It was like a death wish, but I was driven by a power beyond my control to not give up on my dream of becoming a successful writer.

Then, late in 2007, I was approached by a film director named Rehad Desai to co-produce a documentary with the title *Father Inside*. Vaughan Giose of Rainbow Circle Films was to be the cameraman. The story was about Magadien Wentzel, a notorious 28 gangster who had spent twenty-five years in prison and who featured in the book *The Number* by Jonny Steinberg. The problem they had was that there had been a delay of two years, and Rehad and the film crew were too nervous to face Magadien. I had never met him but I had heard of him and his reputation.

Rehad gave me all their notes and a copy of *The Number* to read. I asked him for Magadien's number and I phoned right there and then. When he answered, he was very abrasive, but I needed the money, so I made an appointment with him for the next day. I had to meet him in the gangland of Manenberg. Rehad also gave me a per diem to take the guy for lunch.

Early the next day, I arrived in Kraal Road in Manenberg, also known as 'Die Kraal'. It was an evil place and I was fearful, but fear was my ally. I drove slowly down Kraal Road looking for Magadien's address as the gangsters stared at my car in avarice. I found Magadien leaning on a refuse bin. He was morose and seething with fury as I introduced myself. He went off on me, blaming me for the delay in filming and threatening my life, and I felt a thrill of fear. He looked just like Gums, the perpetrator of my youth. I was unarmed, having stopped carrying a knife some time before, so I took out my ballpoint pen and held it in my hand on the pretence that I was ready to take notes. His eyes flickered at this move, because he knew that the pen was a deadly weapon.

Magadien lived in a Wendy house in the front yard of a council home. I soon realised that I was in the camp of the 28s as gangsters came and went and some hung around. They sabelaed with Magadien and I could see they showed him a lot of respect.

Inside his Wendy, I could see that the cupboards were bare. While I was taking notes, I could feel his eyes on me and the evil radiating from him. He looked at me deep down and said, '*I think I should rob you!*'

I replied, '*That's not what I'm here for. I'm Johnnie and I want to do your documentary.*'

Magadien's fellow gang members chuckled inanely. I had been in these situations before, so I suggested that the two of us should take a drive. We got into my car and I drove to a mall, and instead of taking him for lunch I went to Shoprite and we did some shopping. I bought him enough food to last him a month and he showed me some respect. Back at the 28s' camp, I was welcomed into their fold. I also hired two of the younger gangsters as security on the documentary shoot.

Magadien's story took us on a journey to many 28 strongholds across the peninsula, where I would listen to their stories of crime, mayhem and murder. I was in my element among them, as prison had given me status in this company. Rehad was so impressed that he offered me twice the amount of money that I had bargained for.

That same year, Vaughan Giose of Rainbow Circle Films asked me to co-produce six short films with learners from five Elsies River high schools, so I hired Magadien to be the security. The notorious 28 gangster took to the task like a duck to water. He wouldn't allow me to carry anything. Besides him and Vaughan, the other two members were Nadine Angel Cloete and Kurt Orderson. It was low budget and it wasn't an easy task. At most of the schools, the teachers gave us the worst learners to work with. They were rowdy and some came to school zonked out of their heads. The teachers didn't want them in class, so they happily passed them onto us.

At every workshop at every school, it took me almost half an hour to get their attention, the way they were acting. But as a creative-writing facilitator in prison with youth at risk, my style of working was tried and tested. I identified the leaders in each group and made them the main characters. It worked like a bomb, because whatever they did, the others followed. Each school had to tell their own story, and with our skill and know-how, those kids changed and took their roles seriously. We filmed them in the streets of ganglands in the areas where their story was set, and at the end of the programme we came out with six beautiful short films. We gave those kids the opportunity to rise above the norm of township life. Their films were later screened on Cape Town TV (CTV).

In 2008 I got an invitation from the NFVF to do a follow-up course. To my surprise, there were only six of us left from the previous course. My mentor was Justine Loots, a very tough lady indeed, and we did not hit it off so well in the beginning. Just one steely look from her would put me in my place and remind me that I was a thug. She just didn't get my story or who I really was. My script editor was a young Zulu woman who didn't understand a word of Afrikaans, and progress was slow. I tried to make her feel at ease and told her a couple of jokes. She reported this to Justine and the incident was wrongly interpreted. Words were spoken, and in a moment of fury I decided to quit. I felt that the deck was stacked against me and that I was going nowhere fast.

The next day I got a phone call from Clarence Hamilton, one of the board members of the NFVF, who told me that I couldn't quit now. I asked why, and he just said, '*You can't quit now, John. I'm booking your flight for your next workshop.*' I wondered about this terse message for a while. Then I got an email from David, who motivated me not to give up on my dream, so I returned to the course. They wanted to fire the script editor, but I pleaded her case and she cried with gratefulness. I wasn't there to blow my own horn, but then one of the writers in the group said she had watched my mockumentary *Shooting Bokkie*. It was only then that they realised that I had made some award-winning documentaries before.

I persevered and stayed the course, getting up at four every morning to work on my assignments and hustle to put food on the table, even picking up empty bottles at the beach for resale. I lived the script and walked in the footsteps of my characters. I would change like a chameleon every time I became another character, and people gave me strange looks. One day in November, my son Quinton walked into my office while I was lost in rewriting and asked me, '*Dad, how much do you need to make this film?*'

I replied, '*One million dollars.*' He took out a huge fake chequebook and made out a cheque for a million dollars. I framed it and hung it high up on my office wall. I believed that I was going to get the funding.

Only in 2009 did we get our results, and I had done better than expected, getting the highest marks on the course. There was a note attached from my script mentor Justine Loots that the film should be made. I worked on the script with a newfound vigour until 2010. Armed with those documents and a new draft of the script, David applied for production funding from the NFVF. In 2011 we got an invitation to attend the film market at DIFF (the Durban International Film Festival), where the funding procedures would take place.

Two of my kids lived in Durban, Sonia in Queensburgh, and Clint in Malvern, near the Fruit & Veg City where he was the bakery manager. The day before the festival, I went to visit each of them. I spent the evening with Clint and a couple of friends. We went fishing and chilled on the beach, but on our way back I became more and more uncomfortable with the guy who was driving the car, Regan, a swarthy Indian guy with a boastful attitude. He chattered continuously while cutting in and out of traffic at high speed. During one dangerous manoeuvre, a car next to him closed the gap and ripped off his driver's side mirror. Regan was furious and hell-bent on giving chase. I murmured, '*He's gone, Regan, you won't catch him now.*'

The words of Babba Jan jumped into my mind. '*Be watchful, ever watchful.*' When we arrived at Clint's house, I read Regan the riot act. I got a sense that the guy was dangerous and would resort to violence.

Clint confronted him too, bristling and spitting his anger. I saw myself in him then, and I met him in the mind and told him, '*Let him go, Clint, it's not worth it.*'

Clint said he had got Regan a job in the butchery, so he mustn't come and drive shit.

For the DIFF film market, we had a director lined up, but he never pitched at the market. We didn't succeed in getting production funding, but we got development funding and a script editor, Roshan Cader. I had to rewrite the script under her guidance.

So began another journey of struggle and strife, as we were almost always at each other's throats and she tried to take my story in another direction. I would go with some of her changes, but on others I would not budge. I reckoned the script had been through many phases and changes, so I stuck to my story. I had some money to fall back on, so I wrote and rewrote numerous drafts. It was time-consuming and I sat in my bubble day after day trying to get the script ready so we could apply for production funding. I was determined to make the film happen, even if I had to do it myself. I collected props, wardrobe, scouted for locations and identified my cast. I had a one-track mind.

In April 2012, Clint came home after nine years in Durban. He was very sick with TB and he was hardly able to walk. When he arrived that first day, I told him, '*We are going to help you heal.*' He settled in and Una took care of him. Day after day he would sit behind my back as I worked on the script and he got angry when it was returned with more notes for changes. Four months later he was back on his feet again and he wanted to go back to Durban. Una pleaded with him not to go, as he could easily find a job in Cape Town with his baking skills. But he had fallen in love with Durban and wanted to return to his job at the Fruit & Veg in Malvern. A day after his forty-fourth birthday, we put him on a bus back to Durban. Una left him with a message that she was going to visit him in three months' time.

Three months later on my birthday, 7 October 2012, he phoned me to wish me happy birthday. That same evening, he was ambushed in his house and badly assaulted and left for dead on his lounge floor. The perpetrator stole his new phone, locked him up in his house and fled the scene. Early the next morning, I got a call from my daughter Sonia to say that Clint was in hospital and it looked bad. He died that evening and my world came crashing down. My hatred towards his killer lay like a rusted axe in my heart. It seared through my brain, and my battle cry of 'Don't touch my family' echoed hollowly in my ears. I stopped working on the script.

We could not let Clint be buried in Durban to lie in a lonely grave, so we flew his body back to be buried in Cape Town. He had been so badly assaulted that we did not open the coffin. As a close family, we were completely heartbroken.

As it turned out, Regan, the driver of the car in Durban, was the perpetrator. Accompanied by his mother as his witness, he gave himself up to the police and pleaded self-defence. Their statements were taken, and although he had no marks on him, they sent him home. A detective took over the case and discovered that Regan had sold Clint's cellphone to a female security guard in the parking lot at the Fruit & Veg. Regan went on the run.

My desire for revenge was like a drumbeat in my head, as if prison was calling me back. I became the gangster character of my youth as I plotted and planned my vengeance. The idea was to go to Durban and wait until he appeared in court, where I would cause a disturbance to get locked up for the day. I planned to meet him on the 'front line', down there in the holding cells. Days turned into weeks, but the guy was elusive and eluded the cops for a long time.

I was tormented by the death of my son and there were demands on me to work the script. The script editor Roshan Cader and producer David Max Brown had sent some new notes, but I could not concentrate. I couldn't shake my thoughts of revenge and the hatred gnawed at my soul. Then I heard a rumour that a posse of friends and relatives were planning to go to Durban to seek vengeance. When I heard that Eugene and Quinton were part of it, my heart almost stopped. I could not allow them to walk in my footsteps of violence, so I intervened and nipped their plan in the bud. I told them, 'No more bloodshed.'

It took me a while to get my mind back into the script, so I dug deeper and got lost in the story. The more changes Roshan wanted to make, the more stubborn I became, because for me it was like she did not understand the world of my story. In 2013 she wrote in her report that I needed to stand down because she believed I had project fatigue. She wanted to bring in another writer. My reply was almost a scream of frustration. '*What is project fatigue!?*' I had worked on the script for thirteen years, getting up at four in the morning to write. There was no way I was going to let some other writer take over my story. Two months later, Roshan quit the project and I was afraid that her decision could harm my chances of getting production funding.

Another two months later, David's partner Moshidi Motshegwa came on board. Moshidi had considerable skill with character development from her years as an actress, which she contributed to the script development. She was keen to develop her professional skills behind the camera, so she enrolled on an NFVF/Sediba script-editing course, which ran for a year.

On that course was Henrietta Gryffenberg, who was a commissioning editor at M-Net. Moshidi asked her if she would be interested to read *Noem My Skollie*. Henrietta was delighted to read the script, so Moshidi gave her a copy of the screenplay.

A few weeks later, Henrietta responded that she thought that the script was excellent and that M-Net would surely be interested and she would pass it on. David sent the script by email along with the finance plan and other supporting documentation. Henrietta then sent it on to the head of M-Net movies, Jan du Plessis. Then we waited.

Suddenly, in September 2013, David got a call from Jan, who told him that he'd read the script on his way to the Toronto Film Festival and then read it again on his way back. Jan was convinced that the film had to be made. On my birthday in October, Janine gave me a director's chair as a present. She still kept the faith.

We then had several meetings with M-Net and they sent the script to a panel of advisors who were leading experts in their fields of Afrikaans literature. Scriptwriting, cinema, broadcasting and such like. Their comments were very positive and all of them gave the script high scores on their assessments. They pointed out some issues they felt could be strengthened and other useful critical insights. We discussed the main terms of the sale to M-Net. Then David and Moshidi formed a new company through which to produce the film. They became the joint owners and co-producers of the film.

By this time, Moshidi had progressed with her script-editing course and gave me valuable insight into the possible changes suggested by the M-Net channel. We compared the notes of the NFVF, and David and I rounded off the script. However, just as M-Net confirmed their participation and we settled on the amount of the pre-buy, the NFVF dropped the bomb. Their panel had decided not to support the production of the film. In my mind, I was a protégé of the NFVF and I almost fell off my chair when I got the news.

I knew that David was very disappointed himself, and all I could say to him was, '*David, we stumble but we don't fall.*'

The NFVF panel felt that the film did not conform to the three-act structure and was therefore probably not commercial enough to attract the core coloured audience to the cinema. This challenged the finance structure of the film and threatened the closure of the deal with M-Net.

Fortunately, David discovered an appeals process on the NFVF website called 'Form H', which allows the applicant to appeal to either the NFVF council or the Minister of Arts and Culture. We chose to appeal to the NFVF council on the grounds that the attachment of M-Net to the film was a very strong support that negated the NFVF's worries about the commercial potential. We urged them to reconsider their position on that basis.

Three weeks later the decision was turned around and the NFVF made a financial commitment to the film's production.

At the beginning of our search for a director, I gave the script to a friend and fellow filmmaker, without David's knowledge. I favoured him because he was one of the guys who had followed me and Devious around. We had done quite a few projects together and I figured we worked well together and that we could pull it off. I did not hear from him for a month. Then David sent him the script, and he replied almost immediately. He was enthusiastic about the story and said he and his brother would like to co-direct it, and his partner would do the wardrobe. He pointed out the changes he wanted to make to the script, and he wanted a credit as the co-writer. I had sacrificed thirteen years of my life to write the story and my role in the whole project was not even mentioned.

I was deeply disappointed in my friend, but David's reply to him took him down a peg or two. David thanked him very much for the offer, but he HAD to work with the writer John W. Fredericks. So my friend was out.

The next guy in line, with whom I had worked on the Ikon short documentary series, had a problem pitching at the NFVF in person as he was in America and wanted to do it via Skype instead. I just wanted all my ducks in a row to get the film done. I had learnt to play by the rules and not to jeopardise my film in any way. We moved on.

The third in line was a really nice young woman who had made a couple of films before. She was distant, and when we did some auditions with real-life gangsters at the Joseph Stone Auditorium in Athlone, I sensed that she was all at sea. She was young and out of touch with the reality of the story. She cut her losses and I did not see her again.

Then another director came on board. He was full of fire and we hit it off almost immediately. He insisted that he was not going to change one word of the story and he also wanted me to be the co-director. He bandied this idea with David and Moshidi. I was a silent listener to this conversation. I just wanted my film made. Then the two of us went on a scouting mission and I took him to my old haunts in my hometown. What bothered me about him was that he was always filming me at these gang locations with those gang bangers and I once asked him, '*Why are you always filming me? This is not a documentary.*' He just smiled.

Then he sent me the director's cut and he almost blew my mind. He wanted to make my mother a prostitute in the film, along with other changes that had nothing to do with the story. I could not believe the audacity of the guy. In the ghettoes, swearing or talking badly about someone's mother would lead to fighting or even death. I immediately mailed David that I did not want to see, hear or talk to this guy any more. Once again we had no director.

Then I got sick. After all the years of slogging on the script, I had neglected my health, and I didn't realise how bad it was. I was coughing,

I had no appetite and I was losing weight. Then Gloria, who had returned to South Africa, came to visit and she looked at me as if I was dying. I cracked some jokes with her about my condition, but when she left she had a strange look in her eyes.

Una and the kids badgered me all the time to go to the doctor. My spirit was at its lowest ebb. It felt like all my sacrifices were in vain, and here I was with no job and no prospects.

The turning point came when my siblings and some church brethren decided to come and pray for me around my deathbed. I was shocked out of my reverie and declined their offer. I told them, '*I've got no intention of dying right now, I've still got a film to make!*' Maybe they thought that I was disrespectful towards God, but I believed that He would not teach me to swim just to let me drown. I started to fight back after the doctor diagnosed me with tuberculosis. He put me on a six-month programme and I diligently attended a clinic until the TB cleared up.

By April 2014, we had signed a pre-buy contract licensing the film to M-Net, giving them the African rights to the film. Our other partners were the NFVF and the Department of Trade and Industry. The film was bonded by Hollard and once all the contracting was finalised and the first money was in the bank, the official process of the production went ahead.

Then Daryne Joshua walked into my bubble. He was half my age, so I looked at him deep down. He had a quiet spirit, even his eyes were quiet, and I immediately felt comfortable with him. We were kindred spirits from the townships, as he was a writer too. He understood the concept of the story as he had first-hand knowledge of ghetto life. He knew the different cultures that played a role in the townships, the gangs, the drug dealers and the plight of youth at risk. We met a couple of times after that and I listened to *his* story. I knew then he was the right man for the job and reported back to David. Daryne pitched to the NFVF and he came through with flying colours. He came on board as the director of *Noem My Skollie*.

29

Noem My Skollie

The casting process began well in advance and continued until just before shooting began. Most of the actors in *Noem My Skollie* had performed drama before, and I already knew some of them. I'd met Christian Bennet, who plays Gif, when I worked at CRED, and he was also part of the casting team for the film. I'd met Gantane Kusch, who plays Gimba, at the Artscape when he was performing *Die glas ennie draad*. A week before filming began, I met Dann Jaques Mouton, who plays my character, and Gershwin Mias, who plays Shorty, in the production offices in Woodstock, where all four of them were present. We hit it off immediately as I regaled them with my stories.

Charlton George had volunteered to work for free with me in Pollsmoor under the CRED banner. I liked the guy so much that I identified him as my dad, Philip. The producer wasn't happy with my choice, but I insisted that he could pull it off. I thought that Denise Newman fitted the bill as my mother, but she was always so aloof when I saw her at gatherings and screenings that I never bothered to speak to her and I was surprised when she came aboard as Mrs Lubbe. In the end, my mother was played by Sandi Schultz. I first met Sandi at a church location in Woodstock where she had to perform the role of my mother speaking in a babble of tongues. She found it difficult, and Daryne and I consulted with her in a backroom of the church. This scene was later cut from the film. Mr C was played by Abduraghmaan Adams, who was well known as a character on 7de Laan.

The casting crew tried to make contact with Oscar Petersen, with whom I had worked before, to play Ballie, but they struggled to find him at first. When they eventually tracked him down, he told them that he was taking a break and didn't want to be found, but when he heard that I had written the script, he came on board.

Una's character was played by Tarynn Wyngaard, but in the film her name was Jenny, which is her sister's name in real life. I didn't want to expose Una in the film, so I used a different name. In the film, Jenny works in the library, whereas Una worked as a till supervisor at Shoprite. During the script-editing process, it was decided that the film would play out better that way.

Christian Bennet and the assistant casting director Ephraim Gordon went in search of talented boys to play the younger characters, and they interviewed hundreds of kids from various schools across the Cape Flats. In the end, Austin Rose from Eerste River played the young version of me; Ethan Patton and Joshua J. Vraagom, both from Paarl, were the young Gimba and Gif; and Valentino de Klerk from Elsies River was Shorty. These boys were on fire and played their roles brilliantly.

In March 2015 pre-production began in earnest, and it took two months to prepare for filming.

In May 2015 we went into production. The shoot was scheduled to start on the refuse dump in Baden Powell Drive in Muizenberg. I had to be there at 6:30 a.m. to make the opening speech. That morning I was in a triumphant mood as Una and I set off towards the dump. I believed that nothing could go wrong then. We drove from our house in Strandfontein Village at six in the morning, and as I turned right into the unlighted Baden Powell Drive, my car's headlights cut out. I couldn't see properly and swerved across the road and pulled over to the shoulder. I couldn't see the white lines and I was in a blind panic as we sat there on the dark, dangerous stretch of road.

A sinister feeling came over me, as this had never happened to me before. I phoned my son Quinton, who was second camera on the shoot. I opened the car window, slipped my finger through my key ring and prepared myself for danger. My bunch of keys became a deadly weapon and I was going to use it on anyone who approached my car from the dark. I held onto Una's hand with my left. I had protected her from harm my whole life and I was prepared to die for her. It was an unbelievably scary moment in what was supposed to be the greatest day of our lives.

Quinton arrived to pick us up, but I was unwilling to leave my car there in the dark. He cajoled me to have faith and to go to the shoot.

Reluctantly I left the car, and my nerves were jumping, as I believed that it was a bad sign.

Arriving at the dump was like stepping back in time. They were going to shoot the rape scene and the whole set-up brought back painful memories. The crew and cast gathered. It was a poignant moment as I stood there in wonderment before I delivered my speech. I was introduced to everybody, and at the end of my speech I took a line from a poem that David had written and told them, '*May your dreams also be dreamt in the company of dreamers.*' I stood back and watched as the rape scene unfolded in front of my eyes. Austin Rose, who took on the role of me being raped on the dump site, had lost his grandparents just before the shoot started. Because of the loss of his grandparents, he cried easily and portrayed the part so brilliantly that it was utterly believable. I hid behind a film truck and cried silent tears as the memory flooded back.

I had the opportunity to meet the most brilliant actors from the Cape Flats and surrounds. Many of them were household names and having them acting in my film was something beyond my wildest dreams. I first saw Dann Jaques Mouton playing me on set in Ocean View, and we had a lot of discussions about the character, as I did with most of the other actors in the film during the fifteen days that I was on set. I was still recovering from TB, so I couldn't be on set all the time. Whenever Una and I arrived, Dylan Voegt the line producer would announce, '*John and Una on set!*' – which sent a thrill through my being. *Skollie* had arrived.

Then, on a Sunday night, David Manuel, who was cast as Gums, came onto set to do the prison night scenes. David had spent time in prison and had studied and performed drama while he was serving his time. Now he was out on parole. He arrived with a load of extras from Heideveld and I identified some of them as members of the Junky Funky Kids, a gang operating from Heideveld station. I remembered them because they had once tried to rob me, Devious, Charlton George and Clint at the ticket box at the station. I told them they couldn't rob us of our last money as we still had to take a taxi to get home. I gave one of them a two-rand coin; he was taken aback by my audacity but accepted without further ado.

These guys were for real and they swarmed over the food tables and devoured everything in sight. The eyes of some crew members flickered warily at them. I had never met David before, but I recognised him instinctively as the leader of the pack. I walked up to him and we conversed about respect and discipline. He spoke to the extras and they calmed down. Some of them stuffed their pockets with tea bags and Una reprimanded them. She spoke their language like their mothers would and they showed some respect.

I watched David as he took on the role of Gums, and I was amazed as he changed from the soft-spoken man I had just talked to into the beast who had scared the life out of me when I first entered prison. It was almost surreal as he brought Gums to life, and that night a star was born.

It was winter and quite a few scenes were rained out as we moved to various locations across the Cape. There were plenty of night shoots, and one night my son Quinton approached me on set and asked me, 'Dad, what were you thinking when you wrote all these night scenes?' Yeah, right! The fact is, gangsters operate at night.

Five weeks later, on Father's Day, it was a wrap. The film was in the can at two in the morning. I was dead tired.

David Max Brown suggested that I should take a break now and take Una on a holiday. That was easier said than done. I was on a scriptwriting high. With some money in the bank, I decided to rewrite all my old scripts. With my hard-fought, newfound writing skills, I rewrote four feature-film and four one-hour scripts. Only then did I remove the fake cheque for one million dollars from my wall. I had dreamt the impossible dream. On my seventieth birthday that October, my daughter Janine gave me a replica of an Oscar, which I placed on my desk and I thought to myself, 'Don't limit yourself, dream bigger.'

It took almost a year to complete the editing, music production and grading before the film was ready to be screened. In December 2015 I saw the first cut and my mind boggled as I watched my story unfold. The trailer was made and screened. Alishia van Deventer of Starburst promoted the film and I was kept on my toes running to one radio station after another to talk about it. It was strange being in the spotlight, sometimes doing three interviews a day.

Over the years, I had strained my eyes writing in bad light for long hours but I just carried on. In March I lost the sight in my left eye. It was a huge setback, because now I had to write with one eye and one finger. To give up or lie down was out of the question because I knew I would wither and die.

The first screening of the film to a public audience was on 16 August 2016 in Pollsmoor prison, where it had all begun. The film was screened over three days to convicted male and female prisoners, as well as to a large number of trainee warders. On that first day, David Manuel, who was back awaiting trial on a trumped-up charge, was brought to the screening in shackles. He stood out as he was the only one wearing the yellow clothes of an awaiting-trial prisoner.

There were prisoners serving lifelong sentences, some of them high in the hierarchy of the prison number gangs. A warder pointed out a convict to me and told me he was a general in the 28s, who had caused chaos in prison a few months before. I gave the general a quick scan and he looked like a real tough hombre. At the start of the film, there was a bit of heckling as they identified themselves in the story. As the film continued they became quieter. After the screening, I was invited onto the stage and I spoke to them from my heart. They listened actively as I drew them in with my story, and I had many of them in tears. I locked onto the general and I saw the tears streaming down his face.

Many of them stood up to tell their stories and their hopes for the future. I was moved by the power of *Noem My Skollie*. The next day, David Manuel appeared in court, accompanied by a producer, Ben Overmeyer, to act as a character witness. The magistrate listened to David's story and set him free with the words, '*Go home, David. Go make some more films.*'

The film premiered in August at the Silwerskermfees in Camps Bay and we were nominated for some awards. We didn't win anything, but I felt no pain because deep down in my heart I knew that *my* people of the Cape Flats were going to watch the film. It was released in Ster-Kinekor cinemas in September, and my whole extended family came to the first-night screening at the V&A Waterfront. Many of them, including my close family, were not privy to the dark moments of my past such as the rape on the refuse dump, and I feared they would be greatly embarrassed. They proved me wrong. Two of my grandsons, Shaad and Jesse, were in tears, and Jesse asked me, '*Pa, why didn't you tell us about this ...?*' I had lived with those dark secrets my whole life and my answer to them was, '*How could I ...?*' My children clung to me because only then could they understand who their father really was. They were not embarrassed; they were proud of my achievements.

In its first week, the film was screened in twenty-eight cinemas around the country, and the following week this number increased to thirty-three. It continued on various screens around the country for sixteen weeks, the most popular cinemas being Canal Walk, Paarl Cinemart, Promenade and Parow. It entered the hearts of tens of thousands of people from different creeds and cultures across South Africa.

At the Cinemart cinema in Paarl, it was booked out for three shows a day for eleven days straight. In the second week, I was invited by Lynden Jafta, an events manager in Paarl, to come to a screening. On our arrival at the cinema, there were a lot of high-ranking prison warders, directors and police officials standing in the foyer. I was introduced to everybody present and requested not to go inside until the film had started.

When we entered, the lights were off and the film showing on the screen. I had no idea who was in the cinema. And as at Pollsmoor, the audience was heckling and laughing, and, again, the heckling soon died down. At the end of the film, the lights went on and I stood there on the stage. The audience was deathly silent at the sight of me. They were all gang members from various affiliations. They had been bussed to the cinema at the initiative of a white woman, Aletia Grundling, the CEO of a Christian charity called Monte Christo Miqlat, with the help of the prison warders and police.

I took a line from the film and told them, '*Today I'm going to take you on a boat trip ...*' They were hooked.

I took them on a journey back to my youth and I mesmerised them. When I was done, there was a question-and-answer session. A young man stood up and asked me, '*How can I change? We have made boundaries for ourselves and we are trapped in our own territory.*'

I looked at him for a moment as I searched for an answer. I told him, '*I stay in Cape Town and you in Paarl, so I won't be able to hold your hand … It is in your hands, you decide who you want to be.*'

The next day I got a call from Lynden Jafta, who told me that the mother of the gangster who had spoken up at the screening was in his office. She told him that when her son had got home from the screening he had told her, '*Mom, I'm done with gang life, I want to change …*' My heart almost burst out my chest. As it turned out, the boy, Kurt Vlok, was the leader of the Barbarians in the gang-infested township of Chicago. Kurt made good: he crossed the boundaries with two other gang members and waited an hour on Aletia's porch to tell her they were leaving gang life behind. Kurt had talent as a dancer, singer and playwright. He grabbed his second chance and is currently studying to be a barber. Seventeen of his fellow gang members are enrolled on a rehabilitation programme at Drakenstein prison, where they are doing community work in and outside the prison.

Not everyone reacted positively to the film. David Manuel was working as a car guard outside Mzoli's tavern in Gugulethu, where he was earning a decent living, because a lot of famous and rich people went there and gave him good tips for looking after their cars. Apparently he was attacked by a group of 28 number gangsters for his role as Gums. According to them, the 28s did not rape other prisoners. They were jealous of his role in the movie.

But the accolades kept pouring in as more men, women and youth changed their ways and turned away from lives of crime. I received requests from a number of schools and churches to do motivational speeches, and I got mobbed by the public to take pictures with them, which was quite scary. I'm used to people trying to avoid me, so this was a totally new ball game for me. At schools, learners would burst into tears after my speeches, telling me that *Skollie* had changed their lives. Sometimes I would cry with them. This is my calling.

The NFVF, which had backed *Noem My Skollie* after originally turning it down, went on to support the marketing of the film, which proved absolutely invaluable in getting the news of its release to the public. It also supported the campaign for the film to be South Africa's entry to the foreign-language category of the Academy Awards. In late September, *Noem My Skollie* was selected as South Africa's entry for the awards and was considered alongside films from eighty-five other countries.

Unfortunately, we were not selected as one of the five nominees. The winner was a film from Iran called *The Salesman*. But just being selected as South Africa's entry was an immense honour. I still keep my Oscar replica on my desk.

The first international screening was on 7 January 2017 at the Palm Springs International Film Festival in the USA. The film competed in the foreign-language category, and although we had two sold-out screenings we did not win.

On 1 March 2017, we were nominated for seven awards at the RapidLion Film Festival, competing against other films from Africa, Brazil, Russia, India and China. We won two awards: David Max Brown won the award for best South African film and I won the award for best screenplay. That was the best day of my life. The film was also entered into several other and international film festivals. At the SAFTAS, which took place in Sun City from 16 to 18 March, *Skollie* won five awards: Emma Moss for best wardrobe, Gale Shepherd for best make-up and hair, Warren Gray for best production design, Abduraghmaan Adams for best supporting actor, and Dann Jaques Mouton for best actor. On 3 July, David Manuel won the best supporting actor award and *Skollie* won the best narrative film award at The African Film Festival (TAFF) in Dallas, Texas.

In October 2016, I was approached by Penguin Random House to write the book version of *Skollie*. Una was a bit concerned and asked me, *'Are you sure you can do this?'* She was worried about my eyes and typing it with one finger. I was sure I could do it as this was the highlight of my writer's journey.

So began another adventure. I met with Penguin's managing editor Robert Plummer and I told him about myself and my journey. As I spoke, his eyes lit up and he was so excited that it scared me. I have never written something like this before and I was taking another risk, but that became my motto: *'Take risks. If you win, you will be happy. If you lose, you'll be wise.'* I had six months to write the book, but I finished it in four. If I ever thought that I was a good writer, Robert put me back in school with his editorial changes and suggestions. I am grateful for this opportunity and for the learning curve. I think we met in the mind and I hope the book will be true to both of our expectations.

I don't limit myself, I dream big, because I believe that 'DREAMS NEVER DIE'.

Acknowledgements

This book is dedicated to my wife, Una, who has walked beside me all the way. I also want to acknowledge my children – Eugene, Clint, Sonia, Melanie, Janine and Quinton – for their unwavering belief in my writing and for listening to my stories, sometimes under duress.

Thanks to David Max Brown, who restored my faith in a society that seldom forgives. I learnt to forget the bitter shit and dream my dreams in the company of dreamers.

To Moshidi Motshegwa for rekindling the fires of my waning spirit when hope was almost gone.

To the production team and film crew who worked on the film *Noem My Skollie*, who used a teaspoon to build a mountain.

To Ridaa de Villiers and Jawaad Davids for always being there to fix any IT problems. Without them I would have been lost.

Then to all the people of South Africa who went to the cinema to go watch *Noem My Skollie*. You made it happen.

To the people at Penguin Random House who afforded me the opportunity to write this book, and to my editor Robert Plummer, who helped me to shape it into what it is.

Last but not least I want to thank all the people who I met on the highways and byways of life, in dingy alleys and gangster dives, who shared my dream.

'*I grow in the shadows, I glow in the dark. I am the storyteller, the WEAVER of dreams.*'

JOHN W. FREDERICKS
JULY 2017

Do you have any comments, suggestions
or feedback about this book or any other
Penguin Random House titles?
Contact us at talkback@penguinrandomhouse.co.za

Visit www.penguinrandomhouse.co.za
and subscribe to our newsletter
for monthly updates and news